Phil G. Goulding

Confirm
or
Deny

Informing the People on National Security

HARPER & ROW, PUBLISHERS

New York, Evanston, and London

FOR ANNE,

AND FOR

BARRY, KENT, LAURA, NANCY AND PHILIP

FIRST EDITION

LIBRARY OF CONGRESS CATALOG CARD NUMBER: 79-95958

Contents

Acknowledgments

I owe a debt for this book to several groups of people.

Without a career as a newspaperman I would have had neither the opportunity to serve in the government nor the background to undertake a book. I am especially grateful, therefore, to those who were so helpful to me in my early uncertain years with the Cleveland *Plain Dealer*, and particularly to the late Paul Bellamy, Stanley P. Barnett, James W. Collins, E. P. Derthick and N. R. Howard. That all of these men are now gone from the newspaper business is a loss to journalism and to the people of Ohio. I knew each as an individual of high honor and professional responsibility, and I regarded each as a close personal friend.

Once in government, I could not have survived without the support of the civilian and military personnel with whom I was associated in the Pentagon. Elsewhere I speak of my superiors and the two old friends who were my deputies, but I wish here to thank the personal colleagues who worked most closely with me in our office—my Military Assistants, Major General Donald Cowles and Rear Admiral Shannon Cramer; my Executive Assistants, Colonel Bruce Brown and Lieutenant Colonel Jack Walker; my senior civilian Special Assistant, Orville Splitt, and my two talented and tireless personal secretaries, Mrs. Violet Bryan and Miss Jackie Grant. In naming these few, many of them nonprofessionals in public affairs, I am leaving out dozens of individuals in our Pentagon office and hundreds of loyal officers elsewhere who serve their government and a free press. The dedication of information officers of the armed forces is grossly undersung and their role grossly misunderstood, and I am proud to have worked with them.

I want also to express my gratitude to the Aspen Institute for Humanistic Studies, Aspen, Colorado, where I served as a Scholar-in-Residence while writing much of this book. For six months I lived in Aspen—gloriously isolated from crisis Washington, calmed by the beauty of the Western Slope and the music of the summer-long festival, stimulated by the Institute seminars and comforted in town by long-haired non-Institute friends such as Timothy Walker and Douglas Whitney, whose dislike of the Establishment in general and the Department of Defense in particular was approached only by their scorn for white bread, short-grained rice or brewery-made beer, and equaled only by their openhearted kindness to a lonely stranger. Each member of the Institute staff helped make my stay productive. I particularly thank Board Chairman Robert O. Anderson; Executives William E. Stevenson, Joseph E. Slater and King R. Woodward; Henry Lee, for his good-natured assistance in so many material ways and, most of all, Dan Harris, a sensitive young skiing Yale graduate on the staff who spent scores of unofficial hours at home reading the manuscript and offering valuable detailed recommendations for improving it. I should point out that I was under contract to write the book before becoming affiliated with the Institute, that it was not written under Institute auspices and that the Institute bears no responsibility for its contents.

For immeasurable assistance in organization, writing and the toning down of my irrational prejudices, I am grateful to my editor at Harper & Row, Miss Genevieve Young. From her first attack on the first draft of a rambling first chapter, I have relied heavily upon her skill and judgment—yielding on 95 percent of her recommended changes and knowing this would be a better book if she had won the other 5 percent as well. She is a gem.

Most of all, I thank my family—my mother, father and brother who encouraged me from age ten to follow my desires for a newspaper career, and my wife and children, equally reckless about finances, who would never permit me to give up reporting except for the government. When I began worrying about the future on Jan. 21, 1969, my wife Anne demanded that I take a year to decompress and insisted that a book was the best way to do it. Under this influence, it was my second son, Kent, coming home from his after school job in a suburban shoe repair shop, who summed up the family position: "Since mother and I are both working this year, we see no reason why you should."

Finally, I am indebted to the President who appointed me.

PHIL G. GOULDING

Washington
Aspen
1969

Foreword

Shortly after four o'clock in the morning after the Saturday that 35,000 citizens marched against the Pentagon, Deputy Assistant Secretary of Defense Daniel Z. Henkin left the Army Operations Center where he had been for nearly twenty-four hours, Deputy Assistant Secretary Richard Fryklund quit the news room in which he had been giving periodic briefings, and both joined me in my office for an illicit drink from a bottle of bourbon stashed away for just such an emergency.

Through the windows of Room 2E 800 we could see campfires on the Pentagon grounds, around which were huddled some Americans determined to stay for the weekend protesting the commitment of their country in Southeast Asia.

We were to have three or four hours' sleep on office cots before I checked back with Robert McNamara, Dan returned to the command post and Dick scheduled his next session with the press. Dick was the middleman, supervising the release of official information about the demonstration, receiving facts from a dozen sources and keeping up to date with the most current high-level decisions through private-line conversations with Dan, who was part of the Defense–Justice–White House headquarters team.

While we gulped bourbon and examined a wine bottle—Côtes Debourg, 1964—which had been thrown through a window of Dan's office, just down an inner corridor from mine in the 2E 800 suite, it was Dan who remarked exhaustedly that he was getting a little tired of defending war, violence and catastrophe, and Dick, as we cast about for other potential employers, who first suggested the Tootsie Roll company. Millions of children love Tootsie Rolls, we agreed, and everyone, or nearly everyone, is in favor of the Tootsie Roll itself and the persons associated with it.

No one is in favor of what we were associated with. One of the depressing things about working for the Department of Defense was that it, by definition, must concern itself with weapons of human destruction.

Good News Must Sometimes Knock on the Door of the Tootsie Roll Company, but it never knocked on ours. Seated across the desk, awaiting its turn in the reception room, being assembled on Capitol Hill, speaking at the other end of the phone or, as in this case, camped on the Pentagon grounds, was always Trouble. And nearly always it was instant Trouble. Other Assistant Secretaries of Defense oftentimes could deal with Trouble in an orderly, calm and reasoned manner—sorting it before them, analyzing it, weighing its potential and sometimes even preempting it. But rarely could we do so in our office. We were in the crisis business.

It was crisis around the clock; total traffic in crisis; a torrent of crises, of which hundreds each month were important enough to involve the Secretaries of the Army, Navy and Air Force; scores the Secretary of Defense; and dozens the President of the United States.

In this book I have selected only a few of these misadventures in national security in order to give the reader an insight into how the Defense Department—and by extension the government —actually works. These incidents, arranged chronologically, also provide an informal history of the years we have just lived through. It is necessarily an extremely incomplete history, since I've chosen episodes which illustrate a point and which are also interesting and informative in themselves. Countless incidents have been left out because they were of too little national significance, such as the leper we discovered in the Secretary of Defense's Mess, or because I was not in the government during the time of action, such as the Bay of Pigs or the Gulf of Tonkin. Thousands have been excluded simply by limitations of space, from developments involving the testing of ICBM re-entry vehicles to the surfacing of one of our submarines under a Red Chinese ship. Many crises I still cannot discuss because of the security clearances I held, although in some such cases (United States activity in Laos, for instance) newsmen are free to nibble at parts of them.

Necessarily, one important type of crisis is omitted from this book. These are the crises about which we in the Office of the Secretary of Defense had no knowledge. The appalling massacre of Mylai is one example and unquestionably others of a different nature in other parts of the world will surface next month or next year. I am not at all sure that the tendency to hide instances of corruption, disaster or grievous human error from one's superiors is more pronounced in the military services than in the Department of Agriculture or a giant nongovernment organization, but I do know that it is too great. The Secretary of Defense and we who were his senior colleagues cannot wash our hands of such tragedies as Mylai by proclaiming that we were unaware of them. The final responsibility for operating the Department must rest with the Secretary and his top associates, and during our tenure we must be held accountable for the entire Department—for the tragedies in making war or keeping peace, and for the failures in the system which permitted news of this nature to remain hidden from higher authorities, either in the field or in the Pentagon. The integrity of internal reporting and investigation must be improved in the Department of Defense. I am not proud of the progress made in this regard while we were in office. It is not the subject of this book, which concentrates on external communications to the people rather than internal communications to the leadership, but it is a subject of great importance to any Assistant Secretary of Defense for Public Affairs, particularly as he confronts crisis.

Not all of the work of the Assistant Secretary of Defense for

Public Affairs is concerned with crisis, however, and neither is all of this book. Chapters on the antiballistic missile, the air war in North Vietnam and the stewardship of Clark Clifford deal more with dissemination of information on major defense issues than with crisis management. The participation of the public in matters of national security is mandatory and an important (if neglected) responsbility of our office was to make available information on which the people could base their thinking.

In both areas—telling the story of crisis and explaining the broader defense issues in a nuclear world—conflict with the press was inevitable. (I apologize to others of the news media for pooling them all together as "press" throughout this book.) The press demands yes or no answers, and it is a good thing for the people that it does. An aggressive press is essential to our democracy; the press unquestionably is the most effective single check-rein on an arrogant government. God forbid that it should become docile, however irritating and irresponsible and inaccurate it sometimes is and however often it deliberately breeds controversy.

The press tends to go to extremes, and the responsible press exhibits extremism in pursuit of truth—which is a virtue. The press wants to know everything. It wants to know now. It will not brook a maybe; it insists upon confirmation or denial. In some chapters of this book are examples of this insistence, and where there are not examples the insistence is implicit. Furthermore, when a rumor or report is loose upon the world, the government often responds in confirm-or-deny terms. Once upon a time the phrase "no comment" was neutral, and while sometimes it is still a useful tool of last resort, its meaning has changed. For example:

"Radio Peking says U.S. aircraft overflew the Red Chinese island of Hainan. Did they or did they not?"

"No comment."

For most of the press and the people (and all of the editorial writers, who may not be either) this meant definitely that we had overflown Hainan and preferred not to admit it. More frequently in today's government, therefore, the initial response would be:

"We are checking into the facts. At this time, we can neither confirm or deny the report."

That would not hold the newsmen for long. They would be back in four hours, or twenty-four, demanding the newest information. What about the overflight? Did we or did we not? Yes or no? Confirm or deny. Most of the time we could oblige, although oftentimes we could not—sometimes for the right reasons and sometimes for the wrong ones. It is as legitimate to refuse to confirm or deny on some occasions as it is illegitimate on others, although the government and press will seldom agree on how to judge a given instance.

That is okay. I hope they never do.

The Chateauroux Carelessness

July, 1965

Common sense should play a part in international relationships, especially between two countries whose international relationship goes back to the eighteenth century. Usually it does, but not always, and when it does not, untidiness is inevitable.

It was on July 17, 1965, that the French publication *Le Monde* printed a story alleging that a United States reconnaissance aircraft had been intercepted by a French jet fighter in a prohibited area above the French atomic plant at Pierrelatte, and forced to land at a nearby field.

I was a brand new official of the United States government, having been sworn in only three months earlier as the Deputy Assistant Secretary of Defense (Public Affairs). One of my jobs was to inform the people of our country about matters of this nature.

Newspapermen in both Washington and Paris, needing and wanting informing, requested facts and explanation. While President Charles de Gaulle indulged in certain eccentricities, it was not at all clear that these warranted United States Air Force reconnaissance flights over his nuclear facilities. After conferring with relevant representatives of the Air Force and the Joint Staff, which is the supporting cast for the Joint Chiefs of Staff, and telephoning military headquarters in Europe for additional information, we were reassured. *Le Monde* was all mixed up. There was nothing to worry about. Confidently, we drafted this statement in the Pentagon and released it simultaneously in Washington and Paris:

According to preliminary information from our authorities in Europe, an American Air Force plane on a pre-arranged flight from Ramstein, Germany, to France and return, was forced to deviate by reason of a thunderstorm from the flight plan previously filed.

The information available indicates that the plane did not enter the prohibited zone around Pierrelatte. We also understand that the American plane was not intercepted by the French planes, but that the latter flew off after identifying the plane as American.

I was particularly anxious for that statement to be accurate, simple and straightforward, since this was my first big chance. Assistant Secretary of Defense Arthur Sylvester, my immediate superior, was in Vietnam with Secretary Robert S. McNamara. In Arthur's absence, I was Acting Assistant Secretary, responsible for all public affairs of the Department of Defense everywhere in the world. Having been on the job only three months, this was the first major story I had handled by myself for my government.

It was a calamity from beginning to end.

For openers, my short statement just didn't do at all. France found it both offensive and unacceptable. The Defense Ministry roared back with a news release of its own, bitter in tone and filled with facts to back it up. The United States aircraft, it said, had made not one but four passes over the Pierrelatte plant, had taken 175 photographs, had been detected by French radar and had been intercepted by a Vautour jet fighter. That interception came, added the Ministry for detail, on the second U.S. pass, after which the American intruder broke away by using its afterburners for a quick burst of acceleration and then returned for two more picture-taking runs. Furthermore, said the Ministry, the reconnaissance plane had been identified by its markings, and its home base at Ramstein had been asked to turn in all its illicit film to French authorities.

As further evidence of their displeasure, which after my

original statement now was divided equally between the incident itself and the crass U. S. denial, the French then escalated by bringing in their Foreign Ministry. An oral protest was delivered by their Political Affairs Director to the second-ranking official in our embassy. Specifically, the United States was charged with flying over a forbidden zone, photographing without authorization and photographing a forbidden zone.

I was incredulous. The best information available to the highest levels of the Department of Defense was that the RF-101 had not flown over a forbidden zone, that it had not photographed such a zone and that it had not photographed without permission.

In my old life, as a reporter covering the Pentagon, I had been accustomed to picking up bits and pieces of information which, on occasion, turned out to be untrue. Rarely does a Washington newsman get a major government news story from one single individual determined to "leak" to the press for his own selfish (he might think patriotic) purposes. Sometimes that happens; sometimes a Presidential Assistant or another official espousing his own cause will sneak a favorite newsman a play-by-play account of a top-level conference, or the contents of a top-secret message, but that is most unusual. Most government officials do not know how to say "no" irrevocably, however, and so a good newsman picks up a scrap here and a scrap there, a scrap from the White House, a scrap from State and a scrap from the Pentagon. Out of these he weaves his story, and then he goes to friends in the House or the Senate, sometimes gushing forth all his information in an attempt to give the impression that he knows everything, and thus loosen the tongue of the Senator or Representative, or sometimes camouflaging his larger purpose and seeking only firm confirmation of one critical link.

Operating this way, a reporter is not surprised when one scrap turns out to be inaccurate or one rumor does not check out. So if I had collected a basketful of Pierrelatte "facts" as a newspaperman, flat contradictions by France would not have shaken me. They simply would have warned me that I had not yet gathered together enough good information. But I was not now a reporter; I did not expect to be in the scraps business; I was reading all the classified cables, talking to all the experts, listening to telephone tapes of conversations between the Joint Staff and officers at Ramstein. I had access to anyone in the United States government with information on the subject and had, as well as my official clout, eighteen years of experience as an interrogator to help get it. It was incredible that France was saying that my information was all wrong.

Eagerly I watched for stories over the wire-service news tickers and waited for the new editions of the newspapers. My faith and trust were in the free press. Friends and past associates in the newspaper business, on both sides of the ocean, would ferret out the truth and prove my statement accurate.

Not quite. Everything that I saw in the newspapers and heard on television indicated that things were just as bad as they seemed.

A French official told the *New York Times* in Paris that this was the first plane that had been caught in the act, but that there was no guarantee others had not performed similar reconnaissance flights in the past.

Waverley Root of the Washington *Post* wrote that it looked as if the United States might have another U-2 incident on its hands, similar to the one which had broken up the Four-Power Summit Conference in Paris.

Several newspapers pointed out the inconsistency between my original statement that the plane had deviated from its flight plan because of a thunderstorm and the sunny weather which permitted such outstanding photography over Pierrelatte. Additional reports from France disclosed that there had not been a thundercloud, let alone a thunderstorm, within a hundred miles of the plant.

The Baltimore *Sun* editorialized that the entire episode had the unreal quality of a nightmare. I bought that.

Root had another quote. The communiqué of the Defense Ministry in Paris, he wrote, listed facts which contradicted flatly almost everything American military and civilian spokesmen had said, officially or unofficially, since the incident occurred.

My confidence shattered, I ran for help to Deputy Secretary of Defense Cyrus R. Vance. It is my belief, shared by many others including Robert S. McNamara and Clark M. Clifford, that no American lives today who is more talented in government than Cyrus Vance. He recommended that we retreat with dignity, recheck our information and release this temporizing announcement:

There was no intent to overfly any prohibited area in France. We are continuing to investigate the matter.

That did little to impede the decay of my morale, but it was of significant assistance in impeding the decay of the Atlantic Alliance.

It was just in time. I had been involved in this international crisis for only a day or two, and major newspapers already were editorializing that President De Gaulle might seize upon the episode as an excuse to cut ties with the North Atlantic Treaty Organization.

That Vance should involve himself in the Pierrelatte imbroglio was fitting enough, for he was more responsible than anyone else for my change from Pentagon poacher to Pentagon gamekeeper, from a Washington reporter watching officials to a Washington official watching reporters.

The events leading to that crossover began almost fifteen years earlier, in 1950, shortly after the *Plain Dealer* sent me from Cleveland—where I had joined the paper as a cub reporter after World War II—to Washington. I was the junior man of a three-man bureau headed by the late Walker S. Buel. Walker was a wonderful individual of great talent, warmth and kindness who treated all men with dignity and graciousness. But he, like other veteran bureau chiefs of that time, was inclined to pluck the best reportorial findings of his younger associates for his own Sunday "think" pieces and his prestigious editorial-page columns. This was his indisputable prerogative; he was my superior, and recognized across the country as one of the top writers in Washington. But it was disturbing to a twenty-nine-year-old rookie, and while I dared not challenge Walker or the system, I did cast about for fields in which he had no personal interest. I found two: fiscal affairs and military affairs. Inasmuch as I cannot today clear fractions and do not comprehend a least common denominator, I began in the early 1950s to cover the Department of Defense on a part-time basis. Most of my work was still on Capitol Hill or with national politics, and all three of us in the bureau wrote White House stories, but I would sneak to the Pentagon when free of other assignments. Missiles and rockets were in the early stages of their development; neither the press nor the people knew much about them; their impact on military strategy, defense budgets and interservice competition was becoming gradually evident; and the field was an interesting one to my editors in Cleveland. Walker, who loved and understood politics and Congress so well, thought I was some kind of a nut, but humored me.

By the fall of 1957, when the first Soviet Sputnik rocked Congress and the nation, I was covering military affairs full time except for presidential nominating conventions and presidential campaigns. For months I attended hearings of the Senate Preparedness Subcommittee, which, after Sputnik, was probing into United States–Soviet Union missile and space strength, and there became friendly with Cyrus Vance, a forty-year-old attorney recruited as Special Counsel of the subcommittee by its chairman, Senator Lyndon B. Johnson.

Three years later, the new president of the Ford Motor Company told the new President-elect of the United States that he could not leave Ford because he lacked sufficient experience in military matters to accept the post of Secretary of Defense. After President-elect Kennedy reminded the industrialist sharply that he was aware of no schools for either Presidents or Secretaries of Defense, Robert McNamara finally said "yes." One condition was that he have a free hand in selecting his top people, and among the top people he selected, as General Counsel of the Department of Defense—one of seven jobs at the Assistant Secretary level—was Vance.

In his massive reorganization of the Department, McNamara never hesitated to go to Congress for a new law, but first he wanted to change what he could under existing statute. For advice on how much built-in reorganization power a Secretary possessed, he turned naturally to his General Counsel. The two men worked more closely together on more subjects more rapidly than would normally be the case, and when Secretary of the Army Elvis J. Stahr left in 1962, McNamara recommended to the President that Vance replace him.

This was a natural step up the ladder. All the highest civilian officials in the Department of Defense are appointees of the President, confirmed by the Senate. In descending order from the top, the Secretary of Defense, come the Deputy Secretary of Defense, the Secretaries of the three military services, the Assistant Secretaries of Defense, the Under Secretaries of the three services and the Assistant Secretaries of the three services. Then come Deputy Assistant Secretaries of Defense, but they are appointees of the Secretary of Defense, not of the President.

The power ladder is constructed about the same way, although within their own specialties the Assistant Secretaries of Defense are more influential than the Secretaries of the Army, Navy and Air Force. Recommendations from the service Secretaries to the Secretary of Defense are analyzed for him by his Assistant Secretaries of Defense, who are part of his personal OSD* family, whose entire loyalty is to him, who work intimately with him, who see much of him and whose judgments often are accepted by the Secretary over those of the services.

---

* The Office of the Secretary of Defense includes the Secretary, Deputy Secretary and all the Assistant Secretaries of Defense and their staffs. OSD does not include the four military services—Army, Navy, Air Force and Marine Corps —all of which are part of the Department of Defense (DoD). Because the services like to maintain their identity, often they use "OSD" and "DoD" interchangeably, leaving the impression that they really are not part of DoD—which, of course, they are. Technically, DoD includes all military and civilian personnel in the entire defense establishment, whereas OSD is the Secretary's private family.

Because the reorganization of the world's largest organization is news, I saw more of Vance than Pentagon reporters customarily would of a General Counsel, traditionally a back-room adviser. We renewed our 1957 acquaintanceship on a professional reporter-official basis, advanced it after he became Secretary of the Army and eventually became friendly enough so that in the fall of 1963 he agreed to take me with him on a personal inspection trip of the Army in Hawaii, Okinawa, Korea and Taiwan.

Richard Fryklund, who covered military affairs for the Washington *Evening Star* and had previously been the *Star's* Paris-based European correspondent, came along also. One of my closest friends, he and I had made a similar trip with Admiral George W. Anderson, Chief of Naval Operations, on his Navy plane two years earlier. For reporters, these private trips were quite worthwhile—not so much in the production of news stories en route as in gaining additional military background and developing friendships and professional associations for the future. Dozens of relaxed hours of serious defense conversations in the airplane were perhaps the most valuable part of these expeditions. Dick Fryklund had been responsible for Admiral Anderson's inviting me on that earlier trip; I was responsible for Secretary Vance's including him. In Washington we worked well together as a team. He had many more contacts with the military establishment, which was interested more in the on-the-scene Washington *Star* than in the distant Cleveland *Plain Dealer*, and I had many more on Capitol Hill, which I had covered so long, and in the White House, since I still was working political conventions and campaigns. The Cleveland *Plain Dealer*, a morning newspaper, and the Washington *Star*, an afternoon publication, were not in competition with one another, so for many years Dick and I formed a profitable unofficial partnership, traveling much of the world together. Dick and I were often confused for each other; we were the same age, height and weight; we were both (then) lean with lean faces, and during the working day were almost always together in the corridors or conducting two-man interviews.

Often on trips in the United States and overseas we had a third associate, Daniel Z. Henkin, editor of what then was the *Journal of the Armed Forces*, a weekly newspaper with a large readership and an excellent reputation among the personnel of the Defense Establishment. Henkin had covered military news longer than any of us, worked harder than any of us and was, in my view, the best newspaperman in the Pentagon press room. However immodestly, we three considered ourselves among the best, and were regarded by the Establishment as among the most irreverent in sniffing out secrets.

On something like the Vance trip, however, Dick and I behaved circumspectly, passing up hard spot "inside" news stories which would cause trouble for our host and attempting instead to benefit professionally from our association with him. There always would be time later, under different circumstances, to put to use the information we did not push into print during the trip—although some information, received in con-fidence as a courtesy from Vance, or because we were with Vance, we kept in confidence indefinitely.

As part of the Taiwan visit, Dick and I flew across the Taiwan Straits with Vance for a day on the offshore island of Quemoy, the most heavily fortified garrison in the world, which is closer to the Communist mainland than Alexandria, Virginia, is to Washington. At luncheon with the commanding general, we all three were exposed for the first time to the local beverage called kaoliang. Intending no disrespect to our gracious Chinese hosts, if I am to avoid my own personal credibility gap I must describe kaoliang as a 180-proof blend of turpentine, ammonia and iodine, with an odor of rancid sheep.

Perhaps no single thing, however, played as important a part in the change in my life. In addition to the kaoliang we chug-a-lugged at the luncheon table responding to the "Gom Bai" salute from our Chinese hosts (a dreadfully unfair game, with

each of twelve hosts toasting each of three guests separately, so
that at the end of the luncheon the hosts had chug-a-lugged only
three glasses and the guests twelve), the Chinese gave us each
a bottle to take home.

Shortly after returning to Washington, Dick and Dorothy
Fryklund held a survivors' party at their Virginia home. While
Mrs. Cyrus Vance had accompanied us on most of the trip, the
other wives had not, and Gay Vance had missed the day on
Quemoy. It was inevitable that night that we share the taste of
kaoliang with the ladies, all of whom were too intelligent to
have more than one swallow. Even kaoliang should not be
wasted, however, and it was after having done my share to
prevent such waste, at perhaps one o'clock in the morning, that
I mentioned to Cyrus that it might someday be interesting to
work for a time in the Department of Defense.

Vance later took one more step up the ladder and replaced
Roswell L. Gilpatric as Deputy Secretary of Defense, the Number Two man in the Pentagon. Some time thereafter he telephoned, asking whether I had been serious that night and if I
would have lunch with McNamara and himself.

Out of that luncheon came my personal decision that I would
leave the newspaper business for the Department of Defense,
although the specific position and the timing of the change were
left open. I was not in a hurry to join the government; I still was
enjoying newspaper work, although less so than previously, and
did not intend to quit it for any work other than in the Department of Defense. But in the spring of 1965, when the incumbent Deputy Assistant Secretary for Public Affairs, Nils A.
Lennartson, who had spent years in top-level information posts
in Commerce, Treasury and Defense, under both Republican and
Democratic administrations, left the Pentagon for a lucrative job
in the outside world, I was asked to fill that vacancy by Mc-
Namara, Vance, and Arthur Sylvester.

Vance and I now were strong friends. Arthur Sylvester and I
had been arguing politics as newspaper colleagues since 1950—

he had been Washington Bureau Chief of the Newark News
before the election of his friend, John F. Kennedy. I knew
McNamara only slightly, as any "regular" member of the Pentagon press corps knows a Secretary of Defense. He had heard
me ask questions at news conferences for four years, I had
interviewed him several times in his office and we had chatted
socially at large Washington parties. On several occasions he had
been in our home for private working dinners with Dick Fryklund, Dan Henkin and three or four other Pentagon reporters.

While we had come to know one another better by midsummer, I was not comfortable in our association until after
Sylvester had gone on vacation and McNamara was, of necessity,
dealing with me alone. Our relationship grew stronger over the
next eighteen months and changed significantly after I became
Assistant Secretary in February, 1967. In McNamara's final
eight lonely months, after Vance had left the Pentagon and
Assistant Secretary of Defense John T. McNaughton was killed
in an airplane crash, we became particularly close. Those two
had been his right and left arms for several years, and the
shock of losing both at the same time was a painful one.

But that came later. Kaoliang and Cyrus Vance, more than
McNamara, were responsible for the fact that I was Acting
Assistant Secretary of Defense that July of 1965.

After we had completed the initial review of Pierrelatte
facts which Vance had recommended, our own Department of
State moved in, horrified by the havoc wrought by the Department of Defense in general and the new Deputy Assistant
Secretary in particular. After several days of consultation between
State and Defense officials, in Washington and in Europe, State
issued a statement regretting the United States' inadvertent
violation of French flight regulations that had occurred during a
routine training flight. State announced also that the French
government considered the incident closed.

The temptation to join the diplomats in making believe that
the incident had never happened was towering. I was lying awake

nights, snapping at my wife and children, considering whether a golden retriever was too large to kick and becoming increasingly nostalgic about those halcyon days as a reporter.

But I had not yet been with the government long enough to have learned that you cannot refight yesterday's problems. My reportorial curiosity was too much for me. On reflection, a cowardly compromise appeared the best solution. Publicly, let the incident be closed if State wanted it that way, but privately I would continue to collect facts. We could not be as wrong as the record seemed to show.

While it took time to retrace our steps and start again, we finally pieced together the entire story from beginning to end, and finally I understood why two friendly and honorable governments were so at odds with each other in their public statements.

Among the issues were the thunderstorm, the prohibited zone, our justification for describing the flight as prearranged, whether the plane had been intercepted and why we believed the photography had been authorized.

This is what we learned:

Several years before the Pierrelatte incident, several U. S. military aircraft elements assigned to NATO, including reconnaissance units, were stationed in France. Under agreement with the French, the reconnaissance planes routinely conducted training missions involving photography of the terrain. This procedure was continued, with full French approval, after De Gaulle asked us to vacate the bases and we moved our aircraft to England and West Germany.

Such missions were not covert. Flight plans were filed with French civil aeronautics authorities if the missions were in France, whether the aircraft were based in France, England or West Germany. Similar procedures are followed for our own country, where military as well as commercial aircraft are under jurisdiction of the Federal Aviation Agency.

On July 16, 1965, an RF-101 supersonic jet of the 38th Tactical Reconnaissance Squadron based at Ramstein was scheduled to fly a routine photographic training mission over West Germany. Because of thunderstorms over that target area, that mission was canceled and another planned instead over the Rhone River Valley of France.

In accordance with French requirements, a flight plan was filed three hours before departure. It declared that the pilot would proceed from Ramstein west across the French border to Chaumont, France; on to Lyon, and then to a point at Pierrelatte—44 degrees, 30 minutes North latitude; 04 degrees, 50 minutes East longitude. After conducting north-south reconnaissance runs at low altitude within a radius of fifteen miles from that point, he would retrace the route back to Ramstein.

Normally, that flight plan would have been transmitted from Ramstein to Frankfurt Flight Service, a West German Air Traffic Control Center, for relay to France. But a fire had shut down the Frankfurt facility temporarily, so the plan was telephoned instead to an air base at Chateauroux, France. While the U. S. aircraft formerly based at Chateauroux were gone, the base still was manned by U. S. personnel, who relayed the flight plan to French Air Traffic Control by teletype. Chateauroux was merely a retransmission point, called into emergency service because the fire had disabled the West German center.

But the personnel at Chateauroux erred, though their error was not very big. They simply dropped one sentence of the message they were relaying, and that omission was the major cause of the international incident. What Chateauroux omitted was the sentence taking the reconaissance aircraft from Lyon to the point at 44 degrees, 30 minutes North; 04 degrees, 50 minutes East—the point at Pierrelatte.

Chateauroux picked up the next sentence, advising the French of the plan to fly four reconnaissance sweeps within a fifteen-mile area, and retransmitted the rest of the flight plan accurately. The French who received it could not know that it was incomplete, and the people at Chateauroux, having done their job, did not recheck the outgoing teletype message to France against the incoming telephone message from Ramstein.

And that was why, in the days to come, the United States was so often to say "Yes-we-did" while the French were insisting "No-you-didn't." The news stories were to be splashed over the front pages of the major newspapers of these two countries and many others. The motives of both nations were to be analyzed on network television and scrutinized by the editorial writers. The elected representatives of the people in both were to demand explanations. The responsibility, credibility and common sense of the President of the United States, the Secretary of State and the Secretary of Defense were all to be questioned.

The Chateauroux carelessness was a costly one, and especially so because no one anywhere was aware of it during the first two or three days, when statements were being exchanged and the positions of the two governments were hardening into cement.

Flying his mission precisely as planned, the pilot of the RF-101 made all his flight reports by radio to the French as required. These included a pre-entry check with French military radar, which, he knew, was tracking him the entire time he was in France, as it always did, to help to check the system and train the personnel. En route to Pierrelatte, he knew that the radar had him all the way. He descended from altitude to the training area in clear weather and followed his flight plan as filed, confident that French authorities knew exactly what he was doing, and wholly unconcerned. In this crowded European air, he would have been alarmed, in fact, had he thought French radar and French Air Traffic Control did not know where he was.

One of the four photo runs was over the town of Pierrelatte. The pilot's charts were before him, and neither Pierrelatte nor any terrain beneath his reconnaisance sweeps was shown on them as prohibited or restricted. On his second photo pass he noticed a Vautour fighter plane on his left wing but did not give it another thought. While low, at 2,500 feet, his altitude was safe, and he was not deviating from the filed flight plan. The two pilots did not communicate. (Nor, the American pilot insisted later, did he use his power-increasing afterburner at this stage, despite French charges to the contrary.)

Upon completion of four scheduled runs the RF-101 returned to Ramstein, openly, maintaining all required radio checks with the French ground controllers. He had no cause for stealth; he had been on a routine training flight. Unaware of the flight plan snafu, he was shocked at the commotion he caused. Unaware that there had been a flight plan snafu, the American press was shocked that the United States government had attempted this spying, shocked that it had been caught, shocked that it had then tried to lie its way out and shocked that it had been caught in those lies.

I did not then, and could not now, blame the press. Over the next four years I misled and misinformed the American people a good many times in a good many ways—through my own lack of foresight, through carelessness, through relaying incomplete information which the originators considered complete, through transmitting reports which had been falsified deliberately at lower levels. But I never intentionally deceived the people, and Pierrelatte illustrates better than any incident I know how a series of innocent errors and misunderstandings on the part of two governments can cause a flaming international controversy, and how wrong governments can be when they think they are right.

The first Pierrelatte misunderstanding was over the thunderstorm. Pentagon officers of the Joint Staff, inquiring at my request, were told by Air Force officers at Ramstein that thunderstorms had caused a deviation from the original planned mission. Ramstein meant that storms in West Germany had pushed the mission into France; Washington thought thunderstorms in France had pushed it over Pierrelatte. Human error in communications? Of course. Government inaccuracy? Of course. Misleading of the people? Of course. Deliberate deceit? No.

A second misunderstanding was the flight plan. The French kept insisting, at all levels through their Defense and Foreign Ministries, that our plan had made no reference whatever to Pierrelatte or any point in the vicinity of Pierrelatte. And they were right. Washington kept insisting, after repeated guarantees from Ramstein, that the flight plan told exactly where the aircraft was going, including the Pierrelatte area. And we were right. As dispatched by Ramstein the plan referred to Pierrelatte; as received by France it did not.

This same flight plan mix-up affected the dispute over authorization of photography. Photographic reconnaissance aircraft earn their living in only one way: producing photographs. From our point of view, and in the wake of years of routine operating practices, the flight plan had designated where the plane was to conduct its mission, and we assumed no French objection. From their point of view, approval of the flight plan authorized photography over Lyon, but not over Pierrelatte.

A major misunderstanding, compounded by coincidence and confusion, was over the "prohibited area" issue. Few persons realized—and we did not at the outset—that there were not one but two French nuclear facilities in the Rhone Valley, within twenty miles of one another! One was the Pierrelatte plant, the other at Marcoule.

Pierrelatte was not shown as prohibited or restricted on any chart or publication held at Ramstein, nor on any we could track down later in the Pentagon. Additionally, the Pierrelatte area was not designated as prohibited on the international charts used by commercial airlines; our people borrowed a set from offices at Washington National Airport to check. Commercial airliners, in fact, overflew Pierrelatte routinely on the established French airway between Marseille and Lyon.

Marcoule, however, designated as area "P-59" on the charts, was marked as a prohibited zone.

The RF-101 came no closer than six miles to Marcoule—and did not photograph it. The plane flew directly over Pierrelatte—and did photograph it. Our cameras did take pictures of a French atomic plant, and French charges that we had done so were accurate. Our cameras did not take pictures of an atomic plant in a prohibited zone, and French accusations that we had done so were erroneous. (Because we could not accept France's statements on this point, the apology issued by our State Department regretted general "inadvertent violation of French flight regulations" but did not refer to flying in a prohibited zone.)

The misunderstanding over whether the reconnaissance plane had been intercepted was merely a matter of semantics. Our pilot did not consider that he had been intercepted and, when questioned, denied any interception. The French chose to consider that an intercept had taken place when their aircraft flew briefly alongside ours.

The United States did not want or need photography of the gaseous diffusion plant at Pierrelatte. Whether local Air Force officers should have chosen any atomic facility in a foreign nation as a practice target for reconnaissance is questionable, and had the operations people asked their own information officer, he would have advised them to pick a brick plant instead. Technically, the Air Force could argue that the zone was not prohibited, that its intent had been spelled out clearly in an unclassified flight plan, that it had kept in touch with all necessary French elements according to France's own requirements during every bit of the mission, and that low-level passes of an RF-101 scarcely could be regarded as furtive. Still, a brick plant would have been an admirable target. However valid the Air Force case, it is difficult to see how one nation can improve relationships with another nation by flying over its atomic plants and popping pictures of them.

After discovering all these facts, as a new government official who had jeered full time from the sidelines at Pentagon duplicity for eight years and at the duplicity of the federal government in general for fifteen, I found the Pierrelatte case a shocking experience.

While it is now a humorous memory, as one's first bumbling ski lessons become humorous memories in time, the RF-101 episode was not, in July, 1965, funny at all. For the first time I learned of the enormous difference between speaking for yourself and speaking for the United States government. Every newspaper reporter learns the same kind of lesson in a smaller way when he first sees his opinions or predictions in large type beneath a 72-point, eight-column headline and realizes that writing a story for the world to read is not the same as expressing a viewpoint to friends in a living room. He has committed not only himself but also his publication. As a reporter, I had been dreadfully wrong in very large type. The embarrassment and chagrin on some of these occasions had been great, but not comparable with the lonely, inconsolable feeling of one who has misrepresented the United States government.

And yet, reconstructing the case later, it appeared that the disastrous results had come about despite the fact that we seemed to have done everything right those first few days.

We did not go off half-cocked in the public affairs office, rushing to defend "our" Air Force, "our" Pentagon or "our" government at whatever cost. We did not delegate critical assignments to lower echelons. It was a quiet Saturday, I had not been aboard long enough to be enmeshed deeply in administrative activity, the work-generating Secretary of Defense was out of town and the military world was relatively inactive. The men with whom I worked in the Pentagon, both on the Joint Staff and in the Air Force, were high-ranking officers who were intimately concerned with the problem, and who knew all about our NATO reconnaissance squadrons in Europe and how they trained.

Additionally, we were not combating Communist propaganda. Disputes such as these were always complicated when we were accused of something by the North Vietnamese, the North Koreans or the Red Chinese, because they would not only lie flagrantly but would try to falsify evidence to support their lies. (I found during my forty-five months in the government that the Soviet Union was much more apt to tell the truth in charges of this nature.) But neither the United States nor France deliberately deceived one another or their people over Pierrelatte. Each acted on the basis of information considered reliable. A major problem, of course, was that some of that information, on both sides, was erroneous. It was my first lesson in skepticism about reports from the field. As a reporter covering the Pentagon for years, I had assumed that the vast communications network and the twenty-four-hour-a-day military operation rapidly yielded accurate and complete information to the Department's top officials. How high officials had interpreted that information before giving it to the press had concerned me, but I had given little thought to the possibility that the Secretary of Defense and his top advisers would find information hard to come by—or that it might be wrong.

Much information put before the Secretary of Defense is apt to be wrong, I was to learn, and first reports are always wrong— or are so often wrong that they always must be considered suspect.

By the time all the facts were assembled—in fact, before all the facts were assembled—France and the United States had reached the common agreement that the incident was closed. Many of the details had not been released, but the verdict of both governments was to play the rest in as low key as possible and get on with more important and less inflammatory business. From that point forward, both governments put themselves into a public affairs fairyland and, by their joint silence, sort of made believe that there had never been such an incident. If it had ever happened, surely that must have been a long time ago.

As an official, I could understand that international decision. The United States had erred, had publicly admitted the error and had apologized for it. By closing the case, it was not attempting to avoid responsibility for its past actions or to hide its mistakes. On the contrary, the information that was not disclosed would have helped show that the Department of Defense was not as hapless as France had pictured it.

As a reporter, I would not have accepted meekly that position. I would have argued that the government had an obligation to put all the facts before the American people, whether or not the Foreign Ministry of France and the United States State Department wanted it that way. Mistakes obviously had been made in the Pierrelatte case—perhaps serious mistakes. The public had no way of knowing whether identical or similar mistakes might be repeated, under even graver conditions. The government's duty,

I would have said, was to reveal all the details, along with a list of the actions taken to prevent repetition of the same kind of error. Full disclosure was the major issue, not the temporary temper of our relationship with France.

And as a government official I would have answered the reporter by noting that appropriate committees of Congress, representing the people, were being given all the facts. Congress could ensure that the Executive Branch took necessary steps to prevent this kind of incident from happening again. Making public all the facts at that time unquestionably would have further aroused the French, forced them to reopen the case, brought about another barrage of bitter news releases, inflamed the sensitivities of their people and further irritated an international relationship which then was a tender one—particularly in regard to important NATO decisions directly ahead.

It is my view that the government should weigh such factors in arriving at its public affairs decisions. In determining what information is to be made public, the government must and does take into account the effect the release of that information will have on sovereign states which are friendly to us, allied with us, neutral about us, potentially hostile or outright enemies.

This is a fact of twentieth-century nuclear life. It was true in the Republican administration of President Eisenhower and the Democratic administrations of Presidents Kennedy and Johnson. It will be true in President Nixon's administration and that of his successor.

News media people who demand maximum candor under all circumstances except those which clearly involve "military security" may object strenuously to that truth, but their objections will not change it. "National security," determined at times by the Secretary of State, the Secretary of Defense or the President, will prevail within the government. Not all decisions in this regard will be unanimous. Internal debates will take place over whether the national interest will be benefited more by following Course A and releasing certain information or by following

Course B and withholding it. Sometimes, as when Robert Mc-
Namara decided to release highly classified information on strategic nuclear weapons, it will be judged that deliberate disclosure
of top-secret information will most advance the national interest.
And sometimes, as in the case of Pierrelatte, the government
will attempt to shut the door softly.

Whether the press permits it to do so is another matter, and
this is up to the press. The conflict between press and government is not only natural but essential. But the fact that the
press should keep on fighting for more information does not
mean that the government should always produce it or that the
best interest of the country is always advanced by total disclosure,
when another nation is involved.

From my personal standpoint, the government could not have
stopped disclosing information in the Pierrelatte case at a worse
point. I would much rather have kept it flowing until all the misunderstandings, misinterpretations, communications errors and
facts were before the people. My top-priority private goal those
first few weeks was to establish myself with my long-time friends
in the Pentagon press room and with associates in hundreds of
news bureaus across the river in Washington as the one person
in government who understood their problems, the one person
with whom they could deal, the one person who would try to
shovel out the last grain of unclassified information and who,
through close friendship with Cyrus Vance and proximity to
Robert McNamara, would greatly influence Department of Defense news policies.

It is, I hope, an exaggeration to say that after Pierrelatte no
newsman ever believed me again, but certainly enormous progress
was made in that direction. I had been in office only three months
and, over one weekend, my love affair with the Pentagon press
room had ended. Even Fryklund and Henkin sneered, and I
informed my children, who had listened their entire lives to
criticism of the government and defense of the newspapers, that
the press was no damned good.

Nonetheless, I feel the government acted wisely in agreeing with France that the best interests of both nations were served by considering the Pierrelatte incident closed.

More intense than my newly conceived feelings against my lifelong profession at this time was a sympathy for Assistant Secretary of Defense Arthur Sylvester, a forlorn wish that he had never gone away and a fervent hope for his safe and rapid return. As I viewed the record, everyone had lost by the way we handled the Pierrelatte case in his absence.

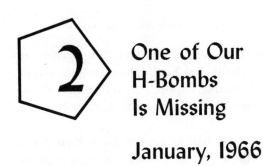

One of Our H-Bombs Is Missing

January, 1966

While the umbilical cord stretching from my career as a newsman to my new life as a government official was cut by the Pierrelatte affair, it was more of a personal disaster than anything else. Additional credibility points were lost by both the Department of Defense and President Johnson's administration, and my virginal reputation was besmirched, but it was not an event which had a lasting national impact.

The chief lessons I learned were that I could not in this new business abandon the skepticism developed over so many years in the old, and that we in our office should resist pressure from any source—press, President or political partisan; friendly foreign nation or potential enemy—to speak out too quickly. I had not learned, however, that at times we would not speak out at all, and that equal or greater dangers to credibility were created by that policy.

Robert McNamara used to say that when he took office President Kennedy gave him two instructions. One was to develop the military force structure necessary to support our foreign policy without regard to arbitrary budget ceilings. The second was to procure and operate that force at the lowest possible cost.

The role that the Secretary of Defense must play in the international issues of the nuclear age leaves him little time to carry out such instructions. A Secretary today must manage the $75- or $80-billion-a-year kingdom over which he reigns, while on his desk are problems involving the war in Vietnam, the situation in the Middle East, crises in Berlin and Korea, decisions concerning NATO and the Nuclear Planning Group, preparations for strategic arms talks with the Soviet Union and ratification of the non-proliferation treaty.

McNamara spent more than half of his day on foreign policy matters in which the Pentagon had an interest, working with the Secretary of State, the President and his own advisers. He was in the Pentagon until after eight o'clock most nights, after beginning the day at an outrageous 7:15 A.M. Saturday was a normal work day.

Because he is so busy, and the decisions before him so important, no Secretary of Defense seeks additional challenges. None needs his name in eight-column headlines or welcomes page-one stories which draw the attention of the Congress, the people or the political opposition to a new problem. When the seventy-five hour Secretarial work week is interrupted, therefore, by an unexpected emergency of some import—the accidental over-flight of a Red Chinese island, the collision at sea of a United States destroyer and a Soviet ship, the bombing of a Russian freighter in North Vietnam, the shelling of an American ship by the armed forces of a friend—it is understandable that the instinctive reaction of any Secretary of Defense as he instructs his Assistant Secretary for Public Affairs is the same: "Play it in low key."

The press believes that the government would like to sweep many of its troubles under the rug, and the press, of course, is right. No one needs more trouble than he already has, and we always had a basketful. A Secretary of Defense naturally feels that the news incident reported in three paragraphs on page 26 is less troublesome than the one stretching across page 1 in 72-point type. In the mind of any Secretary of Defense persists the thought that if only his public affairs office could announce the bad news softly enough—preferably in a sort of whisper—not many would hear it.

The nature of the problem does not affect this reflex reaction to handle bad news in this fashion. The Secretary of Defense knows that the Pentagon must disclose that another F-111 aircraft has crashed, but in announcing it he hopes his public affairs people will play it in low key. A drunken Marine in Puerto Rico has just punched an elderly Congressman in the mouth? Play it in low key. A drone aircraft from Eglin Air Force Base has gone berserk and is headed for Havana? Play it in low key. A submarine in the Gulf of Tonkin has surfaced right under a Communist merchant ship? Yes, we must tell the press—but play it in low key. United States forces are landing in the Dominican Republic? . . .

Incidents of this kind were typical, and a week never passed—indeed, a day rarely passed—when somewhere around the world in the Defense Establishment there was not an out-of-the-ordinary event, seldom as important as the American landing in the Dominican Republic but invariably more important than the assault upon a Congressman by a weaving Marine. On January 17, 1966, we did not know what to expect, but we did know there would be something because there always was.

Certainly Arthur Sylvester and I were not drumming up any new business. Congress was back, a supplemental Southeast Asian defense budget for $12 billion had gone to Capitol Hill and a new record-high military budget for the next fiscal year was soon to be submitted. We were about to announce the development of the Minuteman III intercontinental ballistic missile, a pause in the bombing of North Vietnam was coming to an end, and it was rumored in the press that our commitment of 190,000 men in South Vietnam was being raised to 400,000. A retired lieutenant general named James M. Gavin had an appointment to see McNamara about a new way to fight the war from enclaves. The intelligence community was perplexed over the turmoil in Red China. We had just disclosed the presence of nine North Vietnamese regiments in South Vietnam.

While all of this was rather standard fare, and while it would have been abnormal had not some special event taken place, Sylvester and I were not anticipating that Monday that the United States would lose four of its hydrogen bombs. Curiously enough, our office was nonetheless prepared for just such a bizarre happening.

A public affairs plan for the mislaying of thermonuclear weapons had been drafted and approved, with contributors from the Strategic Air Command, the Defense Atomic Support Agency, the Special Assistant to the Secretary of Defense (Atomic Energy), the Joint Staff, the Air Force Director of Nuclear Safety and our own office.

Precise wording had been worked out to describe the danger—or lack of danger—of a thermonuclear explosion in the event a bomber crashed carrying hydrogen weapons, to explain the types of explosions which could take place on or near the ground from the detonation of fuel elements or other non-nuclear materials, and to define radioactive material. Precise wording also covered such matters as plutonium particles, the hazards if these particles were introduced into the digestive and respiratory tracts and the absence of hazards if they were not.

None of this was propaganda or press agentry. The United States government's obligation to inform the people under such circumstances was clear to all. Every word of every statement had been agreed upon by the scientists, nuclear safety experts and physician specialists. After they had drafted the original statements, their gobbledegook had been translated and rewritten into language the citizens could understand—and that language was then scrubbed up again by the experts to ensure that nothing misleading had crept in during the rewriting.

Our public affairs plan included not only specific approved wording of a great many announcements, but also agreed-upon procedures on which level of government would make which announcements. It was geared to one objective: the delivery of accurate and rapid information to the American people, within security limitations. Not every Department of Defense decision is a wise one, but it would take some kind of special nut to play games with the people over the chances of thermonuclear explosions or the dangers from radioactive particles.

Thousands of man-hours had been spent on the plan, which

was an excellent one. All of it had been accomplished prior to my arrival in the government, so I could view it with some objectivity. And having been out of the newspaper business for only a few months, I was still able to regard it with a critical reportorial rather than fatherly bureaucratic eye.

Unfortunately, our detailed professional public affairs plan on how to inform the people if we lost one or more of our hydrogen bombs, and especially how to educate the people in the immediate vicinity of the loss, was incomplete in one major respect. It assumed that we would mislay them within the continental limits of the United States; it did not foresee that we would drop them into someone else's back yard.

The first announcement of the accident which caused the problem was a short one, released by the Sixteenth Air Force in Spain, after Ambassador Angier Biddle Duke had coordinated it with the Spanish Foreign Office. In it were no hints of real trouble; it said simply, in the lowest key possible:

A B52 bomber from the 68th Bomb Wing at Seymour-Johnson Air Force Base, North Carolina, and a KC 135 tanker from the 910th Air Refueling Squadron at Bergstrom Air Force Base, Texas, crashed today southwest of Cartagena, Spain, during scheduled air operations.

There are reports of some survivors from the crews of the aircraft.

An Air Force Accident Investigation Team has been dispatched to the scene. Additional details will be available as the investigation progresses.

Tragedy for Air Force families was in that announcement, as in any crash where lives are lost, and interest within the Strategic Air Command was high, for B-52s and tankers should not collide during refueling. But it was not regarded as a major news story by the press because there was no mention by the government of the news that was of international import: the bomber carried nuclear weapons, and we had not recovered them. We were not privileged to disclose this information, however, because Spain did not want us to.

From an operational standpoint, the cooperation of Spanish officials for the next eighty days was to be outstanding—cooperation without which we could never have recovered our H-bombs. The Franco government was patient and understanding, despite the misery we had brought upon it. But from the standpoint of informing the public, that government was to be a major problem until the day when the final missing weapon was retrieved from a depth of 2,850 feet 6 miles off the coast in the largest sea-recovery operation in history.

Spain taught us things we had never dreamed of about playing it in low key—most of the time so low that the sound could not be heard at all. And we were stuck with it, for the United States had reached the policy decision that we would handle this matter publicly as the Spanish wanted it handled. The public affairs policy of the United States Department of Defense on a major international news event was controlled to a large degree by a foreign government.

Having been in the Pentagon only a few months, I was at first furious at how we were putting ourselves at the mercy of another government, particularly one which I would not have selected as the global model for freedom of speech, freedom of information and other democratic principles. When I left the newspaper business to work for McNamara, Vance and Sylvester, I was confident that we could defeat the "credibility gap" issue—chiefly by leveling with the press on all occasions. While realizing that there would be times when national security demanded a "No comment," I promised myself that these times would be rare so far as the Department of Defense was concerned. Yet now the State Department was insisting that a Spanish dictatorship have veto power over information disseminated by Sylvester's office on the biggest news story in the world. This was preposterous!

After talking to more experienced associates and listening to my counterparts at State, however, I agreed that the decision forced on us probably was logical and fair—and definitely was unavoidable. The cost to the United States was high, particularly in terms of credibility, but the payment of that price did not mean that the decision was wrong.

So far as I know, the United States is the only nation ever to have misplaced any of its hydrogen bombs. I do not recall any publicity on missing British weapons, but let us assume for a moment that the British were so careless as to drop one or two of their hydrogen bombs in, on or a few miles seaward of the downtown East Ninth Street pier in Cleveland.

Would the Mayor of Cleveland, the Governor of Ohio and the President of the United States stand back and permit the British to handle the announcements as the Prime Minister and his Minister of Defence felt best? Obviously not; Clevelanders were exposed and involved, not Yorkshiremen. The health and welfare of Clevelanders were America's business; America would advise and inform the inhabitants of Cleveland in the time, place and manner of its own choosing—not of Britain's choosing.

Spain demanded the same privilege, and the United States acquiesced, simply treating Spain as we would have expected to be treated if the situation had been reversed. This did not mean that the United States accepted each Spanish suggestion for a news release. Scores of conferences were held in Madrid and Washington; compromises were sometimes developed; our diplomats occasionally were able to move their position from Point A to Point B. While we did agree to make no announcement to which Spain objected, we would not release erroneous information.

For all practical purposes, however, Spain called the shots for eighty days. It was deeply frustrating, and perhaps the most frustrating thing was that we could not explain to the press why we were so close-mouthed and uncooperative. This was because Spain set three objectives for itself during the episode: to soften the concern of its own people (particularly in Palomares), to avert the discouragement of tourism and to present to all nations a picture of close cooperation with America. To help Spain achieve that third goal, Sylvester was asked by his counterpart at State to do everything he could to avoid blaming the Spanish government for our silence. We were not to tell the press that we were releasing only as much information as the Spanish

wanted us to put out about the missing weapons and the search
for them. Finger-pointing of this kind, State said, would destroy
the image of sympathetic understanding and assistance Spain
wanted to create.

While the decision was destined from the outset to reflect
adversely upon the Department of Defense, this was an international matter on which State's view prevailed. It created
some internal administrative problems, since not many military commanders were prepared to take the kind of heat for a
top-level public affairs decision that Sylvester always took, or
that I later attempted to take (with less success, since I was less
courageous). In the military services, information officers usually
do a far better job of protecting Washington on matters of this
kind than do their commanders, because they are more accustomed to abuse from the press, less frightened by threats of
overbearing reporters and less anxious than their star-wearing
seniors to win the goodwill of influential newsmen.

Sylvester's instructions to the military, therefore, simply informed them that no announcements would be made without
prior approval by our office and ordered them to refuse to discuss the episode with anyone. Even in internal classified messages
we did not refer to the fact that the silence ban had been directed
by Spain.

As Deputy Assistant Secretary of Defense, I was not very much
in the line of fire on this one, but Arthur Sylvester honored the
State Department request until the end, never moving to defend himself against press attacks aimed at "our" incredible
policy.

Relative silence on major points was to continue for weeks,
and the information we did not release rapidly to the American
people during those weeks was considerable. Not until three days
after the crash did we even acknowledge that the bomber was
carrying nuclear weapons. Our official secrecy on this essential
point was world-wide. The Strategic Air Command had no comment in Omaha; SAC's Sixteenth Air Force headquarters had no
comment at Torrejón Air Force Base outside Madrid; the Air

Force and the Office of the Secretary of Defense had no comment in the Pentagon. We knew that we had lost four hydrogen
bombs, that we had found three and that one was still missing,
but our answer to all questions about whether bombs had been
aboard was "No comment." We felt terribly foolish saying it.

Our silence did not, of course, prevent news stories from being
written. Reporters could see the search activity going on, and, inevitably, there were some unofficial leaks. On January 19 the
United Press International filed this story from Palomares:

The U.S. Air Force was searching the Spanish countryside tonight,
reportedly seeking an atomic device missing after Monday's collision
of a B52 bomber and a jet tanker.

U.S. officials in Madrid and at the scene refused to confirm or deny
that a nuclear bomb was carried by the B52 which crashed into the
KC135 jet tanker during a refueling mission over Spain.

Hundreds of U.S. troops were searching the scene, some of them
armed with Geiger counters. When asked what the Geiger counters
were for, an information officer said: "What are Geiger counters
normally used for?"

It was understood on good authority that the B52 carried several
atomic devices and that all but one of them had been accounted for
after the crash, which killed seven men.

Other American bombers carrying defused nuclear bombs have
crashed without incident in the past in the United States. Nuclear
scientists have said repeatedly that a nuclear bomb aboard a plane
cannot be detonated until it is armed, even on the impact of a crash.

(In Washington, the Defense Department said: "We have no
comment on the report.")

We sent an immediate message to the Air Force commander
to gag his gabby information officer.

Members of the Pentagon press were disgruntled. They told
Sylvester and me that it was impossible for us to make believe
that the B-52 had carried no bombs or that none was lost when
an army of soldiers and airmen was hauling Geiger counters
through the countryside. We agreed that our position was rather
extraordinary, but we agreed to nothing else.

The newsmen had no way of knowing that we, more than they, were fighting within the government for announcements about nuclear weapons and radiation procedures. They did not know that we kept pressing State, or that State kept pressing Ambassador Duke, or that he kept pressing the Spanish Foreign Office—nor were we to tell them. The international relations of the United States need not and cannot all be conducted in public. It was not the Spanish government which had splattered hydrogen bombs over the landscape, but the United States government. If the method chosen by Spain for handling its people was difficult and embarrassing for us, that was unfortunate. If thousands of man-hours of advance public affairs planning on informing the people about the chances of nuclear explosion, dangers of radioactivity or hazards to health in precisely such a case as this were wasted, that was unfortunate. If the flow of information to the American people was stopped temporarily, that was particularly unfortunate. But it does not follow that the government of this country should therefore have ignored the desires of another government on this issue.

There were, of course, practical as well as ethical aspects to the silence decision. Our primary objective was to recover missing hydrogen bombs lost on or near Spanish soil, and it was impossible to do so without the consent and cooperation of Spain. This was understood by both governments. No one in the Madrid Foreign Office needed to say: "Do it our way or you do not do it at all," but it was an obvious truth. In the background was an additional consideration. Spain was no longer as enthusiastic as it had once been about permitting us to keep our air bases there.

After three days of conferences, concurrence from Spain was obtained finally for one additional paragraph, released by the embassy in Madrid. This contained the first official word that the B-52 had been carrying nuclear weapons, a victory for Sylvester and our office, but in the final version of the announcement no mention was made that any H-bombs were missing, a defeat for our efforts. The statement read:

The SAC bomber which was engaged in a refueling operation off the coast of Spain and suffered an accident with a KC135 tanker was carrying unarmed nuclear armament. Radiological surveys have established that there is no danger to public health or safety as a result of this accident.

As time passed, the wrath of much of the press corps turned into incredulity and the incredulity into disgust. While the reporters had always known that the government was not very bright, rarely had they seen a better example of its arrested development. Everyone in the civilized world knew that we were looking for one or more hydrogen bombs, but the Department of Defense and the rest of the United States government refused to acknowledge it. No possible sense could be made of this. Our bomber had collided with our tanker, our hydrogen bombs had been aboard, some clearly were missing and we owed the people of the United States the facts. To the press, the case was as simple as that.

Sylvester hung on gallantly to protect the government decision, however, and our office continued to remind the rest of the military establishment that the orders were to say nothing. The Air Force, particularly the Strategic Air Command, cooperated commendably. Under the leadership of Secretary Harold Brown, and the Chief of Staff, General J. P. McConnell, the Air Force, in fact, invariably cooperated commendably on public affairs matters.

A second price for our policy of silence, beyond the congealing of the reportorial view that we were arrogant idiots and that the Johnson administration was not worthy of public trust, was the misinformation which appeared in the newspapers and on television.

The Spanish government had not encouraged newsmen to hasten to the scene, nor, of course, had we. No transoceanic press flights were laid on by the Pentagon, and no helicopter missions above the search scene were authorized for the newsmen. We were as low key as a government can get, not only with announcements, but with routine assistance for the press corps. Nonetheless ten to twenty American and foreign newsmen quickly did make their way to Palomares, where they had hotel, food and transportation problems; where officials told them nothing; where the citizenry was filled with misinformation (some from Radio Prague); and where each day they were obligated to send back some kind of a story. Foreign editors, telegraph editors and managing editors do not understand or commend the correspondent who telephones home from the scene of missing hydrogen bombs to say that he simply does not have a story to file that day.

Some days they wrote rumors of their own, and some days they merely reprinted rumors which had appeared in the Spanish press, usually labeling them as such. I did not blame them a bit. News stories will be written about newsworthy events, and if the government leaves a void by its own policy of deliberate silence, it must live with the consequences of that action.

Unofficial reports from Spanish sources that we had recovered three of four bombs which had been aboard the plane were accurate, but another printed report that the fourth was contaminating coastal waters was not. The inability of American officials to comment on that rumor, inasmuch as we were not yet owning up to the loss of any hydrogen bombs at all, enabled the Communists to have a field day. Not only had we killed the fish, thus ruining the livelihood of many fishermen and causing famine for the townspeople; we had also affected the live fish, and it would be dangerous for anyone ever again to eat fish which might have been wintering in that part of the world. Ambassador Duke finally came over from Madrid to go swimming in the Palomares waters. Having eaten mongoose stew for my country, and birds' eyes, I did not feel sorry for him, and possibly many Spaniards slept better at night thereafter.

Military officials on the scene continued to prod the Pentagon for permission to say more; we continued to prod State; officials there continued to prod the Ambassador; he continued to prod the Spanish. What was launched by Sylvester in the Pentagon as a comprehensive statement was released finally in Madrid and Washington on January 24 in this scanty form:

Elements of the United States Navy and the United States Army are assisting Spanish authorities and the U.S. Air Force in a search for wreckage of the B52 and KC135 aircraft which suffered an accident during a refueling operation on January 17. Air Force officials reconfirm that radiological surveys have found no indication of danger to public health or safety as a result of the accident.

We still had not mentioned the missing bomb.

In Washington over the next several weeks, officers in our office worked long hours anticipating problems, drafting statements, clearing them through relevant elements of the Department of Defense and shoving them at the Department of State for approval there and subsequent transmission to the Ambassador and the Foreign Office in Madrid, where they usually died.

While there was little Sylvester's people could do about the attitude of Spain, we felt a need for better on-scene intelligence. If the automatic reaction of top government officials to a crisis is: "Play it in low key," an accompanying reaction in the office of the Assistant Secretary of Defense for Public Affairs is: "Send someone." Dan Henkin, who had joined our office in the fall of 1965, used to advocate painting those words in letters one foot high on a wall of each of our hundred-odd offices in the Pentagon, and so ardently did he champion this practice that it became known in the public affairs offices of State, the White House and the Pentagon as "Henkin's Law."

To receive copies of the official reports by the commander on the scene to the Pentagon is helpful. But the military staffing process is not necessarily a rapid one—nor should it be necessarily. The best way to supplement those reports, to oversee the disclosure of information on the scene, to ensure that Washington public affairs instructions are being carried out, to acquaint the area commanders with the intricacies of Defense–State–White House coordination, and to keep up to date on both substantive developments and public affairs problems on the scene is to send a personal representative.

On rare occasions this means a Deputy Assistant Secretary of Defense, but he is the equivalent in rank of a three-star general, and that much muscle suggests that Washington is taking over the operation. More often we sent a colonel-level professional public affairs officer, armed with credentials as the special representative of the Assistant Secretary.

The American population in Spain concerned with Palomares included the Ambassador, a major general who commanded the Sixteenth Air Force and a rear admiral who headed the search-and-recovery task force. The admiral was reporting to the Air Force general and to the Chief of Naval Operations; the general was reporting to the Ambassador and to the Strategic Air Command; the Ambassador was reporting to the State Department. Also on hand were such people as Dr. Wright H. Langham of the Atomic Energy Commission's Los Alamos National Laboratory in New Mexico, a world authority on radiation health protection.

Part of the Palomares problem was radiation, part search and recovery, part Spanish political and part international. Part involved future agreements with Spain on B-52 overflights and possible reaction by other nations to Spanish decisions in that regard, and part involved Communist propaganda charges, ranging from the allegations about poisoned fish to accusations that we had violated the nuclear test ban treaty.

Clearly the episode demanded the invocation of Henkin's Law, and Arthur Sylvester sent Colonel Donald C. Foster, USAF, his Director of Plans and Programs. After long visits with all top Americans in Madrid, talks with the Spanish, several days on the scene and discussions with information officers and the press, Foster recommended a public affairs plan.

It included releasing fact sheets on radiation hazards, holding joint press briefings by Spanish and American officials, giving newsmen unclassified photography from the Navy task force, scheduling routine briefings on radioactivity clean-up ashore and search efforts at sea, running escorted press tours of both land and sea operations, and establishing an on-site press headquarters manned by representatives of the embassy, the Sixteenth Air Force, the Navy's Task Force 65 and the AEC.

They were all sound ideas, as were other, more confidential recommendations to Sylvester. Adoption of 10 percent of them would have been of enormous value to the credibility of the United States government. But they were not approved, because Spain did not want it done that way.

Back in Washington, the individual most valuable to us in drafting unapproved statements was Lieutenant Colonel James H. Dickson, USA, Chief of Information for the Defense Atomic Support Agency, who was a skilled information officer with enough background in nuclear matters to serve as a strong link between the atomic professionals and the public affairs professionals. Through the entire Palomares period—and two years later when we experienced H-bomb Round Two—Dickson's tact, experience and ability earned him the high praise of both State and Defense.

In mid-February he was the chief architect of a candid, accurate statement on radioactivity in Palomares, drafted as a joint announcement for Spain and Washington. For two weeks it was proposed unsuccessfully in Spain by our embassy. Then parts of it suddenly appeared, word for word, in the Madrid afternoon daily *Informacións* as a press interview with Don José Maria Otero De Navasculés, Chairman of the Spanish Nuclear Energy Board.

While stunned to see Dickson's language which Spain had refused to approve as an official release coming nonetheless from official Spanish mouths, we were delighted. Our objective was not to vindicate ourselves to the press but to get additional information to the public while loyally adhering to government policy. Far better that the facts reach the people in this roundabout way than not at all, even if the independent action in Madrid caused our office to appear more hopeless than ever.

By this time several internal psychological wars had broken out, despite our externally united front. Whenever the Secretaries of State and Defense were involved personally on a major issue, the Assistant Secretaries for Public Affairs of the two departments made their recommendations privately to their Secretaries, heard their decisions, and then supported those decisions in negotiations with one another. But when the two Cabinet officers were not involved personally, more often than not the two Assistant Secretaries shared a common position against other officials of either department who were experienced in their own areas but ignorant of public affairs. The naïveté of most government officials and most military officers in public affairs is frightening. My wife, Anne, is a professional interior decorator in Washington and, in her business, must live daily with the problem I faced for only four years. Nearly every housewife and many husbands consider themselves to be authorities on interior decorating, whereas the natural experts are few indeed. By the same token, nearly every public official brought into State, Defense or the White House for his knowledge of other fields considers himself a public affairs professional, and aside from Clark McAdams Clifford I met none. (Cyrus Vance was coming along nicely by the time he left office; Presidential Assistants are the worst of all.)

In the Palomares case the diplomats were less upset than we about the policy of silence, since Spain was getting what it wanted and a principal role of the diplomats was to keep Spain happy. The technical experts were not as disturbed as we, for their interest centered on search and clean-up. Both diplomats and technical experts were extremely put out, of course, by inaccurate or misleading news stories, but in their ignorance did not realize that the silence policy which they were accepting with comparatively minor protests was the major cause of such stories. Additionally, when they were contributing to drafts of proposed press releases, the tendency of the diplomats was to play down the entire affair as relatively unimportant and of the technicians to play down the potential danger to health—the one because they knew the Spanish sought that low-key tone and the other because they were so familiar with the subject that they honestly regarded health risks as minimal as long as routine safety precautions were taken. Public affairs officials of both State and Defense, concerned by these attitudes and cognizant of the pitfalls inherent in press releases which minimized dangers, were fighting both diplomats and technicians.

The interview of Don José Maria Otero De Navasculés was, therefore, looked upon as a gift from a forgotten set of gods. Seen first by the information people in the embassy in Madrid, who flashed home a translation, it was seized by all public affairs officials as the major breakthrough of our fruitless antisilence campaign. Sylvester and I in the Pentagon, and our counterparts at State, agreed immediately that we would ride the interview as hard as possible, on our own authority, without excessive co-ordination with Madrid or in our own buildings. In the Pentagon, Arthur and I checked with no one. At both State and Defense, the public affairs offices took the position that quasi-verbatim use of our own draft statement by the Chairman of the Spanish Nuclear Energy Board constituted *de facto* approval of that statement by the Spanish government. Arthur volunteered to release a translation of the statement in the Pentagon so that State could blame the bumbling Defense Department if there were diplomatic protests from Spain, but Robert McCloskey, State's first-class Deputy Assistant Secretary for Public Affairs, turned loose the information himself at his daily noon briefing, using this admirable approach:

I'd like to get into one other matter, if I may. Pursuant to the statement by the Chairman of the Spanish Nuclear Energy Board yesterday, I can say that search is being pressed off the Spanish coast for the recovery of material by the two planes involved in the January 17th air collision. . . .

Included aboard the B-52 . . . were several unarmed nuclear weapons, one of which has not yet been recovered. . . .

Now the impact of the weapons on land resulted in the scattering of some plutonium and uranium in the immediate vicinity of the points of impact. There was no nuclear explosion. Built-in safeguards perfected through years of extensive safety testing have allowed the United States to handle, store and transport nuclear weapons for more than two decades without nuclear detonation. . . .

Radiological surveys of the Palomares area and its human and animal population have included detailed laboratory studies by leading Spanish and United States scientists. They have obtained no evidence of a health hazard. These experts say there is no hazard from eating vegetables marketed from this area, from eating the meat or fish or drinking the milk of animals. Steps have been taken to insure that the affected areas are thoroughly cleaned up and some soil and vegetation are being removed. These measures are part of a comprehensive program to eliminate the chance of hazard and to set at rest unfounded fears and thus to restore normal life and livelihood to the people of Palomares.

McCloskey's opening gambit—his use of the phrase "pursuant to the statement by" Otero Navascues—was magnificent, permitting us all to take the position that we were merely repeating to the United States press some information already provided to the Spanish people by their government the day before. Spain could scarcely complain about that.

Before completing his session with the State Department reporters, McCloskey had read into the record the entire interview with the Spanish official, and transcripts were made available to all the press.

One major achievement was the first public discussion of the health hazard. The second, and most important to us in the Pentagon, was Navascues' bland disclosure that the United States had lost a hydrogen bomb. This essential revelation, so long in coming, was tacked on as the last paragraph of the Navascues interview, rather as an afterthought, in these words:

There remains the problem of search for the fourth bomb, which the Americans are very interested in finding because it is exceptionally modern. Hence the presence of the military personnel of that country in the zone.

Forty-four days after the crash, the United States government finally could admit what the civilized world had known for weeks.

Moments after the end of Bob McCloskey's briefing we followed up at the Pentagon with the official disclosure that four weapons had been aboard the B-52, that conventional explosives surrounding the critical core of two blew apart upon impact with the earth, that this scattered small quantities of radioactive material over an estimated one hundred feet, that a third bomb had been found intact and that we were searching for the fourth.

Otero Navascues had said that two thousand people had been exposed to potential radiation, that eighteen hundred had been examined for external contamination, that the results were negative and that refined laboratory procedures had established that not a single person among the inhabitants or postcrash official teams had received a dangerous dose of any kind.

The United States Atomic Energy Commission, which also had been pawing the dirt, announced that same afternoon that fifteen hundred cubic yards of earth and vegetation collected to preclude any possibility of public health or safety hazard were being packed into fifty-five-gallon drums to be buried at the AEC nuclear-waste graveyard near its Savannah River plant at Aiken, South Carolina.

The lid was off, and we took full advantage of it, aware of the possibility that an indignant Spain might clamp it back on again within hours. Briefings were held at the Pentagon and fact sheets provided the press on plutonium and uranium 235. Experts explained that radiation from the particles scattered would not penetrate a sheet of paper, but that physical introduction into the digestive or respiratory tracts would be dangerous. Technicians discussed the safety standards for personnel working in atomic laboratories and plants, outlining yearly tolerable doses and comparing these with the situation at Palomares. Using the single printed interview with Don José Maria Otero De Navascués as the wedge, we finally were implementing, forty-four days late, part of the public affairs plan which had been prepared for just such an emergency.

In the Pentagon we never were certain whether the Spanish scientist had been speaking with the advance approval of his government or whether the interview he granted had resulted from the same kind of internal communications foul-up which sometimes befell the United States. Quite deliberately, we did not ask, since the wrong answer might have turned off the tap again. The Spanish Foreign Office, so far as we knew in the Pentagon, was silent.

Pressures upon us lifted after March 2, both because of the information the government had released and because that episode had demonstrated rather pointedly the existence of our external problems. At State someone decided to talk about those problems. The Associated Press reporter covering the State Department wrote:

Officials said today diplomatic courtesy kept the United States silent on the biggest non-secret in years—the loss of a hydrogen bomb over Spain.

"We couldn't say anything officially until Spain made a move," one authority said. . . .

The reason for U.S. silence, a high official said, was to comply with Spain's desire for no public comment on the matter.

"With Spain perhaps threatening us to remove our air bases, we couldn't very well go against her wishes," this official said. "The fact of the matter is we've had a statement ready to be released by the U.S. Embassy in Spain for the last two weeks."

In time, the full story was now told.

What did happen?

The two aircraft collided at 10:22 A.M. local time at 30,500 feet while flying on course 256 degress at 365 knots. Winds at that altitude were 67 knots, from the northwest. Seven crewmen died and four survived, one of whom was found ashore, badly injured, while three landed in the water.

Several persons saw the crash, some from another Air Force tanker and some from the ground. Included among the latter were a pharmacist in Garrucha, a shepherd, sailors on watch in two Spanish ships and the crews of four fishing boats. The fishermen picked up one survivor eight miles from shore and two others three miles from shore.

Aboard the B-52 were four thermonuclear bombs. A sixteen-foot parachute deployed for one, and members of the Spanish

Guardia Civil found that weapon intact on shore the day of the crash. Two more were found, also on land, the next day by the United States Air Force, although in both cases trigger charges of conventional non-nuclear high explosives had exploded partially on impact, scattering some plutonium and uranium in the area.

Among the fishermen out that morning was Señor Francisco Simo Orts, master of his own boat, who was trawling for shrimp five miles off Palomares. He reported seeing six parachutes—four orange and white, and two white. The latter two came down close to his boat, with something attached to each. One sank immediately a few yards inshore of the vessel; the second, which splashed into the water fifty feet seaward, stayed on the surface thirty seconds before sinking. Señor Orts noted his position, kept his fathometer soundings record chart, completed his trawl and went home to notify the Guardia Civil.

In the weeks immediately after the crash, while silence was maintained, three jobs had to be done. One was to recover a great deal of highly classified equipment in addition to the nuclear bombs, a second to clean up the people and the landscape of radioactive material and the third, of course, to find and recover the fourth bomb.

Little would have been said publicly about the first mission under any circumstances, inasmuch as we did not want to advertise the nature, description or military value of all electronics gear and other equipment built into a B-52. The work was accomplished successfully; the first month after the crash scuba divers working out to eighty feet from the beach recovered more than fifty tons of aircraft wreckage, including the sensitive material.

Dr. Langham and other professionals were rushed to Palomares from the United States to help clean up the radioactivity. Working along with Spain's own nuclear experts, they did all of the proper things for the health and safety of the people, even though we were not then permitted to talk about them as we would have been if the accident had taken place over Ohio.

Nearly five hundred acres of land were cordoned off. The people were scrubbed, their clothes discarded and their urine analyzed. Local problems in communications between the nuclear scientists and the Spaniards of Palomares were considerable, however, and simple fact sheets and announcements such as we had prepared in easy-to-understand language in our massive public affairs plan would have helped enormously. Dealing with such words as "plutonium," "radioactivity," "contamination" and "hazard to health" requires great care if the government is to neither mislead nor unnecessarily alarm the population. But the people-to-people relationship, in which our office normally would have been involved deeply, was out of our hands completely.

Newsmen watching the decontamination action on the scene asked all the obvious questions during those early days. If, as the scanty statements had suggested, there was no evidence of hazard to health, then why were all the soldiers wearing face masks? And why were the bulldozers scraping up tons of land?

In the Pentagon, Arthur Sylvester and I had engaged in some violent arguments with the technical experts over the health-and-safety language of the earlier press releases.

One, issued three days after the crash, ended with this sentence: "Radiological surveys have established that *there is no danger* to public health or safety as a result of this accident." And the next, a week after the accident, included these words: "Air Force officials reconfirm that radiological surveys *have found no indication of danger* to public health or safety as a result of this accident." (Emphasis added.)

The difference between the two sentences was substantial, with the first a flat declaration that there was nothing whatever to worry about and the second a much softer statement that the experts had found nothing to worry about so far.

Sylvester and I considered the earlier announcement both premature and misleading, although the technical people insisted that it was accurate. The final decision on language was not in the Pentagon's hands, however, and the best we could do —and that only because of Sylvester's stubborn and fierce fighting—was to progress from the words of the one release to the words of the other.

Knowing nothing about radiation but a little about what words meant to people, we felt that even the second was questionable and potentially misleading. We asked, as the newsmen did: If there is no danger to public health, why the face masks, the bulldozers and the contaminated land?

In general, the answer by the technical experts went this way: There would have been a hazard to health had not certain steps been taken from the beginning. Since these steps were taken, promptly and efficiently, the potential health hazard had been removed. Both during the clean-up steps and upon their completion, checks for radioactivity were made. Analysis of those checks showed no evidence of hazard to health.

Technically, I suppose, if you spill arsenic across a desk top, turn loose five children to play in the room, re-enter before they have touched the arsenic, clean it all up, remove and scrub their clothing and find in a careful medical examination no traces of arsenic on them, you can make the statement that there is no indication of danger to the children's health or safety.

Information officers in the military services and the Office of the Secretary of Defense play the skeptic's role far more often and to a greater degree than is often suspected. Having been burned over and over again, they recognize the dangers of overstating or half-stating. There is a great difference between the professional military information officer as he actually does his work and the "press agent" or "publicist" or "propagandist" he often is accused of being by his critics.

Weapons development people in the Army, proud of their M16 rifle, confident in it and responsible for it, are much more apt to make extreme statements about it than are Army information officers who have previously suffered a thousand pains over the birth of other new weapons. Test pilots of the F-111 swing-wing fighter plane, who consider it the greatest of all aircraft (as most pilots consider their own aircraft to be), are much more apt to make rash promises about it than cynical Air Force information officers who regard it chiefly as another public affairs problem. Top-level admirals in the Navy, concerned that a mistake will be misinterpreted, are reluctant to acknowledge that a search-and-rescue ship misunderstood a message and steamed in the wrong direction for four hours, but the information officer knows the story will surface eventually and wants to get it out, on the record, before the people, on the Navy's terms instead of as an acknowledgment beaten out of the government by the press.

The experienced information officer knows the press. He knows that extreme statements or phony ones will not hold up; that, for example, the effort to hide a foolish attempt by a foolish Army commander to solicit free whiskey from merchants for a base party will fail. A good information officer always will attempt to tell his commander to face up to the errors publicly and get them behind him. Unfortunately, except at the level of the Assistant Secretary of Defense (and in a few other rare instances because of personal relationships), the information officer too often lacks the clout to make his position stick.

This is even true at the level of the Directors of Information of the services—major generals and rear admirals. They sometimes have acceptable access to their top superiors, but it is a long step from a four-starred Chief of Staff to a young and ambitious two-starred general whose career is in front of him. Not many major generals will pound the desk of their Chief and scrap as a short-term civilian Assistant Secretary of Defense whose lifework is outside the Pentagon will fight with his superior, the Secretary. And even those who do have less chance of winning.

The advice of the good information officer is usually sound, however, and the more experienced he is, the further removed he is from the "press agent"—not necessarily for idealistic reasons, but because he knows his business, is proud of his service and has learned that it cannot win in today's world by employing old-fashioned press agent techniques. The Office of the Secretary of Defense neither encourages nor permits the legendary drum-beating by the Army, Navy, Air Force and Marine Corps, and when OSD's guard slips, as it sometimes does, the press and the Congress move in quickly to blow the whistle.

At Palomares, of course, excessive drum-beating by the services was not a problem. No one wanted to brag about the airplane crash or its results. Military information officers of the services, working under our policy direction, sought precisely what we in OSD sought: a straightforward accounting for the American people. Experienced public affairs officers of SAC, the Air Force and the Navy helped us exploit the March 2 breakthrough after the Navascues interview, and Dickson and other officers knowledgeable about the nuclear side of things were particularly helpful in straightening the record on health hazard due to radioactivity.

But on the debit side remained one major entry. We had not accomplished our third task: One of our H-bombs was still missing. Working from the information of the fishermen, the pattern formed by the debris collected offshore and on land, the negative findings of the land search and the scientific calculation of drop points by technical experts, it was estimated that the weapon was somewhere under the water and, most likely, in an area five miles off the beach within a circle of one-mile radius.

The search-and-recovery job executed by a Navy task force was heroic. Chief search vehicles were the two deep-submergence craft, *Alvin* and *Aluminaut*, and it was in keeping with the entire incredible story that the toylike craft ridiculously named *Alvin* should discover the parachute of our missing thermonuclear weapon. We had been lucky, for the bomb had landed on the edge of a subterranean mountain and left a thousand-foot furrow track as it slid down the mountain face to a point 2,500 feet deep. *Alvin* sighted that furrow March 1, despite the fact that detection ranges on the bottom were rarely greater than fifteen feet. She lost the track, found it again March 13, surfaced because of a tired battery, and on March 15 sighted a parachute enshrouding a cylindrical object of the right size and shape. *Aluminaut* was summoned to rendezvous and baby-sit for twenty-two hours while *Alvin* replenished. The bomb was hooked March 24, lost again and relocated by *Alvin* April 2, 120 yards down the slope and 300 feet deeper.

An even more peculiar-looking gadget called CURV, for Controlled Underwater Recovery Vehicle, took over April 4 and on April 7 fished up the H-bomb which the United States government had lost.

The search cost millions of dollars, required scores of ships and demanded hundreds of thousands of man-hours. It was worth it. We would have felt simply dreadful about leaving a thermonuclear weapon missing in Palomares—especially since we could not be 100 percent positive that it was not in an old mine shaft or on the flat sea bottom nearby instead of in the oceanic mountainous area where it was found. And, enshrouded as it was by parachutes, it might have been recovered from a flatbottom by a single lucky cast of a grapnel by fishermen, by a hostile power or even, conceivably, by an international gang. James Bond's *Thunderball* adventure might have become more than a fantasy.

A final public affairs decision required after the weapon was retrieved was whether we should, for the first time, permit the press to see and photograph one of our nuclear weapons. We decided that we had no choice; a nation which misplaces its hydrogen bombs must maintain a certain public affairs flexibility. It was important not only to recover the weapon but also to convince the world that it was recovered. And while we could not treat it exactly like the Davis Cup, for friends to see and touch, we did nestle it in a wooden cradle, secure it (firmly) to the deck of the submarine rescue ship *Petrel* and permit a hundred newsmen aboard the guided-missile cruiser *Albany* to come within sixty-five or seventy feet of it.

The government's attempt to be honest with the people, finally manifested in the permission to photograph the bomb, was in sharp contrast to the almost nonexistent communications during the first forty-four days of the Palomares incident and the limited communications during the last thirty-six. Certainly I am aware of no other major "public" news event in recent years in which the government concealed such an amount of information from its people. But while we in public affairs were embarrassed by the days of silence, I know of no way that the United States could have ignored the desires of Spain in this instance. We could not have recovered the bombs without her cooperation, and the price we paid for that cooperation was silence. Even those who believe that our obligation to inform our people was more important than our obligation to let Spain handle her people as she felt best scarcely can argue logically that it was more important to keep the people up to date than to recover the bombs.

Of course the path we followed was absurd by our government standards and the standards of the news media in the United States. But our actions were not governed by our standards alone; in this instance, as in many others, sovereign nations elsewhere were attempting to conduct their affairs according to their own best interests. When we are involved with those nations, we cannot always have our way.

It was not to be expected that the press would be sympathetic to our plight. If we had pitched the whole cat on Spain's back or if we in the Pentagon had bucked all responsibility for silence to State, reporters and editorial writers would have been less critical of the Department of Defense. Inasmuch as the entire government did an excellent job up to March 2 of keeping the secret that Spain was responsible for the silence, we had no reason to count on strong support from the news media.

The press hesitates to give the government an inch, for fear that it will take the mile. This is understandable, and their zealousness is essential to our freedom. In an important way, the press fulfilled its responsibilities on Palomares, refusing to accept the outrageous United States position as final. It prodded and poked in Washington and in Spain; it moved to the scene at Palomares; it wrote as accurately as it could. And, by and large, it presented a reasonable picture to the people of the world.

There have been other instances involving foreign nations when the press, in my view, could and should have exhibited

more maturity and understanding in its portrayal of the government to the people. One such instance concerned our aircraft
operations out of Thailand, where admittedly the situation was
grotesque. For months the people of Thailand watched thousands
of take-offs by United States fighter-bombers, loaded with visible
bombs and bound obviously for the war zone. But the government of Thailand, for its own internal reasons, refused us permission to announce that the planes were there.

Everyone in the area could see them there; everyone following
the war knew that they were there; everyone was aware of where
they were going and, as they returned empty, of where they had
been. We never denied their presence; we were, however, prohibited by Thailand from acknowledging it. The position of the
royal Thai government could not have been clearer: these were
Thai bases; this was Thai country; we could use their bases in
their country as long as we made no public announcement of
that use; we could not use them if we did announce that fact
publicly. The United States' choice was also clear: we could fly
from the Thai bases, which we needed, and accept the Thais'
ban of silence, or we could reject their conditions—which would
have meant leaving Thailand, crowding a few of the aircraft on
the overloaded fields of South Vietnam and sending the rest
home.

In many accountings of the credibility of the government during the Kennedy-Johnson years, the Thai base example was used
as evidence of U.S. public affairs duplicity or stupidity. The impression often was left that the government lied to the people
and denied that we were flying from Thailand. Never did I ever
hear such a statement from anyone anywhere in the United
States government, although it is true that some Thai officials
denied both that the aircraft were there and that they were being
used in the war.

All members of Congress knew that our aircraft were based in
Thailand, and nearly all reporters covering the military establishment, the State Department or the war knew it. In off-the-record
sessions with the press, officials in Saigon and Washington dis-

cussed it freely. But we were unable to acknowledge it officially, and, at the request of the Thai government, we asked newsmen not to write about it. Most reporters respected that request initially, until the story was written so many times by the minority and told on television so often that nearly all newsmen considered further secrecy on their part nonproductive.

The Palomares and Thailand cases were almost totally dissimilar. In my view, the government deserved little sympathy or understanding on Palomares, since the press was unaware of Spain's request. It did deserve more understanding on Thailand, and some of the press, I think, themselves misled the people by charging that the people were being misled by the government.

Palomares was an outstanding example of another point—the futility of attempting to play a major news story in low key. We low-keyed ourselves into front-page headlines all over the world for weeks. Out of the incident, as an aside, came a matchless individual low-key statement. Shortly before the March breakthrough, the Air Force security which had been so outstanding slipped just enough for an unidentified Air Force officer in Spain to say to a reporter: "I don't know anything about a missing bomb, but I'll tell you that I believe we have an idea of the location of what I think you think we lost."

We did not lose a single other hydrogen bomb between the Palomares incident in 1966 and January 22, 1968, when a B-52 bomber crashed in Greenland.

NATIONAL CITY PUBLIC LIBRARY

3 The Salisbury Series

December, 1966

In the intervening months there occurred another series of events with which I was involved intimately and which constituted, in my view, the biggest public affairs mistake of the McNamara-Clifford regimes.

To claim sole responsibility for the errors committed by the Executive Branch in this instance would be to exaggerate my own importance. But I felt then and feel now that the fault was more mine than anyone else's, for I was dealing with the public side of the subject more than anyone during 1965 and 1966.

The advance public affairs advice I should have given McNamara and Vance—through Arthur Sylvester, who was busy running a world-wide empire—was wholly lacking. And it is my belief that our failure in this instance contributed markedly to the public distrust of the government which welled up in the mid- and late 1960s, particularly but not exclusively in regard to government statements on Vietnam.

The subject was the bombing of North Vietnam; the mistake was the failure of President Johnson's administration to explain to the citizens of the United States that our bombing inevitably was destroying homes and killing civilians. We permitted the impression to spread that the bombing operations of U.S. aircraft were executed with such surgical precision that we had dropped bombs only on military targets. And when the nation suddenly discovered, largely through the writing of Harrison E.

Salisbury of the *New York Times*, that homes were being destroyed in the North and that civilians were being killed, the nation's reaction was a traumatic one.

While additional loss of faith in the word of the government was the dominant part of that reaction, another part was deeper disenchantment with the war itself. Critics of the United States commitment in Southeast Asia might today applaud any inadvertent government move then which contributed to such disenchantment. My own feeling is that our country unquestionably became overcommitted in Vietnam. While unsure about whether the war was important enough to the security of the United States to merit an initial commitment of ten thousand men and $500 million a year, I am inclined to believe that it was. I am certain, however, that Southeast Asia is not so important to our security as to be worth an absolute commitment. By definition, any commitment that is not absolute can become at some point too great in cost for its potential value. My view is that Vietnam is not now and never has been so important to our security as to be worth 549,500 men, 40,000 lives and $30 billion a year.

That private view, however, is beside the point in a discussion of public affairs professionalism. The role of the Assistant Secretary of Defense (Public Affairs), and his deputies, obviously is not to support those programs in which they believe and to sabotage those in which they do not. In later Pentagon years I enjoyed ample opportunity with Robert McNamara and total opportunity with Clark Clifford to participate in policy-making decisions, but along with the opportunity to express my own views forcefully to the Secretary of Defense I had the obligation to support fully all decisions of the Secretary and all defense policies of the administration. That we had so neglected our professional duties in 1966 as to permit the *New York Times* series by Harrison Salisbury to delude the people cannot be condoned.

My personal feelings about the Salisbury stories are deep and strong. His series—the result of a two-week visit to North Vietnam as assistant managing editor of the *Times* in December, 1966—presented to the American people a reasonably accurate picture of the effect of our bombing in North Vietnam. It had not been presented previously, partly because Hanoi had permitted no other American correspondents to enter the country, although many had attempted to do so, and partly because the United States government had failed to present it. The dereliction of the government was not the fault of the *New York Times* or of Harrison Salisbury. It had itself to blame, and I, as Deputy Assistant Secretary of Defense (Public Affairs) at that time, blame myself.

The issue, however, goes far beyond that. As we read the Salisbury series in the Pentagon, we believed that along with his reasonably accurate picture of the bomb damage Salisbury left a grossly distorted and inaccurate picture of what the United States was attempting to do in North Vietnam, of how well it was doing it and, most importantly, of what it had told the American people. The impact of the Salisbury stories was to present the United States government before the world as a liar and deceiver. That, in my view, was tragic.

My purpose in writing this book is not to snipe at individual newspaper or television reporters. It is not difficult to find errors in the work of any reporter who day after day is turning out five hundred or a thousand words on controversial and complex subjects, writing often on the fly, constantly under deadline pressures and frequently working under intolerable conditions—fighting transportation, communications and, sometimes, language. But the Salisbury case is important enough to demand special attention, and an honest book on the public affairs problems of the Department of Defense and its difficulties in communicating with the people should attempt to meet that demand. No newspaper writing or television commentary in my four Pentagon years so disturbed me, and none so disturbed many of my associates in government.

For Salisbury it began, the *Times* tells us, when the Department of State validated his passport for travel to North Vietnam.

The *Times* said he applied for a visa in the summer while visiting Phnom Penh, the capital of Cambodia, where Hanoi had a diplomatic mission. He was notified in mid-December that his visa had been granted, and he left the United States soon afterward for Phnom Penh, flying then from there into Hanoi aboard an aircraft of the International Control Commission. There was nothing improper about the visit. Some Americans journeyed to North Vietnam without the approval of the United States government despite the statement on each passport that it was not valid for travel to or in Communist-controlled portions of China, Korea and Vietnam, and the additional statement that those who did travel to these countries were liable to prosecution under the U.S. code. Different people have different views on the propriety of visiting the enemy's homeland during a war. My own feelings are mixed, and are not relevant to this case. The point is that Salisbury's trip was approved by his government in proper fashion.

While Salisbury was preparing for his trip, we were experiencing a fierce and frustrating public affairs controversy over the bombing of North Vietnam. The issue involved whether United States aircraft had bombed the capital city of Hanoi. It was a complex situation and difficult to handle from a public affairs standpoint. In an attempt to remove it from the emotional context of Vietnam, let us examine the situation in fiction rather than fact.

You, a foreign nation, deliberately bomb a freight yard in Rockville, Maryland, ten miles from the White House and five miles from the Washington, D.C., boundary.

Have you bombed Washington?

As a Washingtonian, I watched your aircraft fly overhead, heard the distant explosions, saw our antiaircraft guns firing at you, learned from Rockville friends that evening of their terror and viewed television pictures of bomb damage to the freight yard and to a group of nearby residences where several civilians were killed. In my mind you have for the first time bombed my capital city—and in doing so have escalated the war.

You dissent vehemently. You know the orders given your pilots. You authorized no attack upon Washington, either against the population or against a military target in it. Only after the most pressing persuasion did you finally allow your air commanders to go after the Rockville freight yard. You are aware that your pilots had received lengthy orientation briefings and had studied huge reconnaissance photographs of the freight yard. Because Rockville was so close to Washington, only your most experienced airmen participated. Their axis of attack was selected with a view to minimum damage to civilian areas around the target in case of bomb error. The raid was delayed several times because of poor visibility, which might have caused additional civilian destruction. Under no conditions were your pilots authorized to attack targets in Washington—not even antiaircraft guns and surface-to-air missile batteries shooting at them. In addition, they were not authorized to strike any target in Rockville other than the freight yard, no matter what the conditions. A five-hundred-truck military convoy moving down the road was immune from attack. The sole target was the freight yard, biggest in the East.

My allegation that you bombed my capital city—an allegation I phrased so as to leave the impression that you deliberately targeted the White House, Capitol Hill and any civilian structures in between—is, by your reasoning, totally false.

As charges are being hurled back and forth, another point is debated. Even if Rockville is outside the city limits, is it not part of Greater Washington? Both of us check our maps. On the Maryland map on page 25 of the newest Rand McNally Road Atlas, Rockville is shown clearly, just outside Washington. I reproduce this page and distribute it to other nations.

But you find on page 23 of the same atlas the map of "Washington, D.C., and Vicinity." Bethesda, Chevy Chase and Silver Spring, Maryland, are all visible, just north of Washington. Wheaton is shown, a little farther out. One can find a road marked the Rockville Pike, heading north. But Rockville is too far away to be included.

Have you bombed Washington? I say "yes"; you say "no." While we debate, I bring up a damning fact, pointing out that the roof of the British Embassy has been damaged and several houses destroyed by fire on a block just off Massachusetts Avenue. Touring these with the foreign press corps, I repeat my charges that you deliberately have attacked my capital and killed many civilians in doing it.

You are in a quandary, knowing that you authorized no raid against the embassy, the houses or any other target in Washington, but not knowing what the damage looks like or what might have caused it. In time, you will examine it closely in aerial photographs, but you do not want to risk the life of a reconnaissance pilot in this heavily defended area simply to make points in a public debate. Meanwhile, the newsmen in your country are demanding an answer to my latest allegations. You accept the fact that there has been some damage to the embassy roof and the block of houses, but you do not know whether one or more of your rockets went astray, which is one possibility, or whether some of my surface-to-air missiles or antiaircraft fire went astray, which is also a possibility.

While I am condemning your inhumanity and protesting your unwarranted and tragic escalation of the war, you are caught. You want desperately to avoid the blame for something you know that you did not do—deliberately strike my capital, deliberately change your bombing policy, deliberately escalate the war, deliberately kill civilians—but you are unable to issue a categorical denial that you did not "attack Washington."

Your problems are severe, and no matter what you now do, I have succeeded in leaving the impression that you probably bombed Washington but do not want to acknowledge it.

This was the plight of the United States in mid-December, 1966, ten days or so before Harrison Salisbury arrived in Hanoi. On December 13 and 14 the United States had conducted—and announced—raids against two major military targets. One was a large railroad complex at the town of Yen Vien and the other a huge vehicle depot at the town of Van Dien. The immediate

North Vietnamese charge that we were bombing Hanoi and escalating the war was in headlines around the world.

What were the facts?

The Yen Vien target was 5.5 nautical miles (a nautical mile is 6,080 feet) northeast of Hanoi in the Red River Delta plain, in an area intensively cultivated in wetland rice. Several small villages were within one mile. The Van Dien target was five nautical miles south of Hanoi, surrounded by cultivated fields, civilian houses and light industry.

We had not deliberately bombed Hanoi or any target in Hanoi; we had no report from our field commanders of an accidental bombing but could not rule out definitely that a rocket or antiradar missile had gone astray; we knew that neither the two towns nor the targets in them were part of Hanoi on any available maps (French, with Hanoi boundaries clearly marked); we were certain that the targets were of substantial military value; and we knew our bombing policy was unchanged.

For the next two weeks the controversy continued over these raids. The attention was focused on the bombing of Van Dien and Yen Vien—whether they were part of Hanoi, whether we had attacked Hanoi deliberately and escalated the war, and whether any ordnance had hit Hanoi accidentally. McNamara and Sylvester were out of the country at a NATO meeting when the trouble began, and Vance and I spent dozens of hours together, determining what to do next, meeting with the Pentagon press corps, stating the case as honestly as we could, providing all of the information we possessed and seeking to keep the incident in perspective.

Some newsmen were relentless. "Did you or did you not bomb Hanoi?" they asked. "Stop beating around the bush and just give us a straight answer."

There was no discussion during this period of whether we had caused civilian damage elsewhere in the country. The attention of both government and press was on Hanoi, partly because of speculation that we had changed our bombing policy and were escalating the war, and partly on the issue of government credibility. What the people wanted was a bald statement that we had not bombed Hanoi—and we were unable to provide it. But by telling and retelling the story as frankly as possible, we were moving in the right direction until the Salisbury series broke.

For me that story began on Christmas Eve, 1966, when I received a telephone call at home from a member of the *Times* staff. The *Times*, he said, was printing a story written by Salisbury from North Vietnam. Did I care to comment on it?

I replied that I never commented on news stories without having the full text in front of me. Could he send me a copy prior to publication? He said he could not. In that case, I had nothing to say.

Salisbury's pieces stated flatly that we had bombed Hanoi. They also left the impression that Yen Vien and Van Dien were part of the urban area of the capital city, that they were of doubtful military value and that the United States was deliberately directing bombs against the civilian population.

Writing from the scene, Salisbury described the Van Dien target this way: "In fact, there is a large open area with light buildings and compounds that may or may not have been a truck park, lying possibly a quarter mile east of Route One."

How might another reporter have described the target?

The Van Dien vehicle complex was made up of 11 separate areas with a total of 184 buildings. These included 50 structures for vehicle maintenance and storage and nearly 40 barracks with a troop capacity of 4,600. There were also eight administrative and support buildings. It was considered by the Joint Staff in the Pentagon to be a major maintenance and repair area, housing a large stockpile of trucks. The entire area was guarded by troops.

We felt that the American people were left with one impression by the description Salisbury gave and that they would have been left with another had he described the target more fully.

Writing from the scene, Salisbury identified the Yen Vien target simply as a "rail yard." How might he have described it?

It was the largest rail classification yard in North Vietnam. Rail traffic between Hanoi, Dong Dang and Lao Cai was disrupted by attacks on it. Destruction of the yard, the Joint Staff believed, would seriously hamper all rail traffic between North Vietnam and Communist China. The classification yard consisted of fourteen 2,400-foot sidings and four 650-foot sidings. It included also a station, coal storage areas and turning "Y"s. A large warehouse area was at one end of it and a smaller area at the other. Five to ten locomotives and one hundred to three hundred freight cars were working there on the average day. We felt, again, that the description of this huge military target simply as a rail yard left an erroneous impression.

One might ask: Was not Van Dien a truck park? Was not Yen Vien a rail yard? Was Salisbury not reporting accurately?

Technically, I suppose that he was, just as one would be reporting accurately by describing the Empire State Building to someone who had never seen it as an "office building," or the Pentagon as a "military headquarters." But what he left out would have told the story much more fully. We could not charge that his descriptions were false, but in the Pentagon, State Department and White House we were puzzled by their incompleteness.

The United States government had approved the targets after long deliberation. Whether that was a wise decision is another issue; some argue that none of the bombing of North Vietnam was wise. But such missions as these, proposed by the military and considered by the Secretary of State, the Secretary of Defense and the White House, were analyzed in detail—as to their military value, the risk to the pilots, the potential damage to civilians and the possibility of their widening the war. The leadership of the government was not making these decisions lightly; there was no blank-check authority.

Certainly Salisbury was entitled to his own view as to the military importance of the targets, just as the Joint Staff was entitled to its view. It was our feeling in the Pentagon, however, that he would have been fairer to his readers if he had given them a more complete description and allowed them to make their own judgments on whether the targets were worth attacking.

In the wake of the Hanoi controversy, the popular opinion of the military value of Van Dien and Yen Vien was particularly significant. For if they were unimportant—if one, for example, was merely an open area with light buildings that "may or may not be a truck park," rather than a vast complex of 184 structures—then we had no solid military justification for attacking them and additional credence was given North Vietnam's contention that the United States was really bombing the city of Hanoi.

The major issue here was the credibility of the United States government; the important issue was whether we had been lying to the American people, whether our bombing had been killing a great many civilians and destroying a great many civilian houses while we pretended that this was not happening. It was whether we had been directing our attacks against the population and against nonwar industry when we had been pretending that we were directing them only against military targets. It was whether we deliberately had bombed targets in populated areas in big cities without telling the American people that we were doing this.

Given the decision to bomb Van Dien and Yen Vien, we never could have prevented the Hanoi controversy. Unaware of whether a bomb or two or a pair of rockets or an antiradar missile had plowed into the tinderbox dwellings and begun fires which could have leveled an Asian block in thirty minutes, we were always unable honestly to deny the Communist charges that we had "bombed Hanoi." Despite difficulties, however, we were, as I indicated, barely hanging on with the American public until the Salisbury stories. His "new" on-the-scene "evidence," coming when it did and written as it was, pushed us over the cliff.

The people came to the conclusion that the government was lying. And if we had lied about Hanoi, then it was not unlikely that we had been lying about other facets of the air attacks as well. The rest of the Salisbury series, in my view, helped greatly to create the mistaken impression that we had been doing exactly that.

It is my personal belief that the American people today believe that their government misled and deceived them about the bombing of the North. That is the distressing consequence, for I feel deeply that the impressions left by the tone and temper of the Salisbury pieces were erroneous, and I am convinced that they would not have been accepted by the people if the government had not previously failed to communicate adequately on the bombing.

The December 13–14 Hanoi issue was inevitably a loser or a near-loser from a practical public affairs standpoint, regardless of whether U.S. ordnance actually did or did not strike within the city. If we were going to bomb that close to the capital, we had to expect unwieldy problems and do our best to keep the record straight and alleviate them. But despite the approach taken by Salisbury in his stories, the broader, nationwide bombing case need not have been lost and the people's confidence in their government not destroyed in this instance if some of us responsible for public affairs had been more astute in the preceding months.

It took time to research the Salisbury pieces on a line-by-line basis, but as the intelligence and operations people dug into them, they found a great deal which made us feel that the stories were not as objective and analytical as we had hoped and expected. Knowing how to react effectively to counteract the impressions they left, however, was difficult.

For this was an unusual, nearly a unique, situation. This was not the free American press at work, with newsmen competing with one another and doggedly pursuing into corners rumors, half-truths and falsehoods. Our government is accustomed to working in that atmosphere, and it is accustomed in that atmosphere to attempt to keep the record straight. As a newspaperman I could not always keep my own emotions out of the news stories I was writing, but I knew that my telegraph editor back in Cleveland was reading not only my version of the event but also separate stories written by the Associated Press, the United Press International, Reuter's and the *New York Times* news services, all of which the *Plain Dealer* then purchased. All of these were on his desk along with my copy, and the next day my editors would have available two dozen other newspapers with two dozen other versions, plus radio and television reports. Any newsman is bridled by this knowledge. The Associated Press does more than any government public affairs office could do to keep UPI honest, and if the imaginative Washington *Post*, with its predilection for "think pieces" instead of straight reporting, confuses the issue, the reliable Baltimore *Sun* will be on the same newsstands that morning with a more objective version of the same story and the Washington *Star* will come plodding along that afternoon with far more fact than fiction in its account. This knowledge helps keep even the *Post* reporters from getting too far off base, and when they do, the reading public has other choices before it. The system does not work perfectly, nor well enough, in our complex society, but it does work.

This was different. No other American newsmen were in North Vietnam when Salisbury arrived. This was one on-the-scene reporter, representing the newspaper many regarded as the most prestigious of our times, against the United States government.

Among the Salisbury stories which caused the most pain within the administration were those dealing with bomb damage in the city of Nam Dinh.

The North Vietnamese had produced a pamphlet entitled *Report on U.S. War Crimes in Nam-Dinh City*. It was prepared by "The Committee for the Investigation of U.S. Imperialists' War Crimes in Viet Nam of Nam Ha Province, October, 1966." The pamphlet was in English. While I was unaware of its existence, some of the intelligence people in the Pentagon had copies of it.

They first saw it in November, after a North Vietnamese official in Moscow had distributed it to foreign journalists there.

I do not know whether any American journalists then wrote stories based upon it or dismissed it as propaganda. In any case, neither Arthur Sylvester nor I had seen material from it in print, and our intelligence people were unaware of any.

But Salisbury packed it into one of his articles. He did so with no reference to the source, printing the information as though he had established it himself with his own on-the-scene reporting. I have no knowledge of what he told the *New York Times* editors, but when the *Times* subscribers read this material, they were not advised that it was from a Communist propaganda pamphlet.

Some examples of Salisbury's text compared to wording in the propaganda kit are worth reprinting.

In a Salisbury piece datelined Hanoi, December 25, and printed in the *New York Times* of December 27, was this paragraph on Nam Dinh:

The cathedral tower looks out on block after block of utter desolation: the city's population of 90,000 has been reduced to less than 20,000 because of evacuation; 13 percent of the city's housing, including the homes of 12,464 people, have been destroyed; 89 people have been killed and 405 wounded.

And on page 4 of the Communist press kit was this language:

During the 33 above said air attacks against Nam Dinh, they caused many losses in lives and property to the City's inhabitants, 89 persons were killed, among them 23 children, 36 women and 405 wounded, among them 61 women, 44 old men and 41 children. Eight hundred and eighty-one dwelling houses (accounting for 13 percent of the city housing), with an area of 86,847 square meters, were destroyed, leaving 12,464 inhabitants homeless.

Salisbury did not report that the statistics he used came from the Communists. He did not qualify those statistics in any way. He did not attribute them to anyone. He stated them as fact.

There are additional examples.

Salisbury wrote:

Street after street in Nam Dinh has been abandoned and houses stand torn and gaping. One deserted street is Hang Thao or Silk

Street, which was the center of the silk industry. Almost every house on the street was blasted down April 14 at about 6:30 A.M. just as the factory shifts were changing. Forty-nine people were killed, 135 were wounded on Hang Thao and 240 houses collapsed. Eight bombs —Mk. 84s—accomplished this. . . .

And the pamphlet said:

The April 14, 1966, air raid over Hang Thao street was one of the biggest deliberate U.S. attacks on human lives. . . . At 6:30 A.M., when those who had just come back from a night shift were still sleeping, those who were about to work were having breakfast, women were getting ready for their shopping or for their housework, and children were getting ready for their kindergartens or infant classes, two U.S. planes came flying at low altitude along Ninh Binh Highway No. 10 and furtively intruded into Hang Thao, Han Cau, Tran Hung Dao streets and Ben Thoe area, dropped 8 MK 84 bombs, killing 49 people . . . wounding 135 people, and destroying 240 houses. . . .

Salisbury wrote: "Another target in Nam Dinh has been the Dao (Black) River dike. The dike has been hit six times and there have been many near misses. Breaching of the dike would seriously affect the region's agriculture. . . ."

And the pamphlet source: "The U.S. also attacked the dyke surrounding the city in an attempt to sabotage the peaceful work of the population. On May 31 and July 14, 1966, they dropped six bombs on the 2-kilometre long dyke which protects the city against floods, damaging many sections. . . ."

Salisbury: "Most strikes have been carried out by F-105 and F-4s, but B-57s, A-3s, A-4s and A-6As have also been used."

Pamphlet: "In their bombings and strafings of the city, they have used various ultramodern planes such as the A.4A, A.6A, A.3J, F.105, F4H, RB.57."

Even Salisbury and the Times apparently later had second thoughts on their unconscionable reproduction of Communist propaganda, attributed to no one and passed on as fact. The following comment appeared in a story printed in the Times of December 29:

It should be noted, incidentally, that all casualty estimates and statistics of these dispatches are those of North Vietnamese officials. However, descriptions of bomb damage are based wholly on visual inspection.

It was too late. The damage had been done. These two sentences went almost unnoticed. And even this belated confession left much unanswered.

In one piece he wrote: "Two-thirds of the machinery and workers at the big textile plant near Gia Lam have been sent to the countryside." Typically, this was attributed to no one.

He also wrote: "The drone downed on Christmas Day fell 12 or 13 miles northeast of the city [Hanoi]." Who says so? He was not, by his own dispatches, in Hanoi on Christmas Day. How did he know a drone had been downed that day? How did he know it had been "downed" rather than that it had crashed? Did he see it shot down? Or was he again repeating hearsay? The fact is that neither drones nor manned aircraft were downed in the Hanoi area on Christmas Day.

At another point he wrote that a village had been destroyed in a raid on August 13 and that twenty-four people had been killed. Who told him that a village had been destroyed? How did he know the raid was August 13? What source provided the casualty figure?

We were aware in the government of the obvious difficulties in reporting from a Communist country. Salisbury had faced these difficulties before, when he was a Moscow correspondent for the *Times* years earlier. In 1953 *Time* Magazine commented on the problems inherent in covering news for an American publication in a Communist nation, writing in part:

The New York Times, the only non-Communist newspaper in the free world with a staff correspondent in Moscow, sometimes gives as distorted a picture of Russia as the traveling U.S. journalists. Though its correspondent, Harrison Salisbury, files only closely censored stories, the Times prints his dispatches as it gets them, assumes that the newspaper's readers are "intelligent enough" to know they may be reading Communist propaganda.

North Vietnam had denied entry visas to all other American reporters who had sought to come in up to this time, welcoming Salisbury as the first. Among those whose requests had been turned down was Salisbury's colleague on the *Times*, Hanson Baldwin, the newspaper's long-time expert military editor, who was generally regarded as the most competent and experienced journalist in the country on defense matters. He was a hard-liner on the war.

Perhaps the man most incensed by the Salisbury pieces was my immediate superior, Arthur Sylvester, who was shortly to leave as Assistant Secretary of Defense after six years of courageous, sometimes stormy service to his country and six years of total loyalty to Robert S. McNamara. Not always the most diplomatic of men but usually the most frank, Sylvester referred to the reporter in a Chicago speech as "Harrison Appallsbury" and to his publication as "The New Hanoi Times." It was rather a naughty and undignified thing for Arthur to do.

We sought but did not find in the Salisbury pieces mention of how painfully American pilots had worked to avoid civilian casualties, often at added risk to their own safety. Rarely did he present an "on-the-other-hand" view. We were, of course, sensitive, and perhaps overly sensitive, but it appeared to us that the stories were brewed and blended to yield a flavor of indiscriminate destruction executed by the United States.

That would have been more understandable to us if the series had merely chronicled the war damage he observed. But it did not; to his personal observations he added many comments from North Vietnamese suggesting that we deliberately had bombed civilian houses and deliberately had gone after the civilian population. We in the government had seen reconnaissance photography and were aware that houses had been destroyed and civilians killed. An experienced on-the-spot observer should have known that if the United States were on a deliberate people-killing attack, the damage would have been a hundred to a thousand times greater. There was no hint of this, however, from the only American newsman then on the scene, a lifetime journalist. His silence in this regard, his failure to question in print the North Vietnamese conclusions, helped leave the impression that his government had been lying.

It was the most frustrating time of my government service. I could not read Salisbury's stories without feeling sympathy for the civilian bombing victims; on this point I share his reaction. Harrison Salisbury is a compassionate human being; his stories were written with compassion. But, knowing the facts, neither could I read them without bewilderment and intense regret at an impression which I considered unfounded and unfair.

Because, regardless of the tone of the series, on our part we knew certain things to be true. Whether we could now convince or remind the public, coming in, as we were, defensively in the wake of the Salisbury furor, was uncertain. But we reviewed our own position:

One. We knew that no bombing of the civilian population had been sanctioned, that targets had been approved specifically at the highest level of government, and that attacks had been authorized against military targets only.

Two. We knew that requests had come from the military to bomb certain other military targets and that these had been denied for various reasons, one of which was their location in populated areas.

Three. We knew that some higher-priority military targets in several built-up areas had been approved for attack, and (from photography) that civilian structures in these areas had also been destroyed.

Four. We knew that these three points had all been made publicly, that stories about them had apeared in the press, that our announcements in Saigon from General William C. Westmoreland's headquarters had included targets in populated areas and that no effort had been made to keep such attacks secret.

Five. We knew that we had taken the greatest possible precautions to avoid civilian casualties, that never before in warfare

had pilots operated under such tight bombing restrictions and
that never had targets been authorized with such care.

Six. We knew that we had dropped hundreds of thousands
of tons of bombs in North Vietnam, that this had been stated
publicly many times and that this much ordnance could not be
expended without damage to civilian structures and casualties
to civilians.

Seven. We knew there were severe restrictions against bombing military targets in Hanoi, and we knew that no targets in
Hanoi had been authorized for attack.

Nine. We did not know, but we could assume with certainty,
that there had been inadvertent bombing of civilian areas never
reported to higher echelons in the field or to Washington. Our
aircraft were encountering the heaviest anti-aircraft fire ever concentrated against planes. A man takes necessary actions to save
his life. Some men, at some times, panic. Some mistake one
area for another and release their bombs at the wrong target.
Some jettison armed bombs over populated areas when jumped
by MIGs, regardless of instructions not to do so. There had
been some pilot error over North Vietnam and some breakdown
of equipment—and some of both had never been reported.

Ten. We knew that the leadership of North Vietnam recognized that we were not bombing the population deliberately, for
they took advantage of our policy by emplacing military targets
such as radar, troop trucks and antiaircraft sites in the midst of
populated areas. We thought it possible that the people, and
possible lower-echelon officials, unaware of World War II–type
bombing, might not recognize our discriminatory attacks and
might really think we were trying to destroy them all.

As Washington discussed the Salisbury articles, the issues
became intertwined as they always do in any debate over Vietnam.

One set of issues raised by the series involved whether our
country should be in this war in Southeast Asia, whether it was
in our national interest, whether it was worth a commitment of

this size, whether it was just (is any war just?), whether our bombing was intelligent from military and psychological standpoints, whether the attacks were justifiable, whether the bombing was aiding our cause in the South, whether we would reach peace sooner if we bombed harder or stopped bombing.

I am not here discussing any of those issues.

A second set, more factual and less philosophical, involved how we were bombing, what we were bombing and whether we had deceived our people as we conducted this bombing campaign.

Part of the problem in combating the Salisbury series arose from its timing so soon after the December 13–14 raids outside Hanoi. During that controversy, over and over we said that we bombed only military targets, that we had not bombed any military targets in Hanoi and that if there was civilian damage in Hanoi it resulted from accidental strays. Suddenly, however, millions were reading about civilian damage in Nam Dinh and other communities, and many recalled—erroneously—that their government had just denied emphatically any attacks upon military installations in the cities of North Vietnam.

The obvious course of action was to try to straighten the record, to try to point out Salisbury's errors and misstatements.

This would, and did, take time. We could not respond to the story in an issue of the *New York Times* by ten o'clock that same morning. This type of detailed information cannot be gathered that quickly in an establishment as large as the Department of Defense—not if it is to be accurate. And yet the newsmen, including those who believed that the government deserved help and were trying to provide it, wanted and needed the counterinformation quickly. Their editors were not interested in stories which appeared on Tuesday to refute last Thursday's article, especially if their newspapers did not buy the *Times* service and had not printed last Thursday's article anyhow.

This problem of the reporter's desire for instant comment and the government's inability to provide accurate comment that rapidly is one of the more serious barriers to intelligent communications between the government and the people. Given the fierce competition of the American free enterprise system as manifested in the news business, I know of no ready answer.

By the time the government had analyzed Salisbury's stories on a paragraph-by-paragraph basis, the reporters, the people—and the government—were all preoccupied with newer crises. What we needed more quickly than it could be prepared was an analysis of what Salisbury wrote, what impressions his writings left and what the facts were. For example:

NAM DINH RECONNAISSANCE

Salisbury: "Nam Dinh officials attributed the alerts to American reconnaissance which they believed had been continued despite the Christmas truce."

Impression: That the United States was violating the truce on this Christmas Day by sending over reconnaissance aircraft.

Fact: The truce agreement did not ban reconnaissance planes. It had been announced that reconnaissance would continue. Salisbury did not mention that reconnaissance planes were unarmed.

MILITARY VALUE

Salisbury: "Mayor Doan regards her city as essentially a cotton-and-silk textile town containing nothing of military significance. Nam Dinh has been systematically attacked by United States Seventh Fleet bombers since June 28, 1965."

Impression: That there were no military targets in Nam Dinh, but that the United States had nonetheless "systematically"—not "occasionally," despite the lack of military targets—attacked it for six months.

Fact: Nam Dinh is the third largest city in North Vietnam. It is forty miles southwest of Hanoi and a major transshipment point for supplies and soldiers moving south. They came into the city from the north in three ways: by river, by the Hanoi–Dong Hoi rail line, and by Route One, the major highway to the south.

The Joint Chiefs of Staff considered it a major communications hub. In it were four significant fixed military targets, so designated by the Joint Chiefs of Staff. One was a thermal power plant, the second a petroleum-oil storage area, the third a large railroad yard and the fourth a huge storage depot and transshipment facility, for supplies brought in by one means and taken out by another.

The power plant was the only one in the Nam Dinh area. It produced 4 percent of the power capacity of all North Vietnam. The petroleum-oil storage plant accounted for more than 5 percent of North Vietnam's storage capacity of POL.

TEXTILES

Salisbury: "The textile plant, whose most dangerous output from a military point of view would presumably be cloth for uniforms, has been bombed 19 times, but is still operating under great difficulty."

Impression: That the United States was willfully bombing any target it chose, whether it had significant military value or not. Our eager military leaders snatched at straws: they even saw some military value to this harmless textile plant. But the brave North Vietnamese were undaunted.

Fact: Salisbury was correct on one point: the primary industry was textiles. There were three textile plants in the city. He chose not to locate them in relation to military targets—but then he had found no military targets. Two were immediately west of the thermal power plant and the third was halfway between the power plant and the petroleum-oil storage area. Not once was one of the textile plants targeted for attack. Not once was one deliberately attacked. Located as they were, all three had suffered damage. Some of it was severe. His unidentified source for the number of raids was, again, the pamphlet of "The Committee for the Investigation of U.S. Imperialists' War Crimes," which spoke of nineteen attacks by "U.S. piratical aircraft."

CASUALTIES AND EVACUATION

Salisbury: "The city's population of 90,000 has been reduced to less than 20,000 because of evacuation; 13 percent of the city's housing, including the homes of 12,464 people, have been destroyed; 89 people have been killed and 405 wounded."

Impression: That the city had fled the American attackers, who sought to kill civilians and destroy their homes.

Fact: We had no accurate casualty estimates and did not know the facts. Salisbury had no figures of his own either, yet he stated these Communist propaganda figures as fact. I had no basis to accept or reject them, but wanted them properly labeled.

CREDIBILITY AND COMMUNIQUÉS

Salisbury: "No American communiqué has asserted that Nam Dinh contains some facility that the United States regards as a military objective."

Impression: That we were secretly bombing this city and killing the civilians in it even though we ourselves had found no military target sufficiently valid to announce.

Fact: Within hours after the appearance of the article we found and identified for the press three specific earlier public announcements referring to bombing attacks against military targets in Nam Dinh. In them the targets were identified. These announcements had been handed to the press by General Westmoreland's command in Saigon at the routine nightly briefings. Copies had been made available later for the press in Washington. The entire nightly briefing in Saigon was, in fact, transcribed each day, and a copy of it immediately radioed to Washington and taped in the Pentagon, so that newsmen there could hear it if they desired. The fact that we had publicly announced bombing attacks against targets in Nam Dinh could have been ascertained by the *Times* staff, either in Washington or Saigon.

DIKES AND FOOD FLOODING

Salisbury: "Another target in Nam Dinh has been the Dao (Black) River Dike. The dike had been hit six times and there have been many near misses. Breaching of the dike would seriously affect the region's rice agriculture."

Impression: That the Americans, in their cruelty, had been bombing a dike with the intent to destroy it, flood the land and thus wipe out the rice crops needed by the North Vietnamese for their existence.

Fact: A dike bordered the river alongside the transshipment area, where ships unloaded supplies for storage and shipment south. It was not targeted at any time. It was not deliberately attacked at any time. Reconnaissance photography showed that it had been struck a few times. It was made of mud and soil; repair was not difficult. The random accidental hits upon the dike, made during more than sixty-five bombing missions flown against the four targets in Nam Dinh, presented no flood danger whatever, and they presented no danger of destroying the rice. This was in downtown Nam Dinh. How could any observer look at the half-dozen small repaired craters in the dike, check their location in relation to the legitimate military targets, weigh them against the number of attacks and conclude that we were really engaged in an effort to knock out the dikes?

INTENT

Salisbury: "Why have American planes devoted all this unannounced attention to Nam Dinh? 'Americans think they can touch our hearts,' Nguyen Tien Canh of Nam Dinh's City Council said, apparently meaning that Americans thought they could intimidate the populace by continuous attacks. A second suggestion was that the unannounced assault on Nam Dinh was supposed to be an object lesson to show Hanoi what United States air power could accomplish if it were directed more powerfully to North Vietnam's capital."

Impression: That we were deliberately bombing civilians in Nam Dinh, either to destroy their morale and knock them out of the war or as a sample of the people-killing crusade we were capable of launching against Hanoi.

Fact: Even the North Vietnamese casualty figures demonstrate the incredibility of these allegations. The United States flew sixty-five missions against the targets in Nam Dinh. There were one or more aircraft on each mission. For security reasons, the number of sorties—a single aircraft flying a single raid—was not announced, although newsmen used an average of two to three sorties per mission for their own bookkeeping purposes. It was reasonable to conclude that at least one hundred aircraft had been sent against the Nam Dinh targets.

That was a significant bombing effort, spread over a period of months. By Salisbury's own North Vietnamese casualty figures, eighty-nine persons were killed in those sixty-five missions.

We did not then and, when I left the government, still did not have a reasonable reading on the accuracy of the North Vietnamese figures. But one could certainly assume that the enemy was not understating his casualties in a propaganda sheet describing "U.S. Imperialists' War Crimes."

We do know that the North Vietnamese responsible for the defense of their country and the prosecution of the war in the South did consider Nam Dinh important and apparently did not share Salisbury's views, or those reportedly voiced by the mayor, that the city was without targets of military value. The value was of sufficient importance so that more than five hundred antiaircraft guns had been emplaced within a twenty-five-mile air-defense area of the city. Additionally, more than a dozen surface-to-air missile sites had been situated within the twenty-five-mile radius.

To conduct more than 65 bombing missions involving 100 or more aircraft against targets in a city defended by more than 500 antiaircraft guns and 12 surface-to-air missile sites, and to kill no more than 89 persons doing so, must constitute a new peak in precision bombing and must in itself provide certain proof of the care taken by United States planes to avoid civilian casualties.

If these attacks were really an object lesson, U.S. aircraft could have killed a dozen times more people in a single raid—and we considered Salisbury an experienced enough reporter to know it.

And even Salisbury did not use the "eighty-nine" figure as representing purely civilian deaths. He cited it as the total death figure from the bombings, one which would then include men working in the thermal power plant, the rail yard, the petroleum storage depot and the large transshipment area.

I am not here suggesting, nor did we suggest at the time of the controversy, that Salisbury's on-the-scene reports of the damage he saw were all inaccurate. From government reconnaissance photography of these areas, we knew precisely what buildings had been hit a half-block from a target or two blocks away. Neither the Secretary of Defense nor the Assistant Secretary had photographs of Nam Dinh on his desk the morning of Salisbury's story, but they were to be there eventually, blown up to half the size of a Ping-Pong table, together with expert photo interpreters discussing in detail each textile factory.

That there was damage and destruction in areas of Nam Dinh adjacent to the military targets was unquestionably true. And there was damage and destruction adjacent to military targets in areas of many other cities. And, while it was more difficult to locate, since our photography concentrated on target areas for bomb-damage-assessment purposes, there was undoubtedly damage in some areas of North Vietnam which were not adjacent to military targets—damage caused by pilot error or equipment breakdown. No one in government denied such damage. No one had denied it before Salisbury went to North Vietnam; no one denied it while he was there; no one denied it after his return.

Salisbury's curious reporting was not confined to his accounts on Nam Dinh. Other areas included:

PHU LY

Salisbury: "In attacks on October 1, 2 and 9, every house and building were destroyed. Only 40 people were killed and wounded because many people had left town and because an excellent manhole shelter system was available.

"The community had no industry, but lay astride a highway and a railroad line running from Hanoi, which had a couple of sidings in town. Presumably, planes were attacking the railroad.

But in the process they destroyed another residential community."

Impression: That we had leveled this town, that it surely had no war industry, that there were a "couple of [insignificant] sidings," that there was some doubt ("presumably") about what our objective really was and that this was ("another") one of a great many such towns that we had destroyed.

Fact: Salisbury again accepted the Communist version and repeated it as fact. He was not in Phu Ly on October 1, 2 and 9, and had not the slightest notion what happened on those dates or how many persons were killed. Military targets identified by photo interpreters and other intelligence experts in Phu Ly included a railroad bridge, two military storage areas in different parts of the town, a barracks, a set of military buildings adjacent to the barracks, a railroad yard, a control center and a long stretch of port facilities along the river. There were also several antiaircraft sites both in and around the town. The statement that "every house and building were destroyed" was inaccurate.

PHU XA

Salisbury: "The North Vietnamese cite as an instance the village of Phu Xa, a market gardening suburb possibly four miles from the city center. The village of 24 houses was reported attacked at 12:17 P.M., August 13, by a United States pilot trying to bomb a Red River dike. The village was destroyed and 24 people were killed and 23 wounded. The pilot was shot down. . . . It is the reality of such casualties and such apparent byproducts of the United States bombing policy that lend an atmosphere of grimness and foreboding to Hanoi's Christmas cease-fire."

Impression: The United States had wantonly destroyed another town, this one a mere market gardening suburb. One aircraft did the damage; his target was a dike.

Fact: Our most recent reconnaissance photography showed no apparent damage to Phu Xa, which was the location of an early-warning radar site Salisbury did not mention. Nor did he mention military support vans for the radar, camouflaged military vehicles, communications trenches, petroleum drums and anti-aircraft sites, all of which were in Phu Xa. His market gardening suburb, in fact, constituted an outstanding example of the North Vietnamese practice of deliberately mixing military installations and equipment among the civilian population in order to protect from attack things of military value to the war in the South.

Had Salisbury actually visited these towns? Had he seen the railroad bridge, the military storage areas, the barracks, the railroad yard, the control center, the port facilities along the river, the antiaircraft sites, the radar installation, the military vans supporting it, the camouflaged military vehicles, the communications trenches, the petroleum drums?

Did the North Vietnamese take him where they said they were taking him? Did he know where he was? Did they drive him rapidly through one portion of a town and conceal from him the other portions? Had he spent ten minutes or ten hours in Phu Ly and Phu Xa?

We did not know. They were questions of considerable internal importance to the government, since the answers would bear upon how we would attempt to straighten the record and what we should expect next. Aside from that, the answers were really none of the government's business. It has no control over the skills, sympathies, motives and sense of responsibility of reporter or editor, and should have no such control.

There was no telling what was coming tomorrow. In a piece filed from Hong Kong on January 10, Salisbury referred to the hotels which had been bombed out in Ninh Binh. Recall that the *Times* had said, in an earlier story, that descriptions of bomb damage "are based wholly on visual inspection." Yet nowhere did he indicate that he had visited Ninh Binh, and in our minds was the question of whether his statement was, like some of the others, based entirely on what he had been told. We did not know.

He took photographs. One printed by the *Times* was iden-

tified as the ruins of the Catholic cathedral in Phat Diem.
Aerial reconnaissance showed the cathedral in Phat Diem to be
untouched.

He wrote that the North Vietnamese did not seem to place
their antiaircraft sites especially close to civilian housing. This
was simply inaccurate. Hundreds of reconnaissance photographs
refuted it.

Each of the Salisbury pieces was duplicated and distributed
within the government for line-by-line analysis. In the Pentagon,
for example, the Operations Section of the Joint Staff was asked
for the facts on every statement he made on such matters as
numbers of air raids, types of aircraft used, losses of manned
planes or drones and kinds of ordnance expended. All this information was in the computers. The Defense Intelligence
Agency went over the stories to give us their readout on the
matters within their cognizance—estimates of civilian casualties,
descriptions of destruction to civilian structures, details of the
military targets which had been attacked, comments on the
accuracy of statements on how long traffic was disrupted by
the bombing of a specific bridge.

Scores—possibly hundreds—of individuals in the Pentagon
alone participated in this analysis. But, as is always the case,
each had his normal responsibilities to meet. Many were already
working sixty- and seventy-hour weeks. The computers of the
Joint Staff were being used to fight a war, not to combat a series
of newspaper stories. The photo interpreters did not mind coming
in Sundays and working overtime to take us over each structure
in Nam Dinh, before and after the bombing attacks, but they
could not do so until the technical people had stayed nights to
dig into their files, cull out the pertinent photographs and reproduce and enlarge them.

Some information was in our own public affairs files, in the
Pentagon or in Saigon. These are not computerized. There was
no way to ascertain exactly how many times raids against Nam
Dinh had been included in the daily briefings given by the U.S.
Military Command except to go through hundreds of printed re-

ports, one by one. This could have been done, by men already working seven days a week in a war zone, if it had been essential to do it.

In some cases—the target description of Van Dien—the information provided us after the first line-by-line analysis was all that we required. In some—a photographic readout of military targets in the "residential community" of Phu Ly—we asked for additional details. In others—the number of times that the U.S. Command in Saigon had mentioned raids against targets in Nam Dinh—we decided that the information was not worth the time and effort demanded to collect it. If we were to be accurate, it would have been necessary to listen to every thirty- or forty-five-minute taping of every Saigon news briefing for months. It would not have been good enough to have checked the day's briefing against the day of the actual attack, for if an aircraft had been shot down and helicopter rescue efforts had been under way, announcement of that raid might have been delayed a day or two. In this particular case we ordered that the check be run only long enough to ascertain that we had, in fact, made several announcements despite Salisbury's statement to the contrary.

Most of these steps took time. By the time we had compiled all the material needed to make a solid case, it was too late. The fact-gathering effort was continued, because the information possibly would be needed for later testimony before Congressional committees, but the total counterstrike public affairs effort of the government was negligible.

A few statements were put out by the Department of Defense, the Department of State and the White House. The President skimmed by the issue lightly, saying little more than that there had been no change in our bombing policy. State sent a few messages to its embassies around the world pointing out some of the inaccuracies in some of the stories. I wrote two lengthy letters to Representative Ogden R. Reid (R.–N.Y.), who expressed more interest in attempting to get at the facts than most other members of Congress. In them I defined "military target" and offered several examples, re-emphasized that the United States had not approved strikes on textile or fruit-canning plants, noted again that no dikes had been targeted and stressed that none of these statements meant that no bombs had fallen on civilian structures or on nontargeted military installations.

The newspapers and wire services wrote lengthy stories quoting from the letters, and a small piece of the government case was thus made once. But Salisbury was hitting the same theme day after day. He wrote at least fourteen stories from North Vietnam, plus another eight from Hong Kong en route home. He gave speeches and was interviewed on television. He was the eyewitness expert in whom there was news interest; the government had been established as a liar, so many saw little point in talking to it or listening to it. The letters made no noticeable dent.

The Pentagon press was largely sympathetic. It knew and understood our policy, and every experienced military reporter knew that the kind of damage and number of casualties Salisbury was reporting were a tiny fraction of what would have been accomplished by deliberate attacks upon the people. Individual newsmen who came in to talk were given all the information we had—which, the first few days when they had the greatest interest and need, was insufficient. Many of the non-Pentagon press took our lack of immediate information as a sign of guilt.

No genuine effort was made by the President, the Secretary of State and the Secretary of Defense to meet the problem, nor was there a genuine effort by the President's Press Secretary, the Assistant Secretary of State (Public Affairs) and the Assistant Secretary of Defense (Public Affairs). Our government was not set up to operate in the public affairs field in a massive, co-ordinated way—and is not now.

In my four-year tour there was not once a significant organized effort by the Executive Branch of the federal government to put across its side of a major policy issue or a major controversy to the American people. Not once was there a "public affairs program" of State, Defense and White House worthy of the name. The President would occasionally order several of his top officials to hold simultaneous backgrounders on different aspects of the same subject for the newsmen covering the various departments. On the night of his October 31, 1968, speech halting the bombing, for example, three backgrounders were held in Washington—at the White House, the State Department and the Pentagon—and a fourth was called in Saigon. General Westmoreland came home once a year or so for two or three uncoordinated appearances. But these one-shot efforts, always unrelated, scarcely could be called public affairs campaigns.

The Salisbury affair triggers a basic question: How far should the government go in trying to put its case before the people? What is the fundamental responsibility of the government in this field?

I believe any administration recognizes its responsibility to inform the American people. Harsh critics of Republican President Eisenhower contended that he was unaware of this responsibility, or that he rejected it. I covered all eight years of the Eisenhower administration as a Washington newspaperman and dispute that criticism. Bitter critics of Democratic President Johnson made the same charge about him. Having covered part of his administration and served in part, I also dispute that criticism. This is not a partisan political issue. Any man who can be elected President of the United States in our times is aware that he has a responsibility to inform the people and, at the conclusion of his term, hopes that he has done so.

Once that assumption is accepted, three obviously interlinking but nonetheless separate choices lie before the Executive Branch.

One is to aim simply at making the information available. Let us agree that this means making as much information as possible available, within security limitations and within the framework of sensible, orderly government. Security is not the only test; I do not believe that a private internal memorandum from me to the Secretary of Defense listing two potential deputies I recommended hiring should have been made public.

A second, and more complex, objective is to make the information available and to get it to the American people.

A third is to make it available, try to get it to the people and try to ensure that the people understand it.

Basically, the Executive Branch of the government today seeks only to meet the first objective—to release the material, to get it to the press, to get it into the public domain. It does very little about Objectives Two and Three, although there are, of course, a few kindergarten techniques directed toward actually getting the information to the people and even trying to ensure that they comprehend it.

Assume that you are Assistant Secretary and want to issue a government statement that one of our aircraft inadvertently has crossed into Red China. It can be put into a simple news release, printed and distributed to the reporters in the Pentagon press room as a Department of Defense announcement—and you have now put it into the public domain. Or you can accept the invitation of the television networks to read it in front of their cameras, thus making some effort to see that it reaches the people. As a more positive step, you can inform the television people that the Secretary of Defense will appear to read it before their cameras.

If you want to try to ensure that the people understand it, you will call a news conference for the Secretary, who will spend fifteen minutes tracing the background of other such inadvertent border violations. Fact sheets listing them all will have been prepared for the press. Following that session, the Chief of Staff of the Air Force will invite a dozen Pentagon newsmen to his office for a cup of coffee and will provide a professional judgment on how these things can happen in the day of supersonic aircraft.

Your basic responsibility to inform the people has been met when the simple announcement is handed to the Pentagon press, and when you attempt as honestly as possible to answer their questions. From that point on, the tactics are designed clearly to build the story up or to play it down. Some stories cannot be built up unless the President is brought into the act; others cannot be held down no matter how quietly they are announced.

In some instances individuals moved vigorously on their own to set both facts and analyses of those facts before the people, with the hope that public understanding would result, although even these instances have been rare. For seven years Robert McNamara consistently attempted to educate the public on strategic nuclear warfare—and he succeeded to a remarkable degree, chiefly because he tried for so long. Part of that effort was a short but high-powered campaign to explain his antiballistic missile decision in the fall of 1967. McNamara's intensive public exposition on the air war in North Vietnam in August, 1967, was designed to *permit* understanding by the people, but no special effort was made to *ensure* that the people read and understood his case.

If there was a single top-level Pentagon "campaign" to reach the people, it was Clark M. Clifford's intensive effort to win public support for his efforts to de-escalate the war in 1968, which will be discussed in another chapter.

But these are all unusual examples, and none was government-wide. Only exceptionally does the government as a whole try to see that information reaches the people, and almost never does it seek additionally to ensure that the people understand that information.

Internally, there are variations in announcement tactics, and attention is paid to where important disclosures should be announced, or when or by what arm of the government. Should the announcement originate in Saigon, Washington or Paris? If in Washington, should it come from the White House, State or the Pentagon? Should it be made by the President, a Cabinet officer, an Assistant Secretary, a lower-ranking official or by news release?

But these decisions again are related to the immediate impact of that first-day story, and are not followed by a significant effort to see either that the information reaches the people or that the people comprehend it.

Observers frequently marvel that the nation which successfully peddles Coca-Cola to so much of the human race cannot explain to its own people the major policy decisions it makes. Certainly the Kennedy-Johnson administrations did not begin to explain satisfactorily our objectives in Southeast Asia. In the entire Executive Branch of the federal government, for example, not one man had as his sole responsibility the function of explaining the war to the people.

What does the government do to explain our participation in the North Atlantic Treaty Organization in 1969? To inform the people on the issues before the Nuclear Planning Group? To help them understand the balance-of-payments problem? To put before them in an intelligent way the justification for aiding both Arab nations and Israel in the Middle East? It does almost nothing. An occasional Assistant Secretary of State or Defense makes an occasional speech—which is almost always handled in three or four paragraphs by the press, except in the city where the official is appearing. A President or a Secretary of State responds to an occasional news conference question on one of these issues. But there is no plan or program to inform the people.

And if anyone today should develop a sensible plan, bathed in total objectivity, the newspapers would start protesting the government "public relations campaign" and editorialize about "Pentagon press agentry" or blast the White House "propaganda machine." (I am not talking about a plan to persuade the people to agree with the government's objectives, but merely one to explain those objectives.)

The observers who marvel that we succeed in selling Coca-Colas but fail in explaining government policy have not examined the case. Of course we fail. They overlook the fact that we do not attempt to explain the policy, that no apparatus for doing so exists within the federal government, and that any attempt to create even a tenth-rate apparatus would be greeted with hostility both by press and by Congress.

Yet the government must do far more than it has done heretofore. To make the information available is no longer good enough. It does not reach the people, or does not reach them in intelligible form. The present communications system between the government and the people, through the press, will not meet the demands of the 1970s.

Most of the press will argue immediately that the problem will solve itself as soon as the government does a better job of releasing information. While acknowledging a "communications gap" for the last few years, it will contend that this was chiefly the fault of President Johnson. It was the President's responsibility, the press will say, to put across his basic policies to the people. If he failed, it was because he was too secretive, because he played his cards too close to his vest, because he misled even the White House press corps on such simple issues as whether he was going to the Ranch for the weekend. The press will argue that it does its job well enough and that the people will be served well enough if the government concentrates on putting out more of the truth more accurately and more rapidly.

This is precisely the argument I made as a Washington newspaperman for eighteen years. It was valid to a degree, under my own regime in the Pentagon. Too much information which should have been released was not. Too much was classified. Too much which should have come to the surface naturally was rooted out by the press.

The problem will not be solved, however, simply by government improvement in these areas. If the government does a reasonable job of making information available and the press a reasonable job of reporting, then the citizen who expends a reasonable amount of effort trying to keep up with the major issues of his country should achieve reasonable results. In my opinion he does not; he falls far short. Most Americans fall short because they are not interested enough to spend a reasonable amount of time acquiring such information, but even those who are find it almost impossible to keep up.

Some persons in government do much more. It is not unheard of in this nation for an official of the government to expend time and energy to ensure that information is not only released but that it reaches the people and, further, that the people understand it. Millions of official man-hours are spent in pursuit of precisely those three objectives. This is called a political campaign.

The candidate knows that he will reach few voters by one speech, one news release, one television appearance or the publication of one position paper—whether his constituency is a nation, a state or a single city ward. And if he is a winner and becomes an officeholder, he necessarily cuts down on the time spent communicating with the people but continues to use all the campaign techniques to a lesser degree as he immediately begins to get ready for the next election.

Most of us, I believe, applaud the candidate who works especially hard putting his views before the people. We do not condemn him as a propagandist. And while much of the money his campaign costs him does not come from the average taxpayer, we all do pay our share of his salary, office space and secretarial help, and we do not feel he is misusing our funds simply because he exerts extra effort to see that the people understand the information he releases.

I can recall traveling across the state of Ohio for more than two months in 1950 with the late Senator Robert A. Taft, when he was running for re-election against State Auditor Joseph T. Ferguson. Taft had won by only seventeen thousand votes six years earlier. He did not yet know in the fall of 1950 whether he wanted to try again for the presidency in 1952, but he did want to win an impressive victory as a foundation for the future. He wanted, in McNamara Pentagonese, to keep his options open.

At the beginning there were only four of us traveling together —Taft; I. Jack Martin, his administrative assistant; David S.

Ingalls, Taft's cousin and campaign associate; and I, representing the Cleveland *Plain Dealer*. Later the official group grew mightily, dozens of newsmen also joined the caravan and I lost my private seat in the Senator's car.

For eleven weeks we listened to Taft make more than ten speeches a day. He said exactly the same things in each, rarely mentioning Ferguson, running always against President Truman. The issue, he insisted, was liberty versus socialism. He explained why that was the issue. He explained it in every one of the eighty-eight counties of Ohio, in church dining halls, at Rotary lunches, at town squares, in Union League Clubs where he was worshiped, in CIO factories where he was hated. He explained it over breakfast and after dinner, in the rain and the snow, between halves of high school football games, at college fraternity smokers and in seventh-grade classrooms.

It has been nineteen years since that campaign, and I can recite the liberty-versus-socialism speech today. So, until his death, could my dear friend Jack Martin, who was to become an Administrative Assistant to President Eisenhower and a federal judge. Never, except for fresh Brussels sprouts and canned fruit cocktail in World War II, have I become so weary of anything. The burning issue at each stop was whether the schedule would permit the ten-minute version, the thirty-minute version or the forty-five-minute version.

Yet the Senator knew what he was doing. He was reaching the people of Ohio with a message. His words and views appeared in every weekly and every daily newspaper. They were heard over every major radio station in the state and dozens of minor ones. (Television was not yet abroad in our land to any dominant extent.) The people who voted in Ohio in 1950 knew the Taft philosophy, and knew where he stood on all major foreign and domestic issues, because these views were wrapped up in the liberty-versus-socialism speech. He communicated, by repetition and hard work.

Harrison Salisbury and the *New York Times* were practicing skillfully the art of repetition in the bombing stories. The government's puny response of a few letters, a few press releases, a few public statements and face-to-face explanations to a few Pentagon reporters did almost nothing to counter them.

But our basic failure was not the weakness of our response, for by December of 1966 it was too late to recover from the type of stories Salisbury chose to write. By that time, and once he had begun, nothing of substantive value could have been done by the government to save us with the people. Our basic failure, which preceded the Salisbury series by months, was that we had permitted ourselves to get into a position of dangerous vulnerability; and we had done so not by lying but by being exceptionally stupid.

Overly sensitive to the criticism of those who opposed the bombing, we had emphasized too often that this was the most cautious, careful, surgically executed bombing campaign in history. Only a week before the Salisbury series began, the Department issued this statement in response to inquiries from the press:

We have been asked what measures are taken to avoid civilian casualties in air attacks against military targets in North Vietnam. These measures include discrimination in ordnance applied, selection of the most experienced pilots for particular missions so as to achieve maximum precision, specific pilot tactics including the axis of attack, visibility of target and extraordinary pilot orientation on target identification.

Every word was true.

Secretary McNamara had described the targets in general terms dozens of times. Months earlier, on February 2, 1966, at the end of the bombing pause, newsmen on Capitol Hill asked him whether the administration was considering widening the bombing. He responded, in part:

"Our bombing program is directed toward the same objectives today, and will be tomorrow, as it was before the pause. We are directing the aircraft against military targets, only military targets, and those particularly associated with the lines of communications between North Vietnam and South Vietnam over which they are sending the men and equipment which are the foundation of the Vietcong effort to subvert the government of South Vietnam."

Every word was true. But it had not occurred to us that by emphasizing military targets and emphasizing measures taken to minimize civilian damage, we gradually were convincing the people of the United States that all our bombs fell always upon the targets at which they were directed, that we killed no civilians and that we destroyed no civilian structures.

There had never been any secrecy about the amount of bombing we were doing, and we had not even considered the possibility that our citizens would believe that so much bombing could be done without civilian casualties.

The number of missions flown against North Vietnamese targets was announced each day, so that any newsman, by doing his own arithmetic, or by asking the Department of Defense, could learn how many missions had been launched against the North from the beginning.

Similarly, the total ordnance expended in Southeast Asia was made available. On April 14, 1966, more than eight months before the Salisbury pieces, McNamara disclosed that we had used more than 50,000 tons of bombs in the month of March alone. Assuming an average bomb weight of 500 pounds, we had dropped in Southeast Asia in that one month approximately 200,000 individual bombs! The Secretary disclosed at that same time that the total air ordnance tonnage for the year of 1966 alone would be more than 600,000 tons—91 percent of the total consumption for all 37 months of the Korean War.

We had disclosed that we were buying bombs at the rate of 1.8 million a year, air-to-ground rounds (excluding bombs) at the rate of 88 million rounds, air-launched 40-millimeter grenades at the rate of 6.8 million and 2.75-inch rockets at the annual rate of 4.8 million. The people had been told before Salisbury went to North Vietnam that we had flown more than 24,000 bombing missions against the North and that we were well along the route to dropping more bombs in Vietnam than in both Europe and North Africa during all of World War II.

These were not secrets; all of this was public information; all of it had been given the press; all was on the record; all had been written by Pentagon newsmen. Of course there had been damage to civilian buildings. Of course there had been civilian casualties. Not in the furthest corners of the minds of the top officials of the Department of Defense was there a glimmer of belief that the people were developing a different impression.

We should have known better. And I especially, paid by the taxpayers to help keep them informed and trusted by my superiors to alert them to major pitfalls, should have known better.

I should have known that all this information was not being absorbed by the people or the editors, even though it had all been written by the reporters. From my own experience covering the Department of Defense, I should have known that even the newsmen who conscientiously had reported each grain of information, story by story, would not sort it all into logical sequence and conclude automatically that, no matter how deliberate and sincere its intent, no nation could carry out bombing attacks of this magnitude and expend this awesome amount of ordnance without causing destruction to nonwar buildings and death to innocent civilians.

I should have known, but I did not. The newsmen did not have time between assignments and between crises for this kind of logical thinking, and neither did we on the government side. There was always a new crisis, unrelated to bombing and unrelated to Vietnam. When each had passed, or in the midst of each, again the protests would be sounded that the bombing was immoral and that we should not be murdering babies.

And the government would respond, over and over again, that never in history had such care been taken. We would again emphasize the ground rules and the restrictions, again point out that our targets were military, again proclaim that we were not deliberately attacking people, again declare that this was not

London or Coventry or Berlin, again explain that this bombing was unlike any in history, again show that even the axis of attack was planned so that any error would cause the least damage.

I did not then realize that making available the different pieces of the puzzle at different times was not enough. What we should have done was to tell the people what we assumed they knew: despite our target selection and our care, of course we were killing North Vietnamese civilians—not in large numbers, not as civilians have been killed in other wars, but of course we were killing civilians.

We did not do so.

And because we did not, when Harrison Salisbury wrote as he did in December, 1966, a great many Americans became more disillusioned with their government and more convinced that it was lying to them.

It was, in my view, a national disaster. It was also a supreme example of the importance of an intelligent and organized government public affairs operation in today's complex world. Without changing a bomb, without changing a word of Salisbury, the credibility disaster could have been avoided had the government earlier done the job it should have done to explain the bombing effort to the country. We did not fail to make the information available. We did fail to explain it and to see that our explanation reached the people.

The
Attack
on the *Liberty*

June, 1967

In an official Pentagon document dated November 6, 1965, appears this language describing a ship of the United States Navy:

The mission of this ship is to conduct technical research operations in support of U.S. Navy electronic research projects which include electromagnetic propagation studies and advanced communications systems such as moon relay and satellite communications.

The ship was the AGTR-5. A stands for Auxiliary; G for General, and *TR* for Technical Research.

She entered the Mediterranean Sea on June 2, 1967, after taking aboard fuel and provisions at Rota, Spain. Her orders were to proceed at best possible sustained speed to an operating area in the Eastern Mediterranean, north of the Sinai Peninsula, where she arrived June 8.

The Israeli-Arab Six-Day War was in its fourth day.

Once on station, the AGTR-5 was to steam in an area bounded on the north by latitude 32 degrees North, on the east and west by longitudes 34 degrees East and 33 degrees East, and on the south by a curved line following the contour of the coast, 12.5 nautical miles off the coast.

The United Arab Republic claims a twelve-mile territorial sea, Israel six and the United States three. While the United States recognizes claims of only three miles, the operating area of

AGTR-5 was defined to ensure that she would remain in international waters recognized by all parties concerned. Behaving conservatively, she never approached closer than 13.6 nautical miles from land.

She was not hiding, nor did she have reason to hide. At her masthead flew her normal-size American flag, five feet by eight feet, and her distinguishing letters and number—AGTR-5— were painted on her bow. Her name was painted on her stern: USS *Liberty*

She was listed in the international standard naval identification book, Jane's *Fighting Ships*, as a noncombatant, and her configuration was shown in that international book.

Liberty was in a modified condition of readiness three. That meant she had her normal steaming watch on deck, plus one man standing by the forward gun mounts. She carried four pedestal-mounted .50-caliber Browning machine guns—two single mounts on her forecastle and identical mounts on either side of the deckhouse aft of the bridge. Bridge lookouts had been set. Under modified condition three, they would handle the two after guns in case of trouble until the crew manned general-quarters stations.

Her normal speed on this mission was a poky five knots; her normal steaming colors were flown; her normal navigational lights were lighted at night. She did not darken ship at night; she had not even exercised a darken-ship drill during her deployment.

The crew could see the coastline of the Sinai Peninsula. Commander William L. McGonagle, USN, the commanding officer, knew exactly where he was. A conspicuous minaret at El Arish became visible at 9:30 that morning of June 8, helping verify the exact position. Radar ranges were taken on the nearest land on the same bearing as the minaret, which was also identified by radar.

At 10:30, a flight of two unidentified jet aircraft orbited the ship at about ten thousand feet, circling three times, approximately two miles away. *Liberty's* lookouts could not make out the insignia on them. Another aircraft, propeller-driven, was flying at very low altitude, perhaps five hundred feet, parallel to and over the coast in the vicinity of El Arish. It did not approach the ship, staying at a distance of approximately twelve to fifteen miles.

A little later, at 10:56, a fourth plane was sighted crossing astern three to five miles away. After circling the ship around the starboard side, it headed back toward the Sinai Peninsula. Officers and lookouts could see no markings on it and could not identify it. While it made no attempt to signal the ship, each thirty minutes it returned for another orbit.

As the morning passed, *Liberty* chugged along at five knots. At 10:39 she had been on a course of 253 degrees with the minaret at El Arish seventeen miles away; at 11:32 she changed again to 283 degrees. She was now moving in a west-northwesterly direction, away from the Sinai Peninsula.

At 1:10 that afternoon the ship went to general quarters for a routine exercise in chemical-attack procedures, as part of the mandatory training program established by the Commander Service Force, Atlantic Fleet. It was not related to *Liberty's* mission in the Eastern Mediterranean, and at its completion, at 1:48 P.M., the ship returned to modified condition three.

The skipper lingered on the bridge, along with several of his officers.

There was no doubt about the location of the ship. Aware of shoals south of his operating area, the captain checked the radar screen himself, personally sighting the minaret at El Arish on a bearing of 142 degrees at a distance of 25.5 miles.

At 1:58 the lookouts stationed immediately above the bridge reported jet aircraft in the sky. McGonagle looked for himself. He later told a U.S. Navy Court of Inquiry:

I went to the starboard wing of the bridge with my binoculars and there observed one aircraft of similar characteristics, if not identical, to the two aircraft which were sighted earlier in the day and upon which a sighting report had been submitted. It appeared to be on a parallel course traveling in the same direction as the ship. While I observed this aircraft, I did not see it approach the ship directly in a hostile attitude.

Ships of the *Liberty*'s type were accustomed to reconnaissance aircraft. Since the plane was five miles away and more than a mile high, McGonagle, in international waters, felt no special concern. But later he told this story:

Within a couple of minutes, a loud explosion was heard that appeared to me to come from the port side of the ship. I immediately ordered the general alarm to be sounded, and this was done. I went from the starboard wing of the bridge to the port wing to see the area of damage. I immediately noticed that the two 55-gallon gasoline drums stowed on the 01 level, portside amidships, were burning furiously. . . . I ordered the Executive Officer to go to the starboard side of the ship and proceed down to the 01 level, cross over to the port side, and there release the gasoline cans. Lieutenant O'Connor was still on the bridge and he joined the Executive Officer and both proceeded to the starboard wing of the bridge, 03 level.

Approximately the time they reached the top of the ladder to proceed down, the ship received an apparent bomb hit in the vicinity of the whaleboat stowed on the 02 level starboard side, immediately aft of the bridge. Mr. Armstrong, Mr. O'Connor and others in the bridge area were thrown back into the bridge and other personnel in the pilot house were blown from their feet. At this time, I grabbed the engine order annunciator and rang up: "All flank ahead." . . .

I ordered a person, who I believed to be Lt. Bennett [Maurice H. Bennett of Pittsburgh], to report to CNO [the Chief of Naval Operations] via the Highcom [High Command circuit] that *Liberty* was under attack by unidentified jet aircraft and that immediate assistance was required.

Fifty-eight hundred miles away in the Pentagon, we received that word: The USS *Liberty* had been attacked by unidentified jet aircraft. Ten officials from the Navy, the Joint Staff and OSD met immediately in the Secretary's office.

We had no information other than that in the message Mc-Gonagle had sent—which included the *Liberty*'s position.

Two decisions were to be made.

The first and obviously the most important was what to do

for the United States Navy ship which had requested help. Aircraft from two Sixth Fleet carriers in the Mediterranean, the *America* and the *Saratoga*, immediately had been ordered launched and dispatched to the area. Authority was given to use any force required to defend the *Liberty* from further attacks.

Our ignorance in Washington was abysmal: We did not know who was attacking her; we did not know why she was being attacked; we did not know whether she had sunk or was soon to sink.

Robert McNamara later described the uncertainty of that first hour.

When the *Liberty* was attacked, we had a task force in the Mediterranean. We received a flash report here in the Pentagon at the time of attack. We examined the situation. My first reaction—that is the question I immediately posed to the Chiefs and the Joint Staff was: Is it not likely it was attacked by Soviet forces?

We knew the location of certain Soviet forces in the area. Certainly the initial reaction, having known their location, would be to attack those forces. Within a half hour, however, we concluded that a Soviet attack was unlikely.

The next obvious answer was it had been attacked by Egyptians. Who else would have done it if it were not the Soviets or the Egyptians? Well, that too proved in error. It took us a while to find that out.

One possible motivation for the attack could have been the reports which the United Arab Republic had been circulating for several days—reports that aircraft from the *America* and the *Saratoga* had flown to airfields in Israel. This was drivel, and our office promptly had said so, declaring that all Sixth Fleet aircraft then were, and had been, several hundred miles from the area of conflict. Yet we suspected that morning that some U.A.R. commander had taken his own government's propaganda seriously, or that the government itself had arrived at some insane conclusion. Someone, after all, had attacked our ship.

The question of retaliation was raised, but required little discussion, since we could not be certain against whom to retaliate. As a precaution, ships of the Sixth Fleet were ordered to steam toward the *Liberty*, although the nearest was hundreds of miles away.

The Soviet Union also had ships in the Mediterranean. In McNamara's office we discussed what the Russians would think if they were not responsible. How would they react? Their intelligence-collection trawlers would know that we had launched armed aircraft which were streaking toward the war zone (just as they had known earlier that the U.A.R.'s accusation that our carrier planes had helped Israel was false).

Preferring to take no chances, President Johnson used the "Hot Line" teleprinter circuit to inform Premier Alexei N. Kosygin that we were dispatching fighter planes from our carriers in the Eastern Mediterranean to go to the assistance of one of our ships which had been attacked there.

The second major decision before us in the Secretary's office was in my public affairs area, and focused on two questions:

First, should we make an immediate announcement with the scanty information we had, rather than wait for additional facts?

I argued that we should, despite the paucity of information and the overwhelming problems the government would face. We had no other rational choice. Since we were unaware either of the identity of the attacker or of his motive, we had no grounds on which to reach an intelligent estimate of what course his public affairs maneuvering would take.

Had the attack been ordered by a government or was it the work of trigger-happy junior officers? Did the attacker have reason for attempting to conceal his guilt? Would he deny any knowledge of the act? If he tried to do so now, how good was his security? In either the Soviet Union or the United Arab Republic, was discipline so strong that some enlisted man or officer involved would not leak the story to his friends and neighbors? And if that happened, how long would it take the information to reach foreign diplomats and the press, whatever the desires of the government? Or did the attacker plan to take the public affairs offensive? Would he sound the trumpets and announce that a United States warship caught penetrating his territorial waters had been punished severely for her transgression?

We lacked sound grounds even for logical guesses.

Certainly the United States would be at a disadvantage if the attacker chose to announce the episode on his terms. Though he probably would lie, his story would come first, and would be accepted as fact by a significant portion of the world simply because it was said first, said loudly and said clearly. Many nations —not all of them on the other side of the Iron Curtain—are extremely skilled in this art. Combining official announcements with high-level background explanations and low-level distorted leaks, they achieve great success with the more gullible and less sophisticated members of the press, and they plant in the public mind an untruth about us which our government never totally overcomes.

I argued that, despite my inclination to await the receipt of more information, the advantages of speaking out as quickly and clearly as we could were overriding in this instance. We would be telling the American people the facts of the attack as we knew them, and all the facts. We would be leveling with our people to the best of our ability. We could do no more in these first few minutes.

The press, of course, would expect a great deal more—and would expect it far more rapidly than the government would have it to give. Many reporters—not all or even a majority— would take the position that the government was holding back information deliberately. Describing the government's "I don't know" answers to scores of their questions, some newsmen would write: "The Pentagon today refused to say . . ." Pentagon silence and administration duplicity would then be assailed by editorial writers basing their conclusions upon news stories of that tone. The credibility of the Assistant Secretary, the Secretary, the President and the United States government would be questioned.

Many government public affairs decisions would be made differently if the government felt that all newsmen were responsible, or that 95 percent were. We had no such convictions, nor do our successors. In this instance, however, it was clear to me that we would have to accept the consequences of "cover-up" charges and move forward as rapidly as possible to give the American people the information available, however scanty. Confronting us was a major naval tragedy and quite possibly a major international crisis.

I recommended that we draft an announcement of three or four sentences, clear it by telephone with the State Department and White House and release it to the press corps covering the Pentagon as quickly as we could. With the exception of one man, all in the room eventually agreed.

Before proceeding, we had to face up to the second question: how to identify the ship. Should we call her an intelligence-collection ship or merely a technical-research ship? She was, in fact, both.

This was June, 1967, seven months before the *Pueblo* case, and at a time when United States government never had declared officially that certain of its peacetime ships were in the intelligence-collection business. Secrecy about the operations of these ships was not initiated by President Johnson or his Secretaries of State and Defense; these officials were following the practice of all recent Presidents and Secretaries.

On the side of instant identification, this was the argument:

This ship collects intelligence, a fact that will be leaked to the press by the Navy, the State Department, the Office of the Secretary of Defense or the Congress within a few hours. Almost inevitably, it also will be alleged by the attacker. The information then will be a secret no longer—and, indeed, it is nothing but an official secret right now. A tragedy of some kind, still undetermined, has occurred, and its repercussions will cause grief enough to our country in the weeks ahead. The administration need not accept an additional problem. We should take the public affairs initiative, leveling with our people from the beginning. The government need not permit the press to force it into a classified point-by-point discussion of the operations of the ship. We will merely identify it as an intelligence collector and insist that all details of its functions are classified.

On the side of nonidentification, this was the argument:

While we live in the most open nation in the world, there are matters involving the national interest—notably some aspects of intelligence collection—on which secrecy is essential. On these the nation can afford no deliberate violations of security and no involuntary indiscretions. In the Department of Defense alone are nearly five million persons, all of whom know today that they are not to discuss intelligence matters under any conditions. Since they are human they sometimes err, and not everyone lives up to the tight restrictions all of the time, but everyone is aware of the rules. Nothing must be done to change this policy or to suggest a change in it. While the security loss in this particular case might be insignificant, or even zero, the loss in the discipline which must pertain if a world-wide intelligence apparatus is to function might be considerable.

Of course, the argument went on, the *Liberty* will be called a spy ship by the press. But this is not at all the same thing as an official government admission. The difference is a practical operational one. A neutral country will receive in its port a technical-research ship, regardless of how the press describes it. Some of the same countries will not risk the criticism of internal political opponents or the pressures of powerful Communist nations by receiving an acknowledged United States intelligence vessel.

International advisers brought up another point. The governments and peoples of both Israel and the United Arab Republic might be offended if the United States admitted openly it had sent an intelligence ship close to their countries to eavesdrop on their radio conversations. Although legal, the act could be construed as unfriendly. We would gain nothing internationally, they said, by asking officially for such criticism.

As the issue was discussed around the table, Secretary Mc-Namara listened to the Navy, the intelligence experts, the international authorities, Cyrus Vance and me. His personal preference was to support my recommendation to call the ship an intelligence collector in the first announcement, but he yielded to the security and diplomatic arguments of those who felt that we should stick to the official unclassified description of the *Liberty* as a technical-research ship.

With that decision I scribbled out a two-paragraph announcement, to which amendments were proposed by the group. Within ten minutes we had agreed to the following:

A U.S. Navy technical research ship, the USS LIBERTY (AGTR-5) was attacked about 9 A.M. (EDT) today approximately 15 miles north of the Sinai Peninsula in international waters of the Mediterranean Sea.

The LIBERTY departed Rota, Spain, June 2nd and arrived at her position this morning to assure communications between U.S. Government posts in the Middle East and to assist in relaying information concerning the evacuation of American dependents and other American citizens from the countries of the Middle East.

Professionally, this was dreadfully inadequate and the unanswered questions were overwhelming, but it was the best we could do with the available information. The highest officials of the Navy, the intelligence and reconnaissance operations and the Office of the Secretary of Defense were assembled. We were in telephone communication with relevant authorities in the field and had before us, so far as anyone in the room knew, every scrap of pertinent information.

Fortunately, before telephone checks on the announcement were completed with the State Department and the White House, additional information was brought in from both the *Liberty* and State. From the ship came a preliminary report on casualties and on her condition. Even more important, from State came word sent to it by the government of Israel.

After digesting the new information, we added two more short paragraphs to the release:

The United States Government has been informed by the Israel government that the attack was made in error by Israeli forces, and an apology has been received from Tel Aviv.

Initial reports of casualties are 4 dead and 53 wounded. The LIB-ERTY is steaming north from the area at a speed of 8 knots to meet U.S. forces moving to her aid. It is reported she is in no danger of sinking.

While stunned by the incredible news, from my public affairs viewpoint our position had improved immensely. Despite the tremendous gap in our knowledge, we now could provide the public with a rational statement—recognizing, of course, the danger that even these scanty reports invariably are erroneous. A cardinal rule in an establishment as large as the Department of Defense is to assume that first reports are always wrong, no matter what their security classification, no matter to whom they are addressed. Beware of them. Ignore them. File them. Do not, under any circumstances or conditions, share them with the press, for they will come back to plague you. They are the handmaidens of incredibility. Reject them.

But in this instance the dangers of saying nothing overpowered conservatism, for it was essential that we get something to the people. If the reports turned out to be accurate, we had now a skeleton of a story. We could say that a United States ship had been attacked and could pinpoint its location. We knew what it was doing there and what the government had decided to say about what it was doing there. We could identify the attackers and give an initial casualty report. And we had the basic informa-tion on the condition of the ship: it was making way under its own power; it was not in danger of sinking.

Within an hour after the news of the tragedy had reached the Pentagon, the public was given our first report.

During the discussions, I had borrowed the Secretary's hot line to my desk and asked my office to have the Navy pull to-gether as much as possible of the routine background informa-tion newsmen would want: Where was the ship coming from? What was the size of its crew? Who was the commanding officer? What was his home town? How soon would we have a list of the crew, with home towns? Was the ship armed? With what?

While we had agreed in the Secretary's office to use the language of the 1965 unclassified description of the ship in discussing its mission, the "moon relay" phrase sounded too farfetched, and I later deleted it from the description to be read to the press.

A few more facts were flashed in during the next few minutes. Motor torpedo boats and aircraft had participated in the attack. Torpedo damage was reported. We did not know how many torpedo boats, how many aircraft, how many torpedoes, how many bombs or how much strafing, if any.

The Assistant Secretary of Defense (Public Affairs) is sometimes called the "chief spokesman" for the Department of Defense. Possibly that is technically true, although I would assume that the Secretary of Defense actually would be the "chief spokesman." The man who does more speaking for the Department than anyone else is one of the four Directors under the Assistant Secretary, the Director of Defense Information. As soon as the *Liberty* story broke, most of the seventy-one persons working for Brigadier General Winant K. Sidle (my first Director of Defense Information, whom we had stolen from General Earle G. Wheeler, Chairman of the Joint Chiefs of Staff) would be engulfed by questions from the news media.

While the Director of Defense Information and his men are the professionals who deal with news media far more than the two Deputy Assistant Secretaries of Defense or the Assistant Secretary, the most important news announcements were often made by Secretaries McNamara or Clifford, or the Assistant Secretary. On June 8, 1967, I walked to the cluttered room on the second floor in which the regulars of the Pentagon press corps have their desks and read the four-paragraph statement we had drafted upstairs in McNamara's office.

This is not the most efficient way to make an announcement in the Pentagon. Each of the wire services, Associated Press and United Press International, has two men covering the building, and they are highly competitive. Executives of both wire services keep logs on how many newspapers use an AP story, and how many a UPI story, on a particular event. (Many newspapers bought one service or the other; many bought both.) With morning and afternoon newspapers, with each large paper running several editions every day, and with different time zones, some newspaper somewhere is almost always on deadline. In my days on the copy desk of the Cleveland *Plain Dealer* twenty years ago, the wire service which beat the other into the office by five minutes often was the one which made the paper. For the reporter working on a daily newspaper, time is especially important only when he is on a deadline; for a wire-service reporter, time is always important.

When a major Pentagon announcement is read in the reporters' room, the wire services may attempt to get a head start by having one man listen and take notes while the other simultaneously dictates on the telephone to a rewrite man in his main office in Washington. This breeds inaccuracy, it is unfair to the organizations represented by only one man, and it leads to additional hubbub. (A pack of reporters at any time is a noisy enough contingent.)

The work of the government could be performed with a little more dignity if the newsmen were asked to walk a few yards down the hall to the public affairs studio for an announcement, although this would be an inconvenience to some, who take notes on their typewriters during question-and-answer sessions following the reading of a statement. We sometimes went to the press room, sometimes met the newsmen in the studio and sometimes called them to my office. When speed was particularly important, however, the preferred method was simply for one of us to go to the reporters' room and accept the concomitant disadvantages, and on the *Liberty* case I chose that course. Among the questions asked after the announcement were these:

Q: What attacked it?
A: It was attacked by motor torpedo boat or boats, and aircraft.
Q: Was it hit by torpedoes?

A: The report we have indicates at least one torpedo hit.

Q: Did she fire back?

A: She is armed only with our .50-caliber machine guns. I don't have information on whether she fired back.

Q: Were her colors up?

A: Yes, of course.

Q: How big is the crew?

A: Fifteen officers, 279 men and 3 technical representative civilians.

Q: What is her size?

A: 455 feet long, 62-foot beam, 23-foot draft and a full load displacement of about 11,000 tons.

Q: Is it a converted warship?

A: It is a converted liberty ship. . . .

Q: What is the closest Israeli port near there?

A: I don't know. The reported position from the ship itself is 31 degrees, 23 minutes North, 33 degrees, 25 minutes East. That is about the extent of my information.

Q: Is it a communications ship?

A: (*Reading*) The mission of the ship is to conduct technical research operations in support of U.S. Navy electronic research projects which include electromagnetic propagation studies and advanced communications systems such as satellite communications. Technically, it is a technical research ship. It was being used for communications purposes at this time.

Q: Were any of the TecReps* among the casualties?

A: We haven't any idea.

Q: Who was the skipper?

A: Commanding Officer is William L. McGonagle; the Executive Officer Lieutenant Commander Phillip M. Armstrong.

Q: What were the home towns?

A: I don't know yet. I'll get it for you.

We knew no more. Commander McGonagle had been too busy to fire off a play-by-play account of the attack or of his reactions to it. Later he thought that there had been six to eight attacks, with aircraft strafing, firing rockets and dropping bombs. He was to testify:

---

* Civilian technicians.

It seemed to me that the attacks were made in a criss-cross fashion over the ship, with each attack coming at approximately 45-second-to-one-minute intervals. After the starboard bridge bomb hit, I ordered personnel to be organized for a fire-fighting party to put out the fire in the vicinity of the whale boat. The whale boat was burning furiously. . . .

Sometime after the starboard bridge bomb . . . another attack from the starboard quarter was made and I was hit with flying shrapnel. I was not knocked off my feet. I was only shaken up and it made me dance around a little bit, but my injuries did not appear to me to be of any consequence. I noticed slight burns on my starboard forearm and I noticed blood oozing on my trousers right leg. Since I could walk and there was no apparent pain, I gave no further consideration to these minor injuries.

McGonagle estimated that the total air attack took only five or six minutes. The public-address system was destroyed. The electrically powered intercom system was not working. Most of the telephone circuits had been severed. Runners were used to relay his orders to repair parties. A young ensign, David G. Lucas of Virginia Beach, became his assistant on the bridge.

While the commander did not know who or what was attacking his ship, he did know he wanted a record of the assault. Injured, and issuing fire-fighting and damage-control orders, he nonetheless opened the bridge safe, took out a camera and from the port wing of the bridge snapped photographs of the planes as they passed over his ship after their attack.

At 2:24, twenty-four minutes after the first bomb, lookouts saw three high-speed motor torpedo boats approaching from the northeast at a distance of about 15 miles, in a wedge formation, moving 27 to 30 knots.

Commander McGonagle recalled later:

They appeared to be about 150 to 200 yards apart. It appeared that they were approaching the ship in a torpedo launch attitude, and since I did not have direct communication with gun control or the gun mounts, I told a man from the bridge, whose identity I do not recall, to proceed to Mount 51 and take the boats under fire. The boats continued to approach the ship at high speed and on a constant bearing with decreasing range.

After the attack, but before the Court of Inquiry, there was to be a question about whether the United States ensign was flying. In Israel suggestions were dropped to the press that the *Liberty* was improperly marked, that she could not be identified and that the flag was not flying.

The commanding officer addressed that point:

About this time I noticed that our ensign had been shot away during the air attack and I ordered David, signalman, to hoist a second ensign from the yardarm. During the air attack, our normal ensign was flying. Before the torpedo attack, a holiday-size ensign was hoisted.

The holiday ensign was the largest flag aboard—7 feet by 13 feet. Commander McGonagle ordered it flown from the yardarm since the normal flag halyard had been destroyed.

I alerted the crew as best I could to stand by for torpedo attack from starboard. I did not have an accurate ship's position at this time, but I knew that to the left of the ship's course at that time lie shoal waters, and by turning to the left I would be approaching land, closer than had been given in directives which I held in that instant in time. I realized that if I attempted to turn to starboard, I would expose a larger target to the torpedo boats. I elected to maintain a heading of 283 at maximum speed.

And now, for the first time—after the bombing, after the strafing, after the rockets, after the incendiary attacks, and as the motor torpedo boats approached—the commanding officer of the USS *Liberty* got a clue to the identity of the enemy which was killing his men.

When the boats reached an approximate range of 2000 yards, the center boat of the formation was signalling to us. Also, at this range, it appeared that they were flying an Israeli flag. This was later verified. It was not possible to read the signals from the center torpedo boat because of the intermittent blocking of view by smoke and flames.

The air attack had knocked out the *Liberty*'s starboard signal light. McGonagle attempted to signal the motor torpedo boats with a hand-held Aldis lamp. Either it was seen and ignored by the Israelis, or it was not powerful enough to penetrate the smoke pouring from the fires resulting from the bombing.

At this time I yelled to Machine Gun 51 to tell him to hold fire. I realized that there was a possibility of the aircraft having been Israeli and the attack had been conducted in error.

But *Liberty*'s communications had been blasted away by the air attacks. The man in Machine Gun 51, the starboard forward gun, fired a short burst at the boats before he knew what his captain was trying to tell him. Immediately, the aftergun on the starboard side, Mount 53, also opened fire.

The time was now 2:34 for this United States noncombatant ship, still in international waters. The Israelis fired their guns, killing Quartermaster Third Class Francis Brown at the helm. Seconds later one torpedo was seen crossing astern of the ship twenty-five yards away, and within a minute another slammed into the starboard side forward, just below the water line.

All power and steering control was lost. The ship took a nine-degree list to starboard. McGonagle saw oil and debris coming from the starboard side as his ship became dead in the water, but he had no intention of giving it up.

Immediately, I determined that the ship was in no danger of sinking and did not order any preparations to be made to abandon ship. It was my intention to ground the ship on shoal areas to the left of the ship's track to prevent its sinking, if necessary.

It was at approximately this same time that the Israeli attackers apparently had their first second thoughts. The torpedo boat stopped dead in the water five hundred yards away. One signaled by flashing light, in English: "Do you require assistance?" With no effective way of answering by signal light, *Liberty* ran up the international flag signal: "CODE LIMA INDIA: I am not under command" (not able to control movements of the ship). It was meant to convey that the Liberty was maneuvering with difficulty and that the boats should keep clear.

McGonagle was not then aware of the extent of the damage. The torpedo explosion had torn a hole in the side of the ship that extended from a few feet above the water line to below the turn of the bilge. It was shaped like a teardrop, thirty-nine feet across at its widest part. Within an area of twelve frames all compartments on two decks were flooded. Twenty-five men died in the blast.

That was the final attack, although at 3:15 two helicopters approached the ship and circled it a hundred yards away. McGonagle saw the Star of David on their hulls. Having been bombed by Israeli aircraft and torpedoed by Israeli ships, the commander did not know what to expect. He testified:

> It was not known whether these helicopters intended to strafe the ship or not. However, they did not approach the ship in a hostile manner, but kept pointed parallel to the ship as they continued around and never made a direct approach as such. They were not taken under fire by Liberty, nor did they fire at us. The torpedo boats left the general area of the ship at about 1515. About 1537, after they had departed the ship and gone to a range of about five miles, they again headed toward the ship at high speed.
> Their intentions were unknown.
> At about this same time, two unidentified jet aircraft were also noted approaching the ship from our starboard side, in similar fashion to that which preceded the initial attack. All hands were again alerted to the possibility of repeated attacks. No attacks occurred, however, and the jets disappeared from the scene.
> To further assist in identification of the ship, at 1611 [4:11 P.M.], I ordered the ship's international call sign hoisted.

McGonagle was having trouble with the Liberty's boilers and main engines. The ship was dead in the water again. But at five minutes to four he was able to restore communications.

At 1600, a message was sent providing additional information concerning the attack by unidentified aircraft and the fact that the torpedo boats had been identified as Israeli. Preliminary estimate of the number of dead and casualties, as well as the condition of the ship, was also provided.

At the time this message was being dictated to Lieutenant Bennett on the port wing of the bridge, I was lying on the deck with a tourniquet being applied to my right leg at the thigh. A few minutes prior to this, I felt myself blacking out from loss of blood and called for assistance of CTL Carpenter to apply a tourniquet. I had assumed the conn immediately after the air attack and retained the conn until rendezvous was effected with the destroyers about 0630 on the morning of 9 June 1967, leaving the bridge only about three times during the night hours to make brief head calls [bathroom visits] on the 02 level.

The *Liberty's* medical officer, Lieutenant Richard F. Kiepfer of Brooklyn, commented on Commander McGonagle's behavior to the Court of Inquiry:

The commanding officer at that time was like a rock upon which the rest of the men supported themselves. To know that he was on the bridge grievously wounded, yet having the conn and helm throughout the night calling every change of course, was the one thing that told the men "we're going to live." When I went to the bridge and saw this, I should say that I knew that I could only insult this man by suggesting that he be taken below for treatment of his wounds. I didn't even suggest it.

Ensign Lucas told the court:

It would have taken ten men the doctor's size to even begin to get him off the bridge.

He was in great pain. There were several times when he was still walking around, but it was obvious that he was in great pain. He had lost a considerable amount of blood. At several times he felt dizzy. He would not leave, but if he started to get dizzy he would turn to me, or if Mr. Bennett or Mr. Painter were there, he would say this is what course we're on, what speed to make. He would give instructions.

Lieutenant Kiepfer performed one major operation and gave emergency treatment to wounded men, having manned the main battle dressing station in the forward part of the ship. Both stations were packed with seriously injured men, and for a time there was little opportunity to do more than administer first aid. Bleeding was stopped, men received morphine for pain and were treated for shock. Lung wounds were treated to ease breathing. The most seriously wounded were transferred to the aircraft carrier *America* the following day. By that time the doctor and his two corpsmen had been on their feet, giving emergency treatment, for twenty-eight hours. Lieutenant Kiepfer testified:

> Any time we needed one volunteer, we'd get ten. If anything had to be done . . . there were hands everywhere. When we asked for two pints of blood for transfusion, we had people on the adjoining tables who were saying, "If you need some, I have this type." These were people already wounded.

The ship's medical officer and the crew were not alone in their admiration for their captain. The president of the Court of Inquiry, Rear Admiral I. C. Kidd, USN, asked McGonagle this question about navigating the ship out of dangerous waters after the attack:

> Will you please tell the Court how, while lying on your back with no compass except the magnetic compass, and based upon your recollection of your magnetic compass error in relation to the gyro compass book, you used the sun and subsequently the North Star to clear the area?

The commanding officer answered:

> Admiral, after a time on the bridge, when I had received minor injuries, I lost considerable blood and attempts to stem the flow of blood by self-help were unsuccessful, I noticed myself beginning to lose consciousness. I immediately lay down on the deck flat on my back on the port wing and raised the bleeding leg as high as possible, resting it on my port bridge chair, and there a first class communications technician by the name of Jeffrey R. Carpenter and other persons who I don't recall at this time, applied a tourniquet to my right leg which effectively stopped the flow of blood. I at no time lost consciousness and had my full faculties at all times. I realized by that time I had lost considerable amounts of blood because it was sloshing in my shoes and my right leg was completely soaked with blood.

They cut the right pant leg off to get it out of the area of the wounds. I looked at my wounds at that time and they still did not appear to me to be serious and since the flow of blood had been stopped I gave no further consideration to—I didn't consider I had any more problem in that area. I asked them to bring me coffee, fluids, a couple of salt tablets, and so forth. I conned the ship by looking aft and, by being able to see the wake of the ship, I was able to tell after steering which way to apply the rudder and how long to leave it on to attempt to average out the best course that I felt the ship should travel on to stand clear of possible shoal areas. I remained on my back for approximately an hour and a half. I then felt that I had regained sufficient strength that I was able to get up from the deck and conn the ship from the wing of the ship and from the pilot house. I couldn't stay in any one place for too long a period of time. It seemed to me that my remaining on the bridge would be able to lessen the shock that the rest of the crew had received.

There was one more visitation by an Israeli helicopter, which approached the ship, hovered at bridge level approximately thirty feet away at 6:41 that evening and departed after attempting unsuccessfully to communicate.

McGonagle's final testimony included indications of why the Pentagon's official announcements of casualties change in incidents such as this:

Three musters were taken during the night to identify the dead, the seriously injured, and to determine those who were missing. As of 1900 [7 p.m.], 11 June, two of the persons previously reported missing have been recovered [both dead], one by removing him directly from the space on board ship. The other was recovered by the PAPAGO, a Fleet tug steaming approximately six miles astern of the ship on the morning of 11 June. It is not known at this time whether any of the other individuals reported missing have drifted free of the space through the torpedo hole and vanished from the area. It will not be possible to determine until the ship has been dry-docked and the compartment dewatered and remains recovered. Preparation of casualty messages were completed as expeditiously as possible upon the completion of the musters, and necessary message notifications sent.

The ship rendezvoused with the two destroyers on the morning of 9 June. Commander Destroyer Squadron Twelve reported on board to inspect damage and confer with the Commanding Officer. Personnel from the USS DAVIS immediately boarded the ship to render assistance with damage control and treatment of injured personnel.

I have no complaint to lodge against any officer or man on board USS LIBERTY for any acts of commission or omission during the attack and post attack phase. I have nothing but the greatest admiration for their courage, their devotion to duty, and their efforts to save the ship.

In the Pentagon that morning, we knew little of Commander McGonagle's story.

It was Thursday, the regular day for a background meeting between top Defense officials and the Pentagon press corps. Customarily these sessions took place in the Secretary's dining room, usually presided over by the Secretary and Deputy Secretary of Defense, although sometimes either man alone would attend and sometimes either would have with him another high-ranking associate. Under the rules, the reporters could write any material they heard which they considered newsworthy, but could not use direct quotations and could identify the sources only as "Defense officials." McNamara, Vance and I usually lunched together on backgrounder day to discuss the questions most likely to arise. Additionally, a list of the toughest "dirty questions"— known within our organization as "DQs"—and factual information on each were provided the Secretary and Deputy Secretary by my office the evening before. On many backgrounder days we would have another meeting besides our regular morning session and the lunch, and always we three would meet in McNamara's office just before the backgrounder for a last-minute skull session.

Transcripts of the backgrounders were kept on file in the office of the Director of Defense Information, available both to the regular Pentagon newsmen invited to attend the sessions and to all other reporters.

Thought was given to canceling the meeting that Thursday

because we had so little additional *Liberty* information, but the press would have misunderstood our motives so we went ahead. An updated casualty report, received a few minutes before the session, was passed along to the newsmen—ten dead and seventy-five wounded, of whom fifteen were critical. While many questions were asked about the incident, the officials participating had no answers. Credibility points were lost when the officials referred to the *Liberty's* use of the moon as a passive reflector, which drew guffaws from the newsmen. It was my fault; I had forgotten to advise McNamara and Vance that I had deleted the moon reference from the official two-year-old unclassified description read to the reporters earlier that day. Inevitably, George Wilson of the Washington *Post* wrote a story that the Pentagon had reached all the way to the moon to find a cover story to explain why the *Liberty* had sailed into the Arab-Israeli war. We deserved it.

Through the afternoon and the night, we tried to keep the press filled in as more information came in to the Pentagon. Casualty reports were updated. A few details of the attack were received and given out.

In attempting to inform the press and the people rapidly and accurately during a military crisis such as this one, the Assistant Secretary of Defense for Public Affairs encounters several standard problems. They are the same for Republicans and Democrats; they bear no political labels. They belong to the system.

One is the problem of different communications networks and lines of command.

The operational command of our military forces overseas is in the hands not of the individual services but of the Joint Chiefs of Staff, composed of the Chief of Staff of the Army, the Chief of Staff of the Air Force, the Chief of Naval Operations and (on Marine matters) the Commandant of the Marine Corps, and is headed by the senior military officer in the United States, the Chairman of the Joint Chiefs.

The chain of command runs from the President to the Secretary of Defense (and the Deputy Secretary), through the Joint

Chiefs to the four-starred Unified Commanders in different geographic areas of the world, the two most important of which are the Commander in Chief United States Forces in Europe (CINCEUR) and the Commander in Chief United States Forces in the Pacific (CINCPAC). Reporting to these Unified Commanders are the other high-ranking admirals and generals who command the Army, Navy, Air Force and Marine Corps elements in their specific theaters. Many persons do not realize that the operational chain of command thus bypasses the Secretaries of the services.

Assisting the Joint Chiefs are several hundred officers and enlisted men on the Joint Staff in the Pentagon. Ideally, they forget that they are "Army" or "Air Force" men—not an easy thing for them, since they all return to their services for later assignments and, it is to be hoped, career advancement.

One of the tools of the Joint Staff is the Joint Reconnaissance Center, with which we worked so closely on many problems. Another is the National Military Command Center, or NMCC, through which orders from the Secretary of Defense or the Joint Chiefs are transmitted.

But each service has its own communications system as well. When a ship is in trouble, the Chief of Naval Operations wants his information from his own school-tie people, not from a band of interservice, "purple-suited" orphans responsible directly to the Joint Staff and the Secretary of Defense.

On many occasions the flow of different information along the different communications nets contributed significantly to public confusion and credibility problems. In the Liberty case, the proper procedure for the Secretary of Defense, the Joint Staff or the NMCC Duty Officer was to stay within the chain of command and communicate with CINCEUR, then stationed in Paris, or with his deputy, a four-starred Air Force general in Stuttgart, Germany. But the inclination of the Navy in the Pentagon was to work through Navy channels and deal with the top Navy man in the area, an admiral in London. While this admiral reported to CINCEUR on operational matters, his heart was nonetheless with the Chief of Naval Operations in Washington. Information transmitted by a ship in a code message to one headquarters always can be overtaken within ten minutes by additional information given by voice radio to another head-quarters. Back in Washington, conceivably we would see a copy of the first message sent through one channel immediately after it entered the Pentagon, but might be unaware for twenty-four hours or more of the correction or addition in the second arriv-ing through a second channel.

In our office, the Secretary's office or the White House, we never knew how much we did not know. Looming behind us always was the credibility specter of information known some-where in the world, dispatched into some channel, but not yet collated for the highest levels of government. Normally these would not be facts critical to essential decision-making, since the system usually would cough up that kind of material, but they could easily constitute details which later would make a liar out of the government.

A second standard Pentagon problem for any administration involves the unknown error, fallacious assumption, mistaken impression or unwarranted conclusion in the message traffic the first twenty-four or forty-eight hours. Information reported to higher headquarters will often be corrected in a Court of Inquiry or after further informal investigation as the views of additional witnesses and participants become part of the permanent record.

Every nine-year-old televiewer knows that the ten conscientious persons in the bank at the time of the holdup will give ten sworn statements which are dramatically different as to the "facts" of the robbery. Sergeants, lieutenant commanders, brigadier gen-erals and vice admirals are no more perfect. In many cases each is relying upon a lower-echelon imperfect human being for his information. Even Commander McGonagle, with all his cour-age, heroism, poise and leadership, depended upon his junior officers and enlisted men for information in the reports he radioed home. Even in his microcosm of a command, he could not personally check out every fact in every message.

Another eternal public affairs problem is the size of the Department of Defense. We dealt, in our office, with 4.8 million persons. Just as no one can comprehend $75 or $80 billion a year of spending, no one can comprehend an organization of that size. In the Department of Defense are more persons than the combined 1960 populations of Baltimore, Houston, Cleveland, Washington, St. Louis and Minneapolis. The Department is larger than the total populations of Kansas City, Newark, Phoenix, Louisville, Portland, Oakland, Fort Worth, Long Beach, Birmingham, Oklahoma City, Rochester, Toledo and St. Paul. It is larger in population than forty of the fifty states, and has more people than ten states combined. Comparisons with foreign countries are even more graphic. DoD's population is greater than that of Denmark, Ecuador, Finland, Guatemala or Norway. It is bigger than Israel and New Zealand together, or than Ireland and Paraguay together. Of forty-four African nations, it is larger than all but fourteen. Three countries of South America are smaller, and seven countries of Central America.

Among the 4.8 million are thousands of supervisors of varied experience, loyalty, honesty, conscientiousness and intelligence. Secretary of Defense Charles E. Wilson said during the Eisenhower administration that he could improve the efficiency of the Department ten times over if Congress would give him enough money to hand-pick every one of those supervisors. Far below the supervisor level, as the Pierrelatte incident showed, one average American citizen who might have been a twenty-five-year-old bus driver in Evansville twelve months earlier can create international havoc. The Department of Defense is, and will remain, a sluggish, bureaucratic organization. Five million people cannot be called to attention rapidly, and despite military discipline and training, most of those five million most of the time will behave very much like the combined populations of the cities in which they grew up and which are their homes.

All these factors—the different chains of command and communications circuits, the unwitting inaccuracies in instant early reports and the incomprehensible size of the Defense Establishment—combine to produce erroneous or incomplete information for the highest Pentagon officials, even in times of peace and quiet. The problem is magnified in times of crisis—life-and-death crisis, war-or-peace crisis, violence-and-destruction crisis or, not unimportantly, an individual career-at-stake crisis.

In judging the Department of Defense, both the people and the press are apt to overlook these factors. Too often, in any administration, DoD is charged unfairly with deceit or cover-up when it is guilty only of great size and of the human error and human delay that are part of great size—error and delay usually at a level far beneath a President or a Secretary of Defense.

In the Pentagon on the morning of June 9, the day after the attack, the system had produced a reasonable amount of information for newsmen, many of whom had been up all night on the story. Few men work more conscientiously than first-class reporters covering a major news event. They were told by our office:

I have some additional information on the USS LIBERTY.

First, casualties: The latest casualty information we have has nine dead, 22 missing and 75 wounded. During the last 12 hours or so, our time, the LIBERTY rendezvoused with the two destroyers, the USS DAVIS and USS MASSEY, at about 25 minutes after midnight our time. The position then was 33 degrees, one minute north, 31 degrees, 59 minutes east, and that point is about 420 miles east-southeast of Souda Bay, Crete.

Medical personnel from the destroyers were transferred to the LIBERTY after the rendezvous. This includes a physician and a corpsman from each of the two destroyers.

At 4:30 A.M. (EDT) two helicopters from the aircraft carrier AMERICA rendezvoused with the LIBERTY. The position at this time was 33 degrees, 17 minutes north, 31 degrees, 25 minutes east. This was about 380 miles south of Souda Bay. The helicopters immediately began transferring the more seriously wounded from the LIBERTY to the AMERICA. The most recent word we have is that the transfer of the 15 most seriously wounded has been completed. And the most recent word also is that they anticipate transferring a total of 35 wounded and once that has been accomplished they will transfer the bodies of the nine who were killed.

At 5:30 A.M., our time, about one hour after the helicopters met the LIBERTY, the AMERICA rendezvoused with the LIBERTY. I don't have any precise information on whether they established a high line back and forth. But they were together in the same general area.

The LIBERTY and its two destroyers, the MASSEY and DAVIS, are enroute to Souda Bay, Crete. The estimated time of arrival is about 6:30 P.M. tomorrow, and again I am using Eastern Daylight Time throughout. The ships will move at about ten knots. The present position is 33 degrees, 46 minutes north and 30 degrees, 13 minutes east and they are 325 miles east-southeast of Souda Bay.

I do not have any more information of the 22 who are missing, except to say the Commanding Officer of the LIBERTY has reported that he believes that at least some of these missing are in the flooded compartments in the forward part of the ship. The Navy has begun notification of next of kin. It is being carried out as rapidly as the Navy can possibly carry it out, and the names of the casualties will be released as soon as the notification has been completed.

On the day after the attack, the issue of whether the United States had told the Middle Eastern countries that the *Liberty* was taking station in the Eastern Mediterranean became one of importance to many newspapers and television commentators. It had come up at the backgrounder, when Defense officials simply did not know, and newsmen were pressing our office for an answer. Yes or no? Had we notified Israel and/or Egypt or had we not? The reporters regarded it as a simple enough question. Why could it not be answered in five minutes? What was the government trying to hide?

It took a little time for State and Defense together to ascertain that the answer was "no," but the important issue before the government was how that answer should be phrased. A one-word "no" response would not have sufficed; the press immediately would have asked: "Why not?" Before officials in our office could answer, they had to help determine what precedent the State Department wanted to set, and whether that precedent was satisfactory to the Navy, OSD, the Joint Staff, the intelligence community—and the White House. Should the government assume the position that it was obligated to other nations to inform them it would have a ship in these waters? If we did so, did that suggest that in future instances we would again bear the responsibility of fulfilling that obligation? Would a hostile or careless foreign government take advantage of apparent official United States indecision on this point and assume for itself the right to cross into international waters to attack U.S. vessels under tensions of war *unless* we had notified them in advance? How might our answer affect the law of the sea?

Conferences were called, opinions at the highest levels of the State and Defense Departments were sought, the White House and intelligence people were involved and legal experts from various departments of the government were consulted. Before the day ended, this answer had been drafted by the government and was handed the press by a young officer in General Sidle's Directorate of Defense Information:

No countries were informed of the presence of the USS LIBERTY in the Eastern Mediterranean. The ship was in international waters at all times. It is a noncombatant converted merchant ship armed only with four .50-caliber machine guns.

There was no requirement whatever to notify any other nations of the presence of an American noncombatant ship in international waters.

My office was attacked by reporters, columnists, editorial writers and Congressmen for that statement, on the grounds that it was a stupid position, that we were trying to cover up a government mistake by not admitting we were wrong in failing to notify the Middle Eastern nations and that foreign policy was being made by the Assistant Secretary of Defense.

Accepting such criticism, particularly on the last point, is part of the ball game. Newsmen did not know that the short response given out by a desk officer in the Directorate of Defense Information represented hours of internal coordination, nor in such cases could we do very much to explain either the delay or the background of the answer. Handling 35,000 queries a year, General Sidle's office could not spell out for newsmen the degree of internal coordination on each or identify the individuals or elements of government approving each.

Oftentimes government leaders felt that the national interest was served better by a statement from the Pentagon, with military overtones, than by one from the State Department, with diplomatic overtones. Oftentimes the President felt a particular point could be put across more satisfactorily to allies or potential enemies by utilizing the noon briefing of the State Department's talented Robert McCloskey rather than by using his own Press Secretary in the White House. This was his privilege, and there was no requirement to notify the press that McCloskey was making the announcement at the direction of the President. It was none of their business—and, in fact, such notification could have defeated the President's whole purpose.

Not one time in a thousand would the Department of Defense comment officially on international affairs without having coordinated that comment with State. (I am referring to official Pentagon statements or prepared speeches by high officials, not to off-the-cuff remarks of individual officers, whether second lieutenants or four-starred admirals.) In the Liberty case, the legal experts of both State and Defense pointed out internally during the development of our short response that there is established international law, that this country has certain duties associated with it and that so do other countries. Under international law a nation does not have a responsibility to ensure that its ships leave an area of hostilities, or refrain from entering an area of hostilities, or avoid an area adjacent to an area of hostilities.

Nationals of a neutral country who turn up in belligerent territory retain their right of protection by their neutral home state. That is international law. A belligerent must grant to neutral diplomatic envoys—even those accredited to the enemy—the right to quit the territory unmolested. That is international law. In this respect alone a neutral nation has a legitimate and a logical right to dispatch a ship into international waters adjacent to an area of hostilities to fulfill its obligation to protect its nationals. That is international law.

International law does not state that the *Liberty* had a right to be where she was only if we had given advance notice; it states that she had a right to be there, period. And each belligerent, under international law, had a duty to refrain from attacking her.

We did not make this argument publicly, for it is a lawyer's argument, and we were dealing with lost American lives. Perhaps we should have made it to help straighten the record; perhaps we erred in not meeting the point head on; perhaps if we had done so, the main issue of the case would have remained more in focus.

For the main issue was not whether we had notified Israel of our intent to be there, or whether communications went astray, or whether the ship would have been safer forty miles from shore, or whether the attackers mistook her for some other ship, or whether the aircraft commanders knew or suspected that the ship was American when they struck it, or at what level the attack was ordered, or whether the ship was a communications-research vessel or an intelligence collector, or whether the Israelis had asked whether we would have ships in that part of the world.

The real issue could not have been simpler: A United States ship was operating in international waters; it was identified, as are United States ships anywhere in the world, with the American flag, distinguishing letters and number, and name; it was attacked without provocation.

On Saturday, June 10, there moved, on one of the wire services, a news story quoting an unidentified source in the Pentagon as saying that, under the circumstances, the attack was "plausible."

Shortly after this item had been printed on the news tickers that are in the offices of the Washington press corps and the government agencies, Robert McNamara received a telephone call from the White House. Moments thereafter, my hot line rang from the Secretary, who informed me that there was nothing plausible about the attack. The attack was an outrage. At least thirty-four Americans were dead. Seventy-five were wounded. The attack was inexcusable and was not to be brushed off lightly by anyone in the United States government. A Pentagon statement to this effect was to be issued immediately.

I dictated a statement which within twenty minutes was cleared inside the government and released to the press. It said, in part:

We in the Department of Defense cannot accept an attack upon a clearly marked noncombatant United States naval ship in international waters as "plausible" under any circumstances whatever.

The suggestion that the United States flag was not visible and the implication that the identification markings were in any way inadequate are both unrealistic and inaccurate.

The identification markings of U.S. naval vessels have proven satisfactory for international recognition for nearly 200 years.

If the major substantive issue was the inexplicable attack, the major public affairs error was our failure to identify the ship as an intelligence collector. It did not take long for the press to do so. Some references showed up the first day, and they became part of nearly every story after an unidentified officer on the carrier America was quoted by the Associated Press as saying:

To put it bluntly, she was there to spy for us. Russia does the same thing. We moved in close to monitor the communications of both Egypt and Israel. We have to. We must be informed of what's going on in a matter of minutes.

Messages were fired out to the America reminding all hands that they were to pipe down. Denials from the ship that any officer aboard had spoken this way to any newsmen were flashed back. This was to be expected; the traditional response from the field to Washington is that no one out there did anything wrong. As a Washington newsman, I had exactly the same attitude toward queries or protests from the home office in Cleveland. In this instance, as in so many others, there was no real way for the Pentagon to tell whether a sloppy reporter was making up quotes, as they sometimes do, or a sloppy officer was talking out of school, as they sometimes do. It could have been a little of each.

Hundreds of queries were received asking flatly whether the ship had been "spying."

At no time, to my knowledge, did anyone in the Pentagon deny that the *Liberty* was an electronic-intelligence-collection ship. Strict orders prohibiting such denials were sent around the world by my office, with instructions for everyone to answer all questions along these lines with a "No comment." I saw only one news story indicating a violation. An admiral on a ship in the Mediterranean did deny the "spy ship" report, undoubtedly attempting to be loyal to Washington and possibly overreacting to the earlier, tough "All hands shut up" message we had sent. If there were other denials, I was not aware of them. Unfortunately, since the government's position was not to comment on the spy ship issue, we could do nothing officially to inform the press or the public that the admiral was either misinformed or lying. In a weak effort to prevent the responsible members of the Pentagon press from being misled by his denial, and inasmuch as all of them already were writing on their own that the *Liberty* was an intelligence collector, I asked Dan Henkin to tell General Sidle to pass the word quietly and unofficially within the press room that no one should pay very much attention to the admiral's remarks. Officially, on paper and on the record, our response to questions about the admiral's statement remained, "No comment."

The government would have been far wiser to have acknowledged the business of the *Liberty*. This was not a minor incident; Americans had been killed. While we did not know this much at the time of the original meeting in McNamara's office, we knew enough. Those of us who argued in favor of identifying the ship from the outset should have propounded our case with more skill and persuasion—particularly since McNamara's inclination was in that direction. I learned from this incident that decision-makers who are generalists should not hesitate to overrule subordinates who are specialists once they have listened to the specialists' views. Common sense dictated identification of the ship, despite arguments of the intelligence people and the diplomats that we had never identified an intelligence ship before.

It was my view that, while the government was wrong in this

case, it need not be ashamed of that error. The mistake was in judgment, not in motive, and not in lack of consideration for the public's rights. The issue was recognized and discussed at the highest levels of the Pentagon and the decision coordinated with State and the White House at top levels. It was not a low-echelon decision which became automatic merely because senior officials were too busy to pay attention to it. The cover story for the *Liberty* had been selected years before, in time of noncrisis. She was a technical-research ship, performing all the functions she was said to perform, and other functions as well. While we may not like to admit that intelligence operations require cover stories, the fact is that many do. The obvious case would be the U.S. agent who had infiltrated the Kremlin. Few would argue that his true identity should be announced to the world, even if he were caught and exposed. Or if it were necessary to send a submarine poking into the territorial waters of another nation at night for valuable military information, most Americans would agree, I think, that a logical cover story should be used. Not everyone connected with the submarine's voyage, even within the Navy, should know its true destination.

Both of those examples involve illegal operations. It is too bad that we need to engage in illegal intelligence activity in this imperfect world, but it is necessary for our liberty that we do so. The ground rules required for illegal operations need not necessarily apply, however, to the legal and lawful collection of intelligence. The *Liberty* was not a "spy" ship, as my young daughters Laura and Nancy think of spies or as Article 29 of the Hague Convention defines them. To be a real spy, as I read the language of that article, you must do your work in the "zone of operations of the belligerent." Spies slink around under slouch hats; they do not stalk about in the open with the American flag hoisted above their shoulder blades. It may not be gentlemanly to tune in on the radio-message traffic of your neighbor, but surely there is nothing illegal about it—so long as you do your listening from your yard or the street and not from his front step.

The government was wrong in not identifying the *Liberty* after the attack; the press was right in chastising us for our error.

False reports began arriving from every quarter in the days after the attack, confusing the people as false reports always do, and adding to the difficulties of communications between the government and the people.

The Washington *Post*, which justifiably complained about our failure to call the ship an intelligence collector, helped befuddle the Washington readers on the entire episode by spreading and tacitly accepting one of those false reports.

It is not clear [said the *Post* in an editorial on June 17] why the Navy did not quietly alert Tel Aviv to the vessel's presence in waters it had every right to be in. Still more disquieting is a report that the Israelis asked our Naval attaché in Tel Aviv whether any American ships would be in these waters and received no reply.

If this is true, it puts the whole tragedy in a rather different light. If it is not true, then the United States Government owes itself some better explanation of what did happen.

Less than two weeks later, the *Post* repeated the Tel Aviv rumor in much harder terms. Describing the Department of Defense public summary of the Court of Inquiry findings, the *Post* said: "It does not acknowledge or explain what happened to the message reportedly given the American Embassy in Tel Aviv, inquiring about American ships in the area."

We were disturbed by the *Post*'s shifting its gears. On June 17 it mentioned the Tel Aviv report only on an "if this is true" basis. But on June 30 it implied acceptance of the same report. What had taken place between the two editorials to bring about this shift?

To my knowledge, the only thing that had happened was that the United States government several times had denied the truth of the report. In Washington the Pentagon had denied it; in Israel the American Embassy had denied it. The report was a phony, probably planted by the government of Israel. No such query had been put to our naval attaché.

In my opinion, the *Post*'s references to the inaccurate report led the readers of the June 30 editorial into the distinct impression that such a message had been given the embassy in Tel Aviv. Either the Pentagon or State Department reporter of the *Post* could have advised the editorial writer that this was not the case.

My own experience as a newspaperman was that coordination between editorial writers at home and their correspondents in Washington was extremely weak, and that efforts by editorial writers to elicit factual information directly from the government were even weaker. In the *Plain Dealer* Bureau, one man specialized on the White House, one on Congress, one on State and one on Defense. Rarely were we consulted for fact or opinion by the editorial writers in Cleveland, and I know this is true today of many other Washington bureaus.

Israel was floating one self-serving rumor after another. An additional dispatch from Tel Aviv by the Associated Press read:

Israeli naval sources claimed today that U. S. Communications Ship LIBERTY carried no flag when she was attacked by Israel's planes and torpedo boats June 8.

Rubbish. As stated before, she carried one flag until the Israeli aircraft shot it down and then flew a second.

Many stories spoke of the "accidental attack." There was nothing accidental about it. It was conducted deliberately—by aircraft and by motor torpedo boat, by rocket and bomb and torpedo and gun fire. Whether it was a tragic mistake in identity is a separate question, but it was no accident.

On the attack itself, as opposed to the ship's mission, we attempted to pass along to the press all the information we had those first two or three days. General Sidle and his people did an outstanding job. Cooperation from the Navy was excellent. There was still a great deal we did not know, but we kept the newsmen informed on as many details as we received, while rumors continued in the press and on television.

Newsweek magazine reported that "some high Washington officials believe the Israelis knew the Liberty's capabilities and suspect that the attack might not have been accidental."

Newsweek did not identify the officials. The government of Israel roared back:

Such allegations are just malicious. Such stories are untrue and without any foundation whatever. It was an unfortunate and tragic accident which occurred in an area where fierce land and air fighting took place in recent days.

The final sentence of the Israeli reply did little to soothe many angry officers in the Pentagon and was typical of Israel's casual attitude toward the episode, an attitude which suggested from the beginning that it was really our fault for being there in the first place. References to fierce land and air fighting did not justify or explain an unprovoked attack upon a United States ship operating in international waters.

On June 14, Associated Press reporter Seymour M. Hersh, who was later to work as a press assistant to Senator Eugene McCarthy (D.–Minn.) in the 1968 presidential campaign, wrote that many senior military officers believed that the Israelis thought the *Liberty* was Egyptian, masquerading as American. I knew of no officer who believed that, although perhaps Hersh had found one. A reporter who sweeps throughout the Pentagon can pick up an enormous amount of information he would not get from the Office of the Assistant Secretary of Defense for Public Affairs. Much of it is accurate. Much of it is deceptive, passed out by an officer or civilian who has learned a small piece of a story and wants to demonstrate how bright he is by sharing it with a newsman.

The newsman thus misleads the public, who then mistrust their government for denying what had always been inaccurate. Aside from editorial writers, few contribute so much to the breakdown of communications between government and the people as the irresponsible official who is in possession of only half the facts or who, to peddle his own point of view, deliberately gives the reporter only half the story.

After a rash of other misleading and speculative stories appeared early in the week after the attack, I recommended to

McNamara that we clamp a lid on all *Liberty* news until a Navy Court of Inquiry meeting in Valletta, Malta, finished its investigation. He agreed, asking the Navy to handle its inquiry as rapidly as it could so that we could soon give the people an unclassified version of its findings, and I drafted a statement which read, in part:

Many rumors and reports about the attack have been circulating. The Department of Defense has no evidence to support some of these rumors and reports. Others appear to be based on partial evidence. Some appear to be accurate on the basis of present information here, which is incomplete. Until the Court has had an opportunity to obtain the full facts, the Department of Defense will have no further comment.

Fred Farrar of the Chicago *Tribune* termed this "one of the most intriguing pieces of prose that ever came out of the Department's press office."

It was, I agree, ineptly drafted and quite peculiar. I was trying to say this to the Pentagon press: "Some of what you hear is right, some is partly right, some is pure baloney. Hold off for a few days until the Court gives us the facts. Until then, we are not going to foul up the record by confirming and denying leaks and rumors on a piecemeal basis."

One correct rumor was that prior to the attack there had been an unbelievable communications foul-up which prevented the *Liberty* from receiving messages which would have kept it in the area but moved it farther back from the coast of the Sinai Peninsula. The decision to move it had been made in Washington for several reasons—partly for safety's sake, in case the Arabs acted rashly; partly to avoid international wrangling about the presence of the ship in those waters; partly to block false Egyptian charges about United States intervening in the war.

But one message meant for the *Liberty* went to the Pacific instead, bounced back to the Pentagon and wound up at Fort Meade, Maryland. Another was misdirected to a shore station in Morocco instead of one in Ethiopia. *Liberty* was listening to

Ethiopia, not Morocco, and did not receive it when it was broadcast to her. Since she was maintaining normal radio silence, however, neither the shore authorities nor higher headquarters realized that she had not gotten the word.

A basic reason for the failure was that the decision was made routinely and the messages dispatched routinely, with no recognition on anyone's part of a necessity for urgency. A second cause was that the communications nets were overloaded due both to traffic on the war and to messages concerning the seventeen thousand American dependents who were being evacuated under emergency conditions from Middle Eastern countries. The defense system was paying much more attention to them than to a ship in international waters. A third reason was human error on the part of several persons.

The communications failure became a public affairs issue within the Department when Dick Fryklund was working with the Navy on the unclassified report which would summarize the Court of Inquiry's investigation.

Some senior officials, military and civilian, feel that bad news is going to go away if you turn your back on it and make believe it isn't there. This, I acknowledge, is a most attractive idea. To a harassed official, it is even more attractive than playing it in low key—and equally impractical. There are days when everything goes wrong, when one disaster follows another, when we are dropping bombs on a friendly hamlet in Vietnam the same afternoon that we bump into a Soviet submarine in the Atlantic, the day after the West Germans have decided to cut down on their NATO commitment and just prior to the newest attack by Senator William Proxmire on Defense Department procurement polices. This is, inevitably, the same day that the President snaps at the Secretary because of another Pentagon leak and the day that a new prize-seeking reporter makes still another speech blasting our credibility.

On such a day the temptation is strong to say: "Let's not do anything. Maybe it will go away." Unfortunately for Washington officialdom, but fortunately for the public, it doesn't. And nothing could be clearer than the fact that this communications problem involving this ship was not going to go away.

Fryklund insisted that the unclassified summary of the Court of Inquiry proceedings should refer to the communications delay. We did not yet have all the facts since the communications authorities were to hold an inquiry of their own. But Dick wanted to get on the record, in an official statement, that the government had goofed. I concurred completely, and so did McNamara.

The summary of proceedings released to the press on June 28, therefore, included these paragraphs:

Early on the 8th, the Joint Chiefs of Staff had issued orders for LIBERTY to move farther from the coast, even though such a move would partially degrade her mission. The messages were misrouted, delayed and not received until after the attack. LIBERTY's Commanding Officer also had the authority to move farther to sea on his own initiative, had he any reason to believe that his ship was in danger of attack, or for any other cause. The Court found, however, that since he was in international waters, his standard identifications symbols were clearly visible, and foreign aircraft had inspected him three times that day, he had no reason to believe that his ship was in danger of attack. The convening authority specifically concurred that "no indication was received by the ship prior to the attack which would have dictated a need for emergency measures."

LIBERTY continued to carry out her assignment at the location which her Commanding Officer considered optimum for that purpose. The Court reached no judgment on whether earlier arrival of the messages would have reduced the likelihood of the attack.

Alerted by that reference to the communications breakdown, the press zeroed in with hundreds of queries for additional information. Congress involved itself, which was eminently understandable. Many of the details of the communications problems were later released to the public, after the completion of that investigation.

No press criticism of the communications delay could be too severe. The editorial position of the Chicago *Tribune* was seldom one in which I found great comfort, either before or during my career in government, but in this instance the *Tribune* asked a good question: "A warning to the LIBERTY was imperative enough, but what if a great world holocaust demanded an instant warning to the field: Would we find that defense communications failed at zero hour?"

A great many other questions were asked by the press after publication of the Court of Inquiry findings, and there was considerable dissatisfaction with the findings. This was chiefly because segments of the press found it so difficult to accept the fact that the witnesses before the court were all naval personnel from the *Liberty*. We kept pointing out that this was a limited inquiry, that this Navy Court had no authority to summon members of the Israeli government, that it had no jurisdiction over communications dispatched by the Joint Chiefs of Staff, that its mission was not to summon top State, Defense and intelligence officials to discuss why the *Liberty* had been authorized to operate in these waters. It was a Navy Court, finding facts from *Liberty* personnel, and examining the national policy of neither this nation nor Israel. Its president was a young rear admiral—talented, but very junior. While it performed its mission well, it was not a supranational court, nor did it have authority to look into non-Navy matters.

Our office kept making these points, but few listened. The Washington *Star* editorialized June 30 with these questions, under a headline of "Pentagon Cover-up":

Did the attackers, in fact, know that the LIBERTY was an American ship? It seems to us they must have known. If so, why was the attack made and who ordered it? . . . Surely the Defense Department knows the answers to these and other pertinent questions by this time. If it does not, there is something radically wrong in the Pentagon.

Annoyed, we had questions of our own. How in the name of heaven was the Pentagon to learn whether the attackers knew that the *Liberty* was an American ship? How was it to know why the attack had been made and who ordered it? The Israeli government had not offered us its logs or copies of its messages; it had volunteered no witnesses nor affidavits. The basic business between the government of Israel and the government of the United States is carried on through our Department of State, not in a Navy Court of Inquiry. When I left the government, nineteen months after the attack, we still did not have from Israel the answers to why it happened or how it happened or who ordered it or who was to blame. Having acknowledged—rather begrudgingly—its responsibility for the attack, the sovereign government of Israel had not seen fit to disclose details to us. What means did the editorial writers propose to force those details from another nation?

The Washington *News* protested that the report left unanswered the question, "Need it have happened?"

Of course it left that question unanswered. That was another question for Israel. How, conceivably, could Commander McGonagle and his crew have answered it in a Navy Court of Inquiry?

The Washington *Post* charged editorially that the inquiry was "not good enough." The *Post* was wrong again, as it was so often on Defense issues. Not only was the inquiry good enough; it was very good indeed—for the limited purposes for which it had been established. This was understood by most of the Pentagon press, and, as usual, most of the stories by Pentagon newsmen representing major organizations were responsible, fair and accurate. But the editorial writers, having not taken time or trouble to find out what the Court of Inquiry was authorized to do, left the implication that the Navy and the Department of Defense were engaged in a giant conspiracy to deceive the American people.

As weeks and months passed, we gradually picked up informal bits and pieces from various sources in Israel. It was impossible to guarantee the accuracy of most of them, and the government could do nothing with them formally. One could conclude—and I did—that the attackers did not know they were killing Americans and had not acted with malice or deliberation. One could not prove it.

The Israelis behaved with incredible sloppiness, at best. Apparently the Israeli armed forces had received a number of erroneous reports that El Arish was being bombarded from the sea. These reports were wrong in the first instance; El Arish was not being attacked from the sea, by a noncombatant ship of the United States in international waters or by anyone else. But the Israeli Navy and the Israeli Air Force both believed that El Arish was being shelled, and that false belief was the beginning of the tragedy. In war is confusion. Even so, a nation should be able to determine whether one of its cities is being shelled from the sea or whether it isn't before shooting up ships in international waters and slaughtering a crew.

A second tragic error by the Israelis stemmed from standing Israeli orders, which, we heard, authorized attack against any ship which was shelling the shore. The orders further assumed that any ship within the general area of a bombarded shore was the enemy if that ship was moving faster than twenty knots. Through another unbelievable, slovenly and inexcusable calculation, the Liberty was apparently found to be moving at approximately thirty knots—which was just six times faster than she was actually moving and far beyond her maximum top speed. It is impossible to understand how a professional naval officer could believe that any ship looking like the Liberty was capable of such speed.

The Israeli Navy blamed part of the problem on the thick smoke surrounding the Liberty—smoke, it said, which made her difficult to identify. The suggestion left by Israeli Navy officers talking informally to U.S. officers was that the torpedoing might never have taken place had it not been for all of that thick, black smoke. This rationale avoids the fact that the thick, black smoke came from bombs, rockets, and strafing attacks on the U.S. ship by the Israeli Air Force.

There is no question that the aircraft pilots were trigger-happy. There is no question that the motor torpedo boat captains were trigger-happy. There is no question that some officers did hastily misidentify the Liberty as the Egyptian supply ship, El Quseir, to which it bore a very superficial resemblance.

I can imagine the reaction of the Pentagon press if we attempted in this country to foist upon them the story of U.S. aircraft's having confused the Liberty with El Quseir: The Liberty displaced 11,000 tons; El Qusier, 2,640 tons—the Liberty was four times as big. The Liberty's length was 455 feet; El Quseir's was 265—the Liberty was nearly twice as long. The Liberty's beam was 62 feet; El Quseir's was 36 feet—the Liberty was nearly twice as wide. El Quseir was a small transport supply ship and looked like one. The Liberty was jam-packed with communications gear and radar devices and looked like nothing else except another technical-research ship.

No officer of any service could conceivably examine photographs of both ships and confuse one with the other. An officer who did not care enough about human life to take sixty seconds to check his references could assume that one was the other, but he could not check the ship he saw against reference photographs and confuse one with the other.

The Court of Inquiry, working without benefit of information from Israel, addressed this point in an appendix to its findings:

While EL QUSEIR bears a highly superficial resemblance to LIBERTY, she more closely resembles the majority of older tramp steamers operating in ocean shipping. EL QUSEIR is less than half the size and lacks the elaborate antenna array and distinctive hull marking of LIBERTY. The location of the superstructure island, a primary recognition feature of merchant type ships, is widely different. By these criteria as a justification for attack, any ship resembling EL QUSEIR was in jeopardy.

The court also noted rumors that El Arish had been bombarded from the sea, but pointed out that neither the Liberty, with its four .50-caliber guns, nor El Quseir, which is armed with two three-pounders, logically could be suspected of having conducted a shore bombardment.

Addressing the issue of whether the attack was "accidental," the court found that

"from the time of the first air attack onward, attackers were well coordinated, accurate and determined. Criss-crossing rocket and machine gun runs from both bows, both beams and quarters effectively chewed up the entire topside, including ship control and internal communications—sound powered—network. Well directed initial air attacks had wiped out the ability of the four .50 caliber machine guns to be effective.

It is worth saying again: This deliberate attack was no accident —mistaken identity perhaps, but no accident.

Israel had called up a great many naval reservists for the war, a number of whom were involved in the attack, and some of whom had been chided by the Israeli Air Force as being ineffective. They were out to show that they, too, could take on the enemy, and did so by participating in a wholly unjustifiable attack upon a noncombatant ship operating in accordance with international law in international waters.

Our government, I believe, did an outstanding job of putting the record of the *Liberty* case before the public. It was not possible to do it all in the first four hours or the first four days. Even in those early hours, however, we made available the information as rapidly as we received it.

And yet the public, I felt, prodded by the editorial writers, concluded that the government was concealing the truth. This probably was the result of these factors:

One. The decision not to identify the *Liberty* as an intelligence collector from the outset. Already, in the first few hours, the government was engaged in a "cover-up."

Two. The shortage of information the first day. I hope this account has helped establish that a government is not necessarily hiding something simply because it is not revealing something. We had no more information.

Three. The rumors and reports launched in Israel by those determined to make this tragedy the fault of the United States instead of the fault of the Israeli government. Too often the public is apt to accept a charge as truth simply because it appears in a newspaper. So is the editorial writer.

Four. The lack of a swifter report, even in unclassified generalities, on the communications breakdown. The mills of the massive military establishment grind slowly and cannot be accelerated greatly. I believe the national interest is better served if we are patient enough to wait a few days or even weeks for things to be done properly. If our people are told that there has been a communications failure, I consider it relatively unimportant that the unclassified details of that failure are made available to the public July 15 rather than June 22, as long as they do become available.

Five. The uncontrollable absence of information within our government about what went on within the Israeli government or the Israeli armed forces. We could not then and cannot now answer the "why" and "who" questions. Israel was not cooperative.

Six. The reluctance of the public and the reporters to believe in the occurrence of a completely senseless, useless act such as the Israelis committed. Since they could not accept the fact that the Israelis would do such a thing, then clearly our government must have been hiding something.

It was a crisis; dozens of officers and civilians in my office worked around the clock under crisis conditions. Almost unlimited opportunity existed for things to go wrong, but few did, and the dissatisfaction expressed by many editorial writers and a few reporters over the government's handling of the case from a public affairs standpoint was disturbing to us.

Across the world in Southeast Asia a major war was still being waged which demanded most of our public affairs talent and attention. Internally, within the Pentagon and the government, we were engrossed in an all-out policy battle involving the bombing of North Vietnam. And the day after the *Liberty* attack, true to form in the crisis environment of the Office of the Assistant Secretary of Defense (Public Affairs), a new brouhaha was instigated by another strafing of another ship. This time, it was alleged, the United States was the attacker instead of the attacked.

5 We Attack the Russians — and Deny It

June, 1967

One of the days on which I told an untruth to the American people was June 3, 1967.

Worse than that, I also misinformed some 235 million people of the second most powerful nation in the history of the world, the Union of Soviet Socialist Republics. What I did wrong was to tell them, in effect, to cool it and get off our backs because none of our airplanes had strafed their freighter at the port of Cam Pha in North Vietnam, and if someone really had fired at it, they should go talk to the sloppy North Vietnamese antiaircraft gunners. While we could never be absolutely certain in Washington where an individual bomb had landed in Southeast Asia, this time the Russians had claimed that they had been strafed by cannon fire, and the facts showed clearly that our airplanes in that part of the war had done no strafing that day. So I told them so.

As it turned out, it would have been more advantageous to the United States government if I had not. Misleading the puny-armed French a couple of years earlier on our supersonic reconnaissance plane's taking snapshots of their atomic plant was one thing, but walking the Soviet Union down the garden path was something else again. Our associates at State considered it in especially bad taste because the grand Pooh-Bah of the Soviet Union was soon to come to our country for the first time to talk at a special United Nations General Assembly session on the Middle East, and more than likely was going to sit down for black-eyed peas and a side of beef with a President of the United States for the first Summit Meeting in six years.

Of three North Vietnamese deep-water ports, only Haiphong deserves being on the map at all. The other two are Hon Gai and Cam Pha; neither is worth much, and Cam Pha, which strains to handle a few hundred tons of soft coal, almost isn't worth anything. Every now and again, however, a ship from the outside world would drift in to pick up a little coal, and on June 2, 1967, the Soviet merchant ship *Turkestan* was anchored in the roadstead. It had arrived in North Vietnam in April with cargo from Vladivostok, unloaded at Haiphong, made a run to Malaysia and returned to Cam Pha to load coal for Japan. In a formal diplomatic protest, the Russians charged that United States aircraft attacked it in the harbor, dropping one bomb within a hundred yards, strafing the decks, killing one crewman and injuring others.

In the Pentagon, we were astonished by the allegation. United States reconnaissance and intelligence people kept close tabs on all Soviet shipping in and around North Vietnam; our pilots received special briefings alerting them to the presence of Russian vessels in the area and describing those vessels in detail. One of the things we wanted to do least in Southeast Asia was bomb or strafe Soviet shipping, since we saw no way that would lead to a termination of hostilities.

While confident that U.S. aircraft had not attacked the *Turkestan* deliberately, and while we had received no word of an accidental attack, my office could not be 100 percent certain that such information had not been flashed into the Pentagon somewhere without our knowledge. This was unlikely, but not impossible, inasmuch as the first reports of an incident of this nature conceivably could reach the Air Force or Navy through their own communications channels before they came to the Joint Staff and the Secretary of Defense through the National Military Command Center, where representatives from the office of the Assistant Secretary of Defense for Public Affairs were permanent members of around-the-clock teams. Such news should not reach the Air Force or Navy first, but occasionally it did.

When it did, and the Air Force was involved, our office always was notified quickly—certainly by the Secretary of the Air Force as soon as he and the Chief of Staff had discussed it. If it was a Navy problem, however, we were less confident of being read into the picture that rapidly. As soon as the Navy saw fit to notify the Secretary of Defense, of course, he or his office would alert us immediately, but the Navy was not always overly anxious to share its private bad news even with the Secretary of Defense. Embarrassment at the highest level sometimes resulted from this naval shyness, because bad news inevitably leaked out somewhere in the world, to be broadcast on the radio. The President of the United States would hear it, telephone the Secretary of Defense for an explanation, and the Secretary, less addicted to each news broadcast than his senior, would not know what in the world the President was talking about. While instances of this nature were not common, neither were they unique, and rarely did they contribute significantly to an improvement of the relationship between the Secretary of Defense and the Navy. I want to emphasize that I am not unfond of the Navy; I served in it during World War II and some of my best friends are admirals. Navy men are courageous and dedicated, night flight operations on aircraft carriers are impossible acts of skill and we really need the Navy badly. It is simply a little withdrawn from the rest of the world and even a little peculiar.

To be safe on the *Turkestan*, as soon as our office heard the Russian allegation we checked with Secretary McNamara, the Chairman of the Joint Chiefs of Staff, the National Military Command Center and both the Air Force and Navy. No one knew anything about an accidental attack upon a Soviet ship at Cam Pha. As a veteran of Pierrelatte and a hundred similar actions thereafter, however, I moved with conservatism and authorized the release of no more than this:

We do not have any information which confirms the Soviet allegations. We have asked the Commander in Chief, Pacific (CINCPAC), to review the flight paths of all aircraft which might have been in the Cam Pha area at the time of the alleged incident.

Both true and safe, that statement served admirably for a starter. Later that evening, after General Wheeler conversed by telephone with Admiral U. S. G. Sharp in Honolulu, who was running the air war in the North (under policy guidance from Washington), we received the preliminary report that no United States aircraft had been involved. While this was comforting, my faith in preliminary reports had long since been eroded, and I instructed our people not to go beyond the original statement.

In Honolulu, Admiral Sharp received additional information from the Navy and the Air Force the next day and reported it to the Secretary of Defense. On the basis of his report that the investigation was completed, and using much of his message almost word for word, we drafted the following statement and issued it over my name:

Admiral Ulysses S. G. Sharp, Commander-in-Chief, U.S. Pacific Command, has completed his investigation into the allegations by the Soviet Union that U.S. aircraft bombed the Soviet ship Turkestan in the Port of Cam Pha in North Vietnam.

The conclusion of the investigation is that no U.S. aircraft bombed or strafed the Soviet ship. There is absolutely no evidence to confirm the Soviet allegations.

Two flights of four U.S. F-105 aircraft each attacked military targets in the Cam Pha area Friday afternoon, June 2, at the time of the alleged incident.

One of these flights attacked a segment of road more than three miles from the Soviet ship. The second attacked an anti-aircraft site that was also more than three miles from the ship.

The pilots of the aircraft which attacked the road reported that they observed the bombs impacting on the road segment. Strike film taken by the aircraft attacking the anti-aircraft site confirms that the ordnance from that flight detonated on target.

The fact that the Turkestan was at Cam Pha was known by the aircraft crews, who were cautioned to avoid the ship.

There was no strafing by aircraft of either flight at any time.

Both flights reported intense 37mm, 57mm and 85mm anti-aircraft fire. This fire was continuous throughout the 15-minute period of the two attacks—from 4:35 to 4:50 P.M., local time.

It is probable that the heavy North Vietnamese anti-aircraft fire was responsible for any damage to the Soviet ship and any casualties suffered by its crew.

Before the statement was released we were in touch with our allies in the Department of State, who were relying on us to produce the facts upon which they would base their formal response to the Soviet protest. That reliance was not well placed. (Sometimes I felt that the Department of State exhibited commendable restraint in not declaring us sort of a department non grata. We had most of the money, all of the plush aircraft and nearly all of the chauffeur-driven cars; we poked around studying local insurgencies in ways that distressed our ambassadors terribly; we constantly messed up United States foreign relations by bombing a ship or causing a riot or losing an H-bomb or committing some other indiscretion—and on top of all that our Secretaries were inclined, by necessity in today's world, to meddle in international affairs. Beyond those annoying traits, too often we fed them erroneous information on what our servicemen and employees—all 4.8 million of them—were up to around the world.)

On the basis of our facts, State summoned Yuri N. Chernyakov, chargé d'affaires of the Soviet Embassy, to receive from Assistant Secretary of State John P. Leddy the United States note replying to Moscow's protest. That note repeated some of the information in our news release and again suggested that "in all probability" North Vietnamese antiaircraft gunners were responsible. (Some members of the press who had never fought or covered a war habitually reacted scornfully to the military's suggestions that "bombing" incidents in North Vietnam could result from antiaircraft fire or surface-to-air missiles launched by Communist air-defense crews. In World War II it was extremely uncomfortable to be aboard one amphibious ship in a nest of others shooting at enemy aircraft, and at Pearl Harbor U.S. antiaircraft defenders caused a significant amount of destruction to the city.)

Inasmuch as we in Defense had assured State that our hands were clean, the U.S. response to the Soviets was not overly sympa-

thetic in tone. It rejected the Russian accusation and emphasized
that our pilots were under strict instructions to avoid engagement
with any vessels not identified as hostile. Nonetheless, it reminded the Kremlin: "Accidental damage remains an unfortunate possibility wherever hostilities are being conducted and the
Soviet government knows that shipping operations in these
waters under present circumstances entail risks of such accidents."
While regretting the accidental *Turkestan* casualties, State commented pointedly also on the deliberate Communist activity,
noting that hundreds of Vietnamese, American and citizens of
allied nations were dying each week as a consequence of the aggression of North Vietnam against the Republic of Vietnam.

The Russians immediately fired back, rejecting our rejection.
"Facts at the disposal of the Soviet government," they said
sharply, "show irrefutably that the bandit attack by two American aircraft on the Soviet merchant ship, as a result of which one
of the crew members died and several were wounded, was clearly
a premeditated one. There cannot be any doubt that the American pilots were aiming precisely at the *Turkestan*, dropping bombs
on it and strafing it."

In addition to the formal notes, the Soviets wheeled out
Pravda, the Communist Party newspaper, which quoted the master of the *Turkestan*, Captain Viktor Sokolov, as saying that the
attack by two U.S. fighter-bombers came a few hours after the
ship dropped anchor.

"We were bearing all the markings of the Soviet government,"
Captain Sokolov said. "A Soviet flag was flying from the stern
mast. The stack was painted with a red stripe and a hammer and
sickle. The *Turkestan* was about 400 meters from shore. The
visibility was excellent. There is no possibility of talking about an
accidental attack. The American pilots aimed their guns at the
central superstructure where the crewmen live and work."

Within Russia, crews of Soviet merchant vessels on the Vietnam supply run held protest meetings to condemn the attack.
A mob in Leningrad, including many Soviet sailors, spat at American diplomat John Guthrie and his wife, and stoned their bus.

Public meetings were organized throughout the Soviet Union to denounce the "pirate actions of the U.S. military." Demonstraters marched outside an American exhibit in Leningrad. The Soviet news agency Tass charged that officials of the United States were trying to shield the guilty in this provocation against the Soviet Union.

In the Office of the Assistant Secretary of Defense (Public Affairs) we were a little shaky. One upsetting item was a line in Tass that an unexploded 20-mm shell had been discovered during an inspection of the damaged ship and that some "evidence" had been given the Soviet Embassy in Hanoi and the rest taken to Vladivostok. North Vietnamese antiaircraft guns at Cam Pha were 37-mm, 57-mm and 85-mm, but not 20-mm. One could always produce a 20-mm U.S. shell from elsewhere and claim that it came from the *Turkestan*, of course, but it was difficult to see what the Russians would gain by faking the attack and fingering us. Hanoi played those games, and Red China was not above moving airplane wreckage from place to place to support a propaganda ploy, but we could find no logical reason for such Soviet maneuvering in this case.

While publicly we exhibited no lack of faith in the information we had given the world, Dick Fryklund, Dan Henkin (who were both now Deputy Assistant Secretaries of Defense) and I reviewed once again the message traffic from Honolulu. Admiral Sharp was, of course, relying upon the reports given him by the Pacific commanders of the Navy and Air Force; he could not interview each pilot and examine each gun camera himself. All pilot reports were in, and the commanding officers whose pilots had flown sorties targeted against Cam Pha were adamant. Even so, it seemed that the Soviet Union was being very definite about the whole thing, and Dan, Dick and I discussed briefly the possibility that the Russians were right and the United States wrong.

However, we lacked hard evidence on which to urge Secretary McNamara to ask General Wheeler to direct Admiral Sharp to reopen the investigation. Furthermore, the incident was quieting down and becoming yesterday's crisis. A primary problem of public affairs officials of State, Defense and the White House is that no one has time for yesterday's crisis—or, as in the case of Salisbury's Hanoi reports, for planning against tomorrow's possible crisis. Competent officers and civilians at lower echelons do a satisfactory job of public affairs planning for important known actions of the future; a program to withdraw fifty thousand troops from NATO would be staffed and coordinated in advance ad nauseam. It would, in fact, be so staffed and so coordinated among so many persons that inevitably it would leak to the press prior to the announcement. But that is a different kind of issue. We had no time to peer ahead at the unknown, no time to plan for the unexpected or, as in the Turkestan case, no time to look back and recheck. Had we not been swept away in new crises, we might have gone back to CINCPAC saying: "This doesn't make sense. Something is amiss. Are we absolutely certain that the Russians are lying? Why? Could you take another look? We know you are running a war, but this is an important matter, and the Russians are terribly insistent."

But we did put it out of our minds, and the press, swept up in other news events and particularly the Middle East war, did not pursue it. I had forgotten both the incident and our uneasiness when Robert McNamara telephoned me at home on Sunday morning two weeks later.

Was he correct in his recollection that we had said flatly we were not responsible for bombing or strafing the Soviet ship Turkestan?

He was.

Had we left ourselves any out with the suggestion that the investigation was continuing?

We had not. On the contrary, the message from the field had said the investigation was concluded.

Then I had better meet him at the office because we were in a bit of a mess.

The commander of the U.S. Air Force in the Pacific was General John D. Ryan, later to become Vice Chief of Staff during our regime and Chief of Staff in 1969. McNamara informed me in his office that Ryan had discovered on a trip to Thailand that another flight of four aircraft was in the Cam Pha area at the time of the alleged strafing. While their target was a railroad yard sixty-five miles away, these planes had overflown Cam Pha en route home, been attacked by antiaircraft batteries, fired 20-mm cannon back at the batteries and, apparently, struck the Soviet ship. Our information was that the colonel who was the acting wing commander had covered up for his pilots out of loyalty and personal friendship, evidently fearful of the consequences to them.

We had few additional details that Sunday, but inasmuch as the Air Force indicated immediately that a court-martial was planned, few details could have been disclosed publicly in any case without jeopardizing that procedure. In all cases of courts-martial, the Secretary of Defense and his top officials must back off and remain silent, lest something be said prejudicial to either side of the trial. Internal Air Force discipline was not my business, and while in the Pentagon I did not follow the case, although I was generally aware that a general court-martial was held later in the Philippines for the pilots of two aircraft and their colonel.

Months after leaving the government, on April 10, 1969, I read a newspaper story on the incident in the Washington Evening Star. Orr Kelly, the Star's Pentagon correspondent, who succeeded Dick Fryklund when we lured Dick into OSD, had located and interviewed the colonel.

According to Kelly, the pilots of two of the four planes reported the whole story to their commander, the colonel, when they returned to the base at Ta Khli in Thailand. They were strafing one battery of antiaircraft guns when another battery began firing at them. In a normal recovery, one or both would have been killed. So they opened up, throwing everything they had at the ground to force the crews away from the guns long enough for them to get away. It worked. But a ship—the Turkestan—was in the way.

The colonel had been on many missions with his pilots, and

one of the two majors had twice saved his life. Kelly quoted him on his reaction after hearing their report:

I had a choice to make [back at the base]. I could either follow the established procedures and they would be court-martialed for firing on an unauthorized target, or I could do something about it. I stuck by them. I took good care of them. I was fully aware of their situation. I'd been in the same type of situation myself.

Kelly added that the colonel had thought over the problem for several hours and then exposed to light the gun camera film that normally would have been passed to higher headquarters for examination. He quoted the officer further: "I destroyed the film. There was no evidence to convict those two majors of anything."

At the general court-martial, Kelly wrote, the two majors were found not guilty and the colonel was fined $600 and admonished. He is now retired.

The colonel did not know that June day that Premier Kosygin would visit the United States, bringing with him a U.S. Air Force 20-mm shell from the Soviet merchant ship *Turkestan*. An immediate concern of ours in the Pentagon Sunday afternoon, on the eve of Kosygin's United Nations speech, was that he might produce that shell at the UN and blast the lying United States from that forum.

Whether the Summit Meeting with President Johnson at Glassboro, New Jersey, would have taken place—it was not yet arranged—if General Ryan had not turned up the new information and we had not retracted our denial is an open question. In any event, the *Turkestan* case provides two significant lessons.

One is the importance to the United States government of an isolated action in the field by a pair of young majors and a lone colonel in this day of instant world-wide communications and sensitive international maneuvering. Consider the consequences: American diplomats stoned, public protest meetings called throughout the Soviet Union, demonstrations held in Leningrad, the probability posed of an attack on the United States by the

Soviet Premier at the United Nations, a deterioration of relations at a time when we wanted fervently to discuss nuclear de-escalation and a strong possibility raised of denying the entire world the potential benefits of a Summit Meeting.

The second lesson is that in this age what is said and how it is said can often be more important than what is done. The real problem in this instance was not that we had strafed the Soviet ship, because the Russians knew they were assuming some risk when they moved into the harbor. It was not as if we had attacked it in international waters, which would have been a hundredfold more serious. While we were not bombing the actual port facilities at Cam Pha, we were hitting other military targets in the area, and the master of any ship in the harbor realized the possibility of an accidental shell. In one short note of regret, the strafing might have been explained satisfactorily. Far more grave was the fact that our government had rejected a legitimate and accurate Soviet charge, misled our own people and, from the Russian standpoint, first lied and then tried to cover up the lie.

In the Pentagon that Sunday, our next move was obvious. As rapidly as the Department of State could inform the Soviet Union, we would release the new information to the American people. The State effort enjoyed the top priority; we were all agreed that Premier Kosygin should learn the truth through diplomatic channels rather than from the evening television news or the morning newspaper. To keep the government in step, the words of our public news release were coordinated with the language of State's formal note. This was standard operating procedure, sometimes time-consuming since often the Secretary or Under Secretary of State was personally involved in approving the final language of both the State note and the Pentagon release. Frequently the Washington press could not understand an eight-hour delay in producing a five-paragraph statement, and we were not free to tell them that we were waiting for an Assistant Secretary of State to telephone back the clearance from his superior. The Secretary of State did not always drop everything to tackle a press release. On the other hand, on many occasions he did drop everything, and frequently clearance was expedited by person-to-person telephone calls between McNamara or Clifford and Secretary Rusk, or our Deputy Secretary and their Under Secretary. Sometimes the Department of Defense was criticized in the press for delays when we were waiting for State, or they were criticized when waiting for us, but reportorial pouting is to be expected and one tries to learn to ignore it. On this occasion we had first to find language agreeable to both departments and then to await presentation of the note to the Soviet Union.

Sevreal hours passed before I could authorize the Sunday clerical crew which had been called into the Pentagon to reproduce and distribute the statement. That it was a Sunday crew, and that it worked hastily once given the "go" signal, are the best explanations I have for the fact that both "regarding" and "*Turkestan*" were spelled incorrectly in the first run, which read:

A report containing additional information on the incident regarding the Soviet ship TURKISTAN was received today from General John D. Ryan, Commander of the U.S. Air Forces Pacific.

New information disclosed that in addition to the two flights of U.S. F-105 aircraft, previously described, which conducted strikes against military targets at Cam Pha on June 2, a third flight of U.S. F-105 aircraft passed through the area at the general time of the incident.

The target of the third flight was the railroad yard at Bac Giang, about 65 miles from Cam Pha.

As previously reported, there was no strafing by the aircraft of the first two flights. However, it now appears that there was 20mm suppressive fire against a North Vietnamese anti-aircraft site at Cam Pha by aircraft of the third flight, and that some of this fire may have struck the TURKISTAN.

Investigation of the incident is continuing. The Soviet Government is being informed of this latest report.

Perhaps because Premier Kosygin was arriving in the United States to lead the Soviet delegation to the UN, the Russians accepted our reversal with better grace than some of the American press. We winced when we saw the Los Angeles *Times*, which said editorially: "The credibility gap of the United States government—its record of supplying inaccurate information on Vietnam—has been enlarged by this incident."

We misled the people on the *Turkestan*, as we had misled them another time when we denied that a U.S. sentry at the Guantánamo Bay Navy Base had shot a Cuban. The young sentry, afraid to admit what he had done, had lied to his sergeant, who unwittingly reported a clean bill to his superior, and soon the United States government was spouting an untruth to the world. That one was also corrected as soon as we learned the facts.

If the present administration has not already misled the public and told an untruth, it soon will—because the system involving nearly five million persons demands it. The more slowly the government is permitted to react, the less it will misinform, but neither the press, the political opposition, the Congress nor the President encourages the Pentagon to react as slowly as it should.

Too often, I felt, the government was accused unfairly of being untrustworthy. In the Department of Defense we should have been held responsible for a sloppy system which misinformed the people, for the errors we made, for the poor judgment we exercised. If those charged with disseminating news to the people fail to do so responsibly, accurately and reliably, they should be replaced. The people need not accept a second-rate government, but they should recognize the differences between error or faulty judgment and deliberate attempts to mislead or lie. In the Pierrelatte overflight the government misinformed the people because of a series of misunderstandings and human errors. At Palomares the calculated silence of the government encouraged speculation which confused the people. Lack of government foresight led the people into erroneous impressions of the bombing of North Vietnam. In denying attacking the *Turkestan*, the government itself was misinformed.

In all these cases the consequences were unfortunate, and in some they were grave. But in none was deliberate deceit involved; in none were the government of the United States, the administration of President Johnson or the Department of Robert McNamara attempting to delude the people. In none was there government trickery or double-dealing.

That fact does not excuse the government of its shortcomings. It is, however, a fact of immeasurable importance, for I believe many Americans today have lost faith in the word of the government because they have not distinguished between error and sham. Undoubtedly the government must do better, but I do not believe that it tries to mislead, whether the man in the White House is a Massachusetts Democrat or a Texas Democrat or a California Republican. I know that Robert McNamara and Clark Clifford did not deceive the American people deliberately, and I do not believe that Melvin Laird and his successor will do so.

Deliberate deceit aside, a serious error was made in the *Turkestan* affair, and it was made principally because Dick, Dan and I did not have the time to pursue the question further. A legitimate question at this juncture might well be: what *did* we spend our time on then? It might be worthwhile to discuss further the internal responsibilities on which the Assistant Secretary and his deputies spend their time. In June, 1967, when it might have been wise to re-examine the reports received from the field on the *Turkestan* charge and described by Pacific commanders as "final," some of the matters demanding the personal attention and professional action of the Assistant Secretary of Defense (Public Affairs) included:

The war between Israel and the Arab states, the issue of U.S. intervention in the Middle East; Israel's attack on the USS *Liberty*; Red China's explosion of a hydrogen bomb; the forthcoming visit of Premier Alexei N. Kosygin to the United Nations; preparations for a Summit Meeting which McNamara would attend; dozens of messages to Southeast Asia regarding a trip on which I would accompany the Secretary; the Army court-martial of Captain Howard R. Levy, who regarded the war as "diabolical" and claimed he was being court-martialed for

"heresy" and "witchcraft"; the criminal stupidity of another
Army performance in which a young soldier died during an
alcoholic "prop blast" ceremony celebrating completion of his
paratroop training; the Pentagon announcement of a major and
controversial change in the force structure of the Army Reserve
and Army National Guard; a national "policy statement" by
a rear admiral in the Tonkin Gulf which was at odds with the
policy of the President of the United States; erroneous reporting
by CBS that McNamara was urging the President to call reservists to active duty; a Senate subcommittee report damning the
Army's rifle procurement program since World War II; false
charges that U.S. aircraft in the Mediterranean Sixth Fleet were
flying to Israeli airfields; allegations by Chairman John Stennis
of the Senate Preparedness Subcommittee that we were "down
to the nub" in military manpower; wide rumors that General
Westmoreland was asking for another 250,000 troops for Vietnam; publication of two more tell-it-all articles in national
magazines on our favorite aircraft, the TFX; a rhubarb over the
sale of 20,300 M16 rifles to Singapore when South Vietnamese
troops did not yet have the M16; another rough series of attacks
by Congress on the weakness of the M16 (if it was no good, why
did anyone care if we sold it to Singapore?); news stories that
we were building a $3.5 billion electronic barrier across South
Vietnam; additional anti-American agitation on the military-
governed island of Okinawa; reports from Europe that an
international ring was smuggling GI deserters into Communist
Eastern Europe; renewed criticism from several sources of the
Military Code of Justice; baseless North Vietnamese charges
that we were deliberately attacking their dike and irrigation
system; another blast by Senator William Proxmire on Mc-
Namara's incompetence as a manager, this time on his inability
to halt apparent profiteering on war contracts; a major move
forward in the McNamara-Vance program to desegregate housing
around military posts; the coming election in South Vietnam
and the necessity of preventing the U.S. government from over-
selling it—and countless time-consuming nit-pick items such as
another attack on his superiors by Hyman Rickover and demands

from the press that we provide names of Congressmen flying overseas on a chartered military aircraft, countered by harsh instructions from Congress that under the law the Department of Defense served only as a carrier on any such trips involving Congressmen and that it was none of the Pentagon's business who was aboard on any trip which had been authorized by the appropriate committee chairman.

Each of these items and dozens more required communication with the Secretary of Defense—sometimes simply to alert him to them, sometimes merely to acquire the latest highest-level information so that our office could plot an intelligent course. My communications with McNamara were various but always informal. We began each day with a meeting at 7:50 attended only by him, the Deputy Secretary and me. On most days I would walk into his office several times for quick two-minute conversations which I initiated, and he would telephone me once or twice on the hot line between our desks to ask me to join him. Usually there were several additional telephone calls back and forth on matters not requiring face-to-face conversations, and often I would write him short memoranda which would be hand-carried to his office. He also frequently dictated two-sentence memoranda to me, nearly always beginning with the phrase "Would it not be wise to . . ." and ending with a specific date and time for completion of action on his "suggestions." I was invited to attend all major meetings in his office or in the dining room adjacent to it, whether the subject was the antiballistic missile, a new troop request from Vietnam or preliminary planning for the new budget. Just as time did not permit a back look at the *Turkestan* case, frequently it did not allow me to take advantage of these invitations, and Dick or Dan would substitute for me. They did not have the time either, but it was essential that one or all of us who were running the public affairs operation be advised of all major defense activities from their conception, and not merely called in, without background or knowledge, for counsel on how to handle publicly the crash landings. Because of this close contact with the Secretary, we knew his thinking on the issues and could conduct much of our business without specific checks with him on each detail. However, both McNamara and Clark Clifford after him personally approved and often helped rewrite the major press statements of the Department of Defense, whether these were released under their names, my name or simply as DoD statements.

Most matters which are before the Secretary of Defense must also be before his Assistant Secretary for Public Affairs. This fact of Pentagon life is a major reason why my job was, in my view, one of the half-dozen most interesting in the federal government. The most secret government secrets are shared on an internal "need to know" basis, and the need to know of the Assistant Secretary for Public Affairs is nearly total. Generally, the more secret and sensitive the issue, the more important that he be aware of it so that he can help safeguard the information in his world-wide formulation of public affairs policy.

Occasionally Dan, Dick and I would ponder how much simpler our jobs would be if we were limited, as were other Assistant Secretaries and their deputies, to special fields—International Affairs, Installations and Logistics, Manpower or Research and Engineering—or if we were involved only in the across-the-board activities of a single service. But we were concerned with all of these, and all took time. Merely to keep informed and up to date consumed several hours a day and could be done only by night reading at home after a thirteen-hour Pentagon stint. The major policy meetings in McNamara's office took time; reading the Central Intelligence Agency, Defense Intelligence Agency and National Military Command Center daily reports took time; scanning the most important overseas messages, even after they had been précised, took time. It was maddening for a lifelong newsman to have in front of him a lengthy cable from the American Ambassador in Moscow reporting on a meeting with Premier Kosygin, and not have time to read it because it did not deal with a current Defense problem. The State Department's message traffic came into my office, and among the hundreds of cables each day were always a dozen or more extremely sensitive and interesting ones which were available to only a handful of men in Washington. Yet I had no time to read more than a quick summary even of these.

Time was always the enemy. Everything, no matter how important or engrossing, was pushed aside by today's crisis and today's special project. These statements about demands on my time are not meant to be self-serving; they are simply facts. My predecessor was caught in the same trap, and so is my successor. This lack of time would later permit the development of another dangerous and damaging situation during my tenure: The Secretary of Defense was following one set of objectives for the air war in North Vietnam while the Commander in Chief of our forces in the Pacific and the chairman of the Senate Preparedness Subcommittee were stating publicly a different set.

Awareness of such cross-currents and recognition of them as a potential public affairs disaster for both the administration and the people must be one of the prime functions of the presidential appointee who is serving as Assistant Secretary of Defense. He must provide policy recommendations to the Secretary—and through him to the Secretary of State and the President—when public misunderstanding threatens the successful pursuit of national objectives. Similar recommendations must come to the three principals from the Assistant Secretary of State for Public Affairs and the President's Press Secretary.

These are the types of matters on which the Assistant Secretary of Defense (Public Affairs) must spend more of his time—not answering routine questions from newsmen or even assuming personal charge of handling the public affairs sides of such incidents as the *Liberty* and *Pueblo* episodes. The list a page or two ago of world-wide actions in which our office was involved with the Secretary of Defense was neither imaginary nor unusual, nor even complete; pick your own ten-day period and the incumbent Assistant Secretary can send you a comparable list—or read the headlines and make up your own. Whoever is sitting at that desk in today's world will work seventy to eighty hours a week in the

Pentagon if he conscientiously tries to serve the President, the Secretary, the people and the press—and his top associates, both military and civilian, will be working by his side.

To best utilize those seventy or eighty hours, he must free himself from so much fire-fighting. He also must recognize that his personal relationship with the press is one of the least important parts of his job, and learn to ignore newsmen critics who feel otherwise. Unlike the President's Press Secretary, who has a staff of only a half-dozen including secretaries, who personally meets daily with the White House press and who is the main link between the President and the people, the Assistant Secretary of Defense basically is an administrator with a world-wide organization to run. He will be successful if he runs it well, from Saigon to Stuttgart, and a failure if he runs it poorly. Whether he gets along well with the reporters who cover the Pentagon has almost nothing to do with his job. I was on excellent terms with some members of the Pentagon press corps, on atrocious terms with some, and, at the end, could not recognize perhaps one-third of them. At a farewell cocktail party given by Clark Clifford, I had to ask the Director of Defense Information to introduce the reporters individually to the Secretary; many of their faces were not familiar to me.

Undoubtedly the Assistant Secretary of Defense's most difficult and important administrative responsibility, aside from this special crucial function of alerting and advising the Secretary on areas of extreme public confusion or potential confusion, is to ensure that the special interests within the military establishment do not misinform the public by their own parochial and incomplete pleading.

The authority of the Assistant Secretary in this area is colossal, a result of potent feelings by his superiors in the Executive Branch—the Secretary and the President—and of powerful chairmen of powerful committees of Congress over the last decade that there be strong central control over the words spoken by the millions of men and women in the Department of Defense.

This means strong central control over the information policies and all other public affairs activities of the Army, Navy, Air Force and Marine Corps.

You will not hear many public speeches by the ASD (PA) about this gargantuan portion of his job, because inevitably any discussion of this issue triggers news stories that he is advocating "muzzling" the military or demanding that the entire Department "speak with one voice." Essentially that is exactly what he is doing, but those color phrases require that he then present a lengthy defensive explanation of the difference between encouraging internal debate and prohibiting the sabotaging of presidential policy once it has been made, and to make that distinction, in public, is always a no-win proposition.

Paradoxically, in addition to charging that the Assistant Secretary muzzles the military, critics accuse him also of operating the world's largest propaganda machine on behalf of the military. He does, in fact, rule the biggest public affairs kingdom on earth, which is one of the reasons time forces him to turn his back on the *Turkestan* cases, but persons concerned about militarist propaganda err gravely when they urge elimination of the Office of the Assistant Secretary of Defense (Public Affairs) or advocate a significant reduction in its strength or size. My predecessor, my successor and I all will guarantee the people worried about the power of the military establishment, the dangers of the military-industrial complex, the magnitude of the military budget or the influence of the military on foreign policy that one of the worst things that could befall their cause—aside from abolishing the Secretary and Deputy of Defense—would be the elimination of the Office of the Assistant Secretary of Defense for Public Affairs.

Remove the central control over the dissemination of news, over the review for security and policy of all statements reaching the public, and over the liaison of the military with the veterans organizations, the unions and the Chambers of Commerce; remove the central control governing coordination with the networks on their documentaries or with the authors on their books and magazine articles; remove the central control over tours con-

ducted for the American press in this country and abroad, or
tours of this country by the overseas press, over policy guidance
messages sent by the services to their commands around the
world, or over a hundred other service activities which were restricted by the Office of the Assistant Secretary of Defense for
Public Affairs in January, 1969, and the result would be a propaganda nightmare.

In ninety days the Department of Defense would be an old-
fashioned public relations shambles.

Each service would pull from its bottom-drawer files the sales
programs for its favorite weapons. Dozens of admirals and
generals would march across the country to peddle their favorite
national and international policies. (The ten smartest ones would
march, instead, to the *Today Show* and its television competi-
tors.) Advocates of special projects previously considered desirable but not essential would rush to Capitol Hill and, with current policy restrictions removed on the testimony they are allowed
to volunteer, would torpedo the President's budget as inadequate
and present heart-rending sales pitches to sympathetic Congressional committees. Network television cameramen would be
swarming over ships, aircraft and military camps. Artists' sketches
of drawing-board weapons essential to national security at only
$10 billion each would begin to appear in defense-contractor
magazine advertisements. The Air Force would fly ten Washington newsmen to every other football game at the Air Force
Academy in Colorado Springs; the Army would run monthly
press tours to its chemical warfare laboratories and ABM test
sites; the Navy would shuttle the press across the Caribbean on
nuclear-powered frigates. Each time an Air National Guard transport aircraft left for Vietnam 10 percent of its passengers would
be local editors and owners of local television stations. Defense
Department participation in the Paris Air Show would be increased 300 percent. Military bands would appear at the major
fund-raising luncheons of the B'nai B'rith and the local Chambers
of Commerce. Seventy-five billion dollars a year would be the
prize, and the armed services would be in hot pursuit of it.

I have seen it from both sides. For years as part of the press herd I watched the services operate with their pet newsmen in Washington and their pet Congressmen on Capitol Hill. The dangers of increased military spending and influence unquestionably are worthy of the public's attention, but they are reduced significantly by a strong Secretary and Deputy Secretary of Defense, supported by strong Assistant Secretaries of Defense. Strength is particularly desirable in the two Assistant Secretaryships some of Congress and many of the military object to most vocally—Systems Analysis and Public Affairs.

Military people in the armed forces of the United States will follow orders, which is one of the great differences between the Department of Defense and the Department of State, and the cooperation I received from all four services (even the Navy) was always at least fair and often good. From the Air Force it was usually excellent. Mutiny is not encouraged by the system, and military officers do not feel obligated, as do many top-level Foreign Service officers in State, to save the inexperienced Secretary from his unwise policy decisions. Instructions, if clear, usually will be obeyed—as long as the military understands that the man giving them really means it. In my four years in the Pentagon, I knew of very few deliberate and organized efforts by one of the services or high-level groups within one of the services to disobey orders.

But they will go right up to the wire. They will take advantage of indecision and move rapidly into the voids. They are capable of both power plays and end runs, and will bend regulations right up to the breaking point. The Navy would not attempt to issue policy statements in Saigon, realizing that the colonel or brigadier general who headed the U.S. Military Information Office, and who received his policy guidance from the Assistant Secretary of Defense, would shoot them down. But they would try to float current Navy policy into "insignificant" home-town press releases sent to a local paper in Kokomo about Petty Officer Robert Jones, or the Army would try to push policy into "internal" troop information bulletins, which are not under the control of the Assistant Secretary of Defense (Public Affairs). The in-experienced ASD (PA) who is unaware of these ploys and a thou-sand others, or who believes that the services are tamed or who thinks that the central discipline applied by McNamara is now an unalterable part of the system, will not long survive with effectiveness.

A monumental advantage enjoyed by Dick, Dan and me was that we had been on the other side so long and confidants in earlier years of so many officers of all ranks, including Chiefs of Staff. From fifty combined years of experience covering the Pentagon as newsmen, we knew that the services really would rather run their own business than have the Office of the Secre-tary of Defense run it for them. Military officers do not fight civilian control; they are brought up on it and believe in it. But in their heart of hearts they prefer to be controlled by their own civilians, over whom they exercise more influence. They want civilian Secretaries for their Army, Navy and Air Force—civilians who are part of them, who share loyalties to a particular service, who fight for them on Capitol Hill. And they accept, unhesi-tatingly, the authority of the Commander in Chief. Life for them would be so much more pleasant, however, without that extra layer of civilians composed of the Secretary of Defense and his meddling Assistant Secretaries.

Interservice competition for the budget dollar, for the assign-ment of a mission in space or for a short-range air-transport role is not a myth. While the military generally will abide by the system when they know that the unblinking eye of the Secre-tary or his bird dogs is upon them, it must be recognized that each year budget submissions from the services to the Secretary of Defense total $20 or $30 billion above the final figure he sends the President. If these billions represented worthless spending or obvious waste, the dangers would be slight, but they do not. The requests have been approved by the civilian Secretary of the ser-vice and his Chief of Staff for projects they deem necessary for the continued security of our nation. The service Secretary and Chief, who have already pared down significantly the submissions to them from their own people, believe deeply in the budget they propose to the Secretary of Defense—and they are not stupid or frivolous men. Because they feel so strongly that this money is needed for their country's safety, they are prepared to fight for it. Remove the central control which prevents them from fighting for it in public, eliminate from the Office of the Secretary of Defense the restraints which prohibit each service from rocketing off on its own, and it would be Katie Bar the Door.

Robert McNamara made order out of chaos in a hundred different ways. None, including his five-year programing, the establishment of his sophisticated Systems Analysis operation or his insistence on across-the-board budgeting (Air Force long-range missiles should compete for the budget dollar against Navy long-range missiles, not against Air Force helicopters), was more important in establishing order than the central control he and Assistant Secretary of Defense (Public Affairs) Arthur Sylvester clamped over the information policies of the four services.

As the war has grown more unpopular, the urban problems more acute and the people more unhappy about defense spending, it has become fashionable to requote Dwight D. Eisenhower's 1961 warning about the military-industrial complex. Reporters writing about the military-industrial complex invariably count up how many retired officers are working for how many defense contractors, or how many men on the staffs of the Armed Services Committees hold reserve commissions, or how many military installations have been built in the states of the committee chairmen. This is fair enough, but the newsmen overlook the main event. Eliminate from my old office the Directorate for Security Review, which read and cleared each speech destined for the public and each word prepared for Congressional testimony of every officer and civilian in the Pentagon, and return to the services the right to review and clear the public addresses of their own people in any manner they choose, and the pressures for increased military spending would increase many times more rapidly than could be brought about by all of the retired officers, staff reservists or irresponsible, constituent-pleasing Congressmen working in a coordinated effort.

Any significant reduction in the strength of the Directorate for Security Review would be tragic. Charles W. Hinkle, a retired officer who runs it as a high-level career civil servant, would reorganize and continue to operate a more efficient shop than many others in the Pentagon, but his smaller staff would necessarily be less alert to the nuances of the propaganda campaigns at which the services are always nibbling, and more pressure-building statements from the admirals and generals would slip by his watchdogs and into the public domain.

After lengthy hearings some years ago, the chairman and members of the Senate Armed Services Committee recognized this point and directed Arthur Sylvester and McNamara to strengthen the Security Review Directorate. Yet of the hundreds of news stories I have read about the military-industrial complex, I cannot recall one which concentrated upon the braking power of the forty men in the Directorate for Security Review in the Office of the Assistant Secretary of Defense (Public Affairs). Nowhere else is there a single antimilitary propaganda force that approaches it in power and importance.

While the Assistant Secretary is not involved personally in 95 percent of the work of the Security Review Directorate, the most sensitive problems do come before him. In our regime, when Hinkle's people scented trouble in speeches or testimony submitted by members of the Joint Chiefs of Staff, a service Secretary or Under Secretary or another Assistant Secretary of Defense, they would call it to his attention and he would bring it to Dan Henkin or Dick Fryklund. If our efforts to negotiate a satisfactory change in language failed, we would put the matter before the Secretary and/or Deputy Secretary. Issues of this type took more of my time than conversations with newsmen, largely because it was essential that they be handled with tact and courtesy. If our people were too dictatorial in their attitude toward a speech to be given by the Chief of Naval Operations, his staff might leak to the press both the offending statement and the fact that the Secretary of Defense was attemping to "muzzle" the admiral. The system is unchanged as this is written. The military editor of the New York Times or the managing editor of the Washington Post may resent it today when his telephone calls to the Assistant Secretary are returned by a Deputy Assistant Secretary or a major general, but if the incumbent Assistant Secretary is working with the Secretary of Defense to prevent the Commandant of the Marine Corps from saying something in Honolulu that might affect adversely peace talks in Paris, the priority of the military editor or managing editor simply is not high enough. The newsmen, naturally more interested in their own problems than in those of the government, will sulk, which is regrettable but not calamitous.

Critics might acknowledge after study that our office effectively opposed most propaganda efforts of the services, but then offer in rebuttal that we nonetheless acted as propagandists for the Secretary of Defense. Clearly we were in a position to do that. But persons fighting for lower military spending—the objective of most who complain about Pentagon propagandists—should realize that over the last eight years the Secretary of Defense was their strongest ally against the alleged military-industrial complex and was the strongest curb on higher military spending, even if his final budget was far larger than they desired. He does not feel pressure from contractors or constituents as does a Senator; he is not looked upon to provide morale and leadership to a million men as is a Chief of Staff or a service Secretary; he is not a zealot in a specialized field as is an anti-submarine warfare admiral. His objective is to get the job done in the cheapest and most effective way; it is of no concern to him which service does it or whether it is undertaken by one of the across-the-board organizations McNamara established, such as the Defense Supply Agency or Defense Communications Agency. The Secretary of Defense is responsible only to the President, and invariably a President beset with domestic problems will plead for the lowest practical defense budget.

McNamara for years fought off the services with one hand and

Congress with the other; he frequently said he was the only Minister of Defense in NATO whose problem was too much money from Congress rather than too little. A review of his fights on Capitol Hill shows that in nearly every instance the legislators were trying to push upon him weapons he did not want or to prevent him from making money-saving mergers he considered more efficient. Vietnam aside, McNamara's most vehement critics for seven years were those who wanted more nuclear power for surface ships, more money for a new manned bomber, more spending for antiballistic missiles, more divisions for the Army, more and bigger and better intercontinental missiles. Proponents of lower military spending might logically, albeit erroneously, have accused the Office of the Assistant Secretary of Defense (Public Affairs) of being propagandists for their side, but to consider it as part of a military-industrial complex seeking higher and higher defense expenditures makes no sense whatever. Of course it supports the President's budget, and of course that budget is much higher than is desirable. Basically that has to do with our foreign policy and the military force required by that foreign policy, not with excesses achieved by a military-industrial complex.

I have noted that our office usually did no more than make information available, seldom went so far as to try to see that it reached the people and rarely did anything to ensure that the people understood it. "Propaganda" is another color word which to me suggests sugar-coating information so that the public swallows it, or deliberately repeating a false concept so often that the public accepts it. I have seen no Assistant Secretary of Defense engage in propaganda of this description, either in my four years in government or in fifteen years as a Washington newspaperman, and I know of no evidence supporting any charge of this nature.

In January, 1969, the Office of the Assistant Secretary was structured properly to permit him to begin to function as he should. His organization was sound, the directives giving him necessary power over the four services were strong, the essential relationship with the Joint Staff was outstanding, cooperation from Unified Commanders around the world was good, liaison with the Secretary and Deputy Secretary of Defense was perfect and, for the first time since the establishment of the Department of Defense, the Assistant Secretary had almost enough top-level hands and heads to manage his world-wide organization and to do his job. When the war in Vietnam ends, in fact, he could accept a 10 or 20 percent reduction in Pentagon personnel on his own payroll. What he needs critically, however, is two additional Deputy Assistant Secretaries immediately beneath him.

When recruited into the government by Sylvester, Vance and McNamara, I was the only Deputy Assistant Secretary for Public Affairs, although most of the other Assistant Secretaries had four or more deputies in their offices. We later added a second and, just before McNamara departed in 1968, he approved my recommendation to introduce two more. In those last months of a presidential election year we were unable to find men of the caliber Henkin, Fryklund and I wanted, and as this is written the positions have not been filled by the new administration. One is needed as Director of Defense Information, occupying the slot now earmarked for a brigadier general. Newsmen and the people would be served better if this man were more senior, with the same access to the Secretary and Deputy Secretary of Defense that I enjoyed under Sylvester and that Henkin and Fryklund had with both McNamara and Clifford. The second new man should work more with the Secretaries of the services and other Assistant Secretaries of Defense. Any serious manpower study of the organization would point up the need for the two; it is asinine in a $75 billion operation to refrain from spending $60,000 or $70,000 more a year for necessary top-level talent. Preferably both should be professional newsmen from the Pentagon press room as Henkin, Fryklund and I were, at least one should have network experience and their political affiliation should be ignored. I was a lifelong Republican and such an admirer of Senator Robert A. Taft in my younger days that when I left Cleveland for the *Plain Dealer's* Washington bureau in 1950 my associates in the city room wrote on my farewell gift: "Mr. Republican, Jr., goes to Washington." All Washington newsmen are offered political jobs from time to time, and over the years opportunities were offered me to work with Taft, the Republican National Committee, a Republican Governor and several Republican Congressmen. McNamara and Vance both were aware of my Republican background when they hired me in 1965, and so was President Johnson when he appointed me Assistant Secretary two years later. A friend once introduced me at a dinner as "the only Taftite for Kennedy in the Johnson administration." (It is true that I preferred President Johnson to Senator Barry Goldwater in 1964, but no one ever asked me that question when I was invited to join the government.)

As this is written, pressures to cut military spending are mounting, which is admirable. McNamara used to say that the services chose new weapons systems as women choose perfume, on the basis that the most expensive and most exotic necessarily are the best. Congress should be much more hardheaded about the defense budget. In my view, the expenditure of another $1 million a year to recruit a talented professional staff for a Congressional appropriations committee—a staff composed of Rhodes Scholars and men of comparable intelligence, such as Alain Enthoven attracted to the Pentagon, blended with experts with practical experience—would save the taxpayers hundreds of millions of dollars each year. (Although only changes in our foreign policy will bring about a $40 billion defense budget instead of $75 billion. Even when the Vietnam war ends, neither internal nor external experts will find enough "waste" or "water" to achieve reductions of that magnitude.) History indicates, however, that an early victim to budget cutting by meat ax is the public affairs operation of any government department. This concerns me greatly, not only because communications with the people will suffer at a time when it is essential that they improve, but also because a weakening of the muscle of the Office of the Assistant Secretary of Defense (Public Affairs) inevitably will result in looser control over the services, a more intense internal brawl for the budget dollar and increased pressures for higher defense spending.

McNamara's Fight for De-escalation

August, 1967

Historians may never decide whether the United States pursued the right course in bombing North Vietnam—whether we should have begun the bombing, whether we hit the right targets, whether the gradual escalation was sound, whether the raids should have been cut back or stopped before 1968 or whether President Johnson erred in stopping them then. No historian will have access to all the records, especially personal communications which are a crucial part of those records, and no historian will be aware of important head-to-head conversations of which no records exist. After four years in the government, I have become skeptical of written history which analyzes why something happened as it did. Too much of value appears in no printed record or is otherwise not available. Even a Secretary of State writing a candid memoir may be unaware of an informal Sunday night supper conversation between a President and a Secretary of Defense; even the most objective memoirs can tell the story only from a limited vantage point. Within the government too many cables are drafted for eventual public consumption or for the historian or to safeguard careers, even if they are marked "Top Secret," "No Distribution" or "For the President's Eyes Only"—or even "Literally Eyes Only for the President."

Incomplete record-making takes place consistently in the government, at all levels, for a number of reasons. One is that the high-ranking subordinate does not want to be overruled formally. Another is that both subordinate and senior want to avoid a record which would encourage the press and the Congress to play up their difference of opinion as a "feud" or "controversy" or to publicize internal division, and so oral agreement is negotiated before written recommendations are submitted. Most persons in government are team players, and few want to drag far behind the leadership or stalk far out in front of it. In addition to the records hedged deliberately, some are of questionable value because of the predilection of the record-keeper. An Air Force study on the effect of the bombing campaign against North Vietnam, however honestly attempted, yields conclusions different from those in a study by the Central Intelligence Agency.

As an aside, too often the press and the public receive only fragments of one viewpoint, based on incomplete analysis and leaked to them by proponents of it. While Congress learns more through its investigations, unfortunately most Senators and Representatives—and their staffs—conduct much of their business with think-alike members of the Executive Branch. Doves in the State and Defense Departments feed Senator J. William Fulbright of Arkansas and his Foreign Relations Committee; Hawks feed Representative Mendel Rivers of South Carolina, chairman of the House Armed Services Committee. When either staff is preparing for a hearing, most—not all—of the witnesses called will offer evidence to support the position the chairman and the staff have already reached.

Historians weighing the air war in the North, however, will possess one major advantage, and perhaps two, over participating decision-makers. They will be able to study the settlement and its impact on both North and South Vietnam, and they may even also have some important information we lacked on Hanoi's internal reaction to the bombing. Our information on the thought processes of Ho Chi Minh and other North Vietnamese leaders was negligible. The intelligence community produced outstanding statistics on the capacity of North Vietnam's logistics system to move supplies or the dollar value of imports from Communist China, but it really did not know beans about

Hanoi's thinking. This is not a criticism exclusively of the Central Intelligence Agency, which turns out the most professonal staff work I saw in Washington. No one in our country knew beans about Hanoi's thinking. In 1969 the American who probably was the most knowledgeable about the North Vietnamese and best understood their leadership was Cyrus Vance, then a private citizen and lawyer in New York. But his knowledge came late in the game at the Paris peace talks, between May, 1968, and February, 1969.

Robert McNamara used to lament our ignorance of the Vietnamese, particularly when he compared our maneuvering in Vietnam with the management of the Cuban missile crisis. Our estimates of what the North Vietnamese might do next—or, indeed, what the South Vietnamese might do next—were always estimates only and often wrong. In contrast, McNamara would recall, during the Caribbean crisis Soviet experts Llewellyn Thompson and, until he left to be the Ambassador to France, Charles "Chip" Bohlen predicted each Russian reaction and response with astonishing accuracy. McNamara believed that this deep understanding of how Kremlin minds operate was crucial in carrying us through the crisis. We had no Tommy Thompsons or Chip Bohlens on Southeast Asia.

It has been suggested that the "computer-like" McNamara was frustrated because the war in Vietnam "defied reason." Such statements indicate ignorance of both McNamara and the war. He does not believe that reason is applicable to all areas of life and would cite faith and morality as two immediate exemptions. Beyond that, however, he would deny that the Southeast Asian conflict did, in fact, "defy reason."

"Many people," he said one day, long before leaving the Pentagon, "attack reason without attacking the application of reason. The problem in Vietnam is simply that there are a number of factors on which it is very difficult to obtain information. The attitude of the North Vietnamese is one example. Reason can be applied to this war, but it must be applied imperfectly because we lack certain facts."

The McNamara-computer image, incidentally, is another phony. He would far rather discuss existentialism or Rouault, climb up a mountain or ski down one, play squash or drink a martini than crank out statistics on the number of air sorties flown against North Vietnam. And he was able to spout the figures and percentages not because of a superhuman memory but because he worked harder than almost anyone else, did his homework better than almost anyone else and anticipated the questions he would be asked by the press or Congress more diligently than almost anyone else. He would spend four or five hours in preparation for each hour as a witness before Congress. To be sure, his memory was well above average, even in the last year or so when he began to wear out, but it had not nearly so much to do with his mastery of facts as simple hard work.

Measured by lives lost, equipment utilized, personnel committed or dollars spent, the air war in the North represented only a small fraction of the total United States effort in Vietnam. Yet it undoubtedly created the most public controversy and was the most emotional part of the war, both to our own people and to the people and governments of other nations. It also became one of the two major measuring sticks of "escalation" or "de-escalation," the other being the size of American troop deployments to the South.

Our memories of the Vietnam war are now colored by events of 1968: President Johnson's speech of March 31, his decision not to run, the bombing limitation, the campaigns of Senators Robert F. Kennedy and Eugene J. McCarthy, protests on the campuses, the antiwar clamor at the political nominating conventions and the bombing halt. In 1967 and before, however, the apparent national mood was different. While there was highly vocal opposition to the bombing, centered around such Senators as Fulbright and such publications as the *New York Times*, and while opposition to the war itself was growing steadily, through the summer of 1967 and into the fall the heaviest pressures upon the administration, by far, were for escalation of the war in the North. Perhaps the people were beginning to move ahead of their government by then; some antibombing signs indicated that this was so, and those who did oppose the bombing were deeply committed and emotional. But both within the leadership of the Executive Branch and within the Congress, the Doves were still far outnumbered by the Hawks. The overriding pressure was in favor of additional action against North Vietnam so that the war would end more quickly. It was for the government to use our kind of weapons—heavy air power—and to stop meeting the enemy on his terms, in the delta and the jungle. This pressure came chiefly from three sources: certain members of the Joint Chiefs of Staff and most of their subordinates within the armed forces; citizens unaccustomed to limited wars who regarded strikes against the enemy's homeland as the natural way to fight a war; and members of Congress who believed that the harder we hit the enemy, the quicker the war would end and the fewer casualties we would suffer.

The issue of whether the bombing was moral was debated outside the administration to some degree, usually as part of the issue of whether this was strictly a civil war or whether it also involved aggression from the North against the South. Some of this debate was stirred up by Harrison Salisbury's stories. But in and before 1967 the number of Americans demanding that the President stop the bombing unilaterally, or even that he reduce it, was in the very small minority.

I am not qualified to discuss the morality or immorality of the air attacks on North Vietnam. My layman's view is that it would be difficult to pluck out the bombing from the rest of the war and conclude that the commitment of 549,500 troops was moral but the bombing of the enemy immoral. My personal interest as a citizen was whether the attacks would shorten or lengthen and expand the war. My professional interest as Assistant Secretary of Defense was to support the case of the Secretary of Defense.

Part of that professional responsibility demanded that we in OASD (PA) help explain the air war in the North to the people. We did a poor job. Our people did not know what their government was attempting to accomplish in bombing North Vietnam, and the major reason was that the government as a whole did not know. Incredibly, there was no such thing as a government-wide bombing policy, understood and accepted by the Pentagon, the rest of the Department of Defense, the State Department, the White House and the Congress. When in the spring of 1967, three or four months after moving up to Assistant Secretary, I suggested to McNamara that we should adopt new tactics to do more to explain the policy to the people, he responded that the problem was more than a tactical one since he had never obtained agreement on the bombing objectives within the Department—as for example, he had hammered out an agreement on the nuclear-test-ban-treaty objectives some years earlier. The result was that on the bombing issue honorable and intelligent Americans were consistently talking past one another in confusion. The press accurately reported this confusion to the people, and the people did not have a chance.

While not in the government at the time of the test-ban pact, I knew that McNamara regarded it as one of the two or three most important achievements of the Kennedy-Johnson administrations. Had it not been for the work he did within the Pentagon, there would have been no treaty, inasmuch as some of the Joint Chiefs fought it vigorously at the outset and it was inconceivable that the Senate would approve a treaty banning nuclear testing in the atmosphere if the nation's senior military officers opposed it on national-security grounds.

Convinced that the key to the treaty was to get the Chiefs aboard, McNamara undertook to do so by laborious exploration of every point of their disagreement. As he explained the process to me later, he summoned them to the conference table in his dining room and invited them to place on the table for discussion every point with which they disagreed. The sessions took many hours each day; they lasted several days. McNamara conducted them personally, directed the conversations in the most minute detail. Every premise raised by every participant was explored, all evidence bearing on each premise examined. Not

until there was understanding and agreement around the table
on one point did McNamara permit the discussion to move on
to the next. Gradually, all false premises were destroyed. When
they were finally finished, the Joint Chiefs agreed with Mc-
Namara's own basic position—that the treaty carried with it
certain risks, but that the alternative risks of continued atmos-
pheric testing were far more grave, both from the moral standpoint of the health of unborn generations and from the hard
military standpoint that unlimited testing on both sides was allowing the Soviet Union to narrow the gap. It was agreed that
new risks were being assumed, but it was also agreed that old
risks were being avoided.

Our objectives in bombing North Vietnam had not been
agreed upon in this way. While hundreds of meetings on the air
war were held in Washington, Saigon and Honolulu (home of
CINCPAC), to the end there was disagreement on what the
bombing had accomplished and what it was capable of accomplishing. Secretary McNamara had listed his own objectives publicly often enough, but we had failed to get them across to the
people, he had not convinced others in the government that his
objectives were the right ones and many high officials in the Executive and Legislative branches kept citing objectives that were
quite different. Without agreement on what the bombing was
supposed to do it is not surprising that there was disagreement
on what kind of bombing was required to do it—or whether any
was required.

McNamara's own feelings had been formed for a long time.
Six months prior to our conversation that spring, he had told a
visitor in his office: "The bombing hurts, but not badly. Eighty-
five percent of the gross national product of North Vietnam is
agriculture. The infiltration of five thousand men a month could
be kept up for many, many years. The cost of the war by any
measurement to North Vietnam does not, therefore, have any
significant effect upon them."

A little earlier, in September, 1966, he had told another visitor
that the bombing could never stop the flow of men and equip-

ment. He said then also that the enemy could not be bombed into submission and that history showed no example of a nation's will being broken by bombing. Politically, physically and psychologically, he declared, North Vietnam could go on indefinitely under the bombing.

That was in the fall of 1966, a year before the San Antonio formula which was designed to halt the bombing; a year before McNamara undertook the most serious public analysis made of the bombing; eighteen months before it was cut back and two years before it was stopped.

At no time, either in 1967 or later, did the public or even the Congress receive a full explanation of McNamara's own complete position on the bombing issue. Even that August, when he was to outline precisely what he thought the bombing could and could not accomplish, and what targets he thought should not be struck in the future, he would not disclose his prior recommendations to the President.

Very few persons in Washington were aware of those recommendations. In the Pentagon, McNamara would discuss them only with the officials who had worked on them. And if they were rejected, he would not report the President's conversation or the presidential reasoning to anyone, not even his associates who originally had helped frame the memoranda to the White House. We knew that McNamara had lost because the President took Path X when Path Y had been recommended, but the Secretary held no Pentagon post-mortems on the presidential meetings—except with his Deputy Secretary, and not always with him. This refusal of the Secretary to quote the President even to his innermost advisers often made it extremely difficult to operate within the Department, but McNamara would have it no other way.

He possesses a stronger sense of loyalty than any man I have known. In regard to close friends, it is an emotional loyalty, and one which sometimes enables associates of those friends to take advantage of him for their own gain. In regard to the President of the United States—either President—it was emotional to the man and rational to the position. In regard to an organization, it is purely rational. The type of organization is not important in this concept; it can be a church, an educational institution, a large corporation, the World Bank, a department of government or a government.

If an organization of any nature is to succeed, the men in it must establish certain basic objectives. They will not move toward those objectives, McNamara feels, unless each man is loyal to the organization—and by definition, therefore, to the objectives. When anyone substitutes his judgment for the leader's, fragmentation is the inevitable result, and the inevitable result of fragmentation is failure to move at all. A basic tenet of McNamara's philosophy of management is that it is preferable to inch in the direction of an objective, even if you must head a few degrees off-center, than to stand rooted waiting for exactly what you want. He believes further that the moment you move reluctantly, the moment you express resentment for, indecision about or objection to a decision the leader has made—even in a private talk with closest friends—you make achievement of the goal more difficult. Departments of government which function most effectively, he thinks, are those which hew most closely to this principle. The individual—a Secretary of Defense, a Secretary of the Army, an Assistant Secretary of Defense—must subordinate his views so that the entire organization can proceed toward the common goal.

This clearly does not prevent that individual from stating his case internally and fighting for it within the government before the President has made up his mind. But once a presidential decision was reached on any issue, including the bombing, McNamara would support it loyally, with never a public and rarely a private hint that it was contrary to his own best judgment or his private recommendation. While this was sometimes unsatisfactory, it was preferable to the fragmentation and subsequent stalemate resulting from an every-man-for-himself philosophy in the Executive Branch.

From a standpoint of dealing with the press and public (as well as from his own personal standpoint), this sense of loyalty and concept of organizational progress put McNamara in a particularly difficult position in the spring and summer of 1967, when internal and external pressures were mounting to expand the war in the North. What neither the public nor the Congress ever knew was that he was attempting to move the country in precisely the opposite direction at this time, having recommended strongly that the raids in the North be limited to the southern portion of North Vietnam, specifically to the Panhandle south of the 20th Parallel. This was in the spring of 1967, almost a full year before Clark Clifford helped convince the President to cut back the bombing in exactly that manner. McNamara believed that the cutback would be more effective in interdicting the flow south, less costly to our pilots, less apt to widen the war and more consistent with the efforts of our government to move toward negotiations.

The Pentagon in the spring and early sumer of 1967 was split three ways, with most of the military favoring a significant expansion of the air campaign, some civilian leaders arguing for a slight step-up and a very few key civilians joining McNamara for restricting the bombing to the southern part of the North. Chief among the latter were Vance and the late John McNaughton, then Assistant Secretary of Defense for International Security Affairs. Their view was supported by Secretary of the Navy Paul Nitze, who was soon to succeed Vance as Deputy Secretary of Defense. Sharing this position also was Paul C. Warnke, who moved from General Counsel to McNaughton's post after John's death and was perhaps the most anti-Vietnam high official in the building.

A handful of others in the Pentagon were aware of the McNamara position, but our number was very small. The secret was well kept. Months after he proposed the restriction, a few news stories appeared reporting some sentiment within the government for a 20th Parallel limitation, but none that I saw then or later attributed to McNamara himself the prime support for this de-escalation.

This was not the first time that the Secretary of Defense had favored easing off on the bombing. Eighteen months earlier, in the fall of 1965, he had recommended the Christmas pause which was to last thirty-seven days. From private, indirect contacts with Hanoi at that time, there was reason to believe that North Vietnam would begin peace talks if we halted the attacks. McNamara saw risks in the pause, aware that Ho Chi Minh might pick up the option to talk through the Soviet Union and then filibuster while continuing full infiltration. But the possible gain of working toward a negotiated settlement was, he thought, worth the risk.

Now, in the spring of 1967, while recommending a partial halt, McNamara was also still prepared to stop the bombing completely if North Vietnam was willing to pay a satisfactory price, even if the payment came after the cessation. There had been no indication during the thirty-seven days that she was willing to pay any price at all, and there was no indication during the spring and summer. By this time—actually, before this time—McNamara had become convinced in his own mind that the major value of bombing was the blue chip it represented to lure the North Vietnamese to the negotiating table.

He believed nothing could have been more damaging to the war effort than overt conflict and controversy between the President and himself. And yet he was also worried that advocates of air power would build up such a case for expanding the bombing and win so many advocates to the "easy victory" route that the President would not be able to maintain the flexibility to cut it back or stop it—even if McNamara's advice not to increase it was heeded. Convinced that bombing North Vietnam could not conceivably end the war, that no military means could end it within a practical time frame, that it was eventually going to be settled through negotiations or a gradual cutback of action by each side, and that there could be no serious negotiating or reduction in action while the air war in the North continued, McNamara looked upon possible national acceptance of the hit-them-harder-and-win theory as catastrophic.

(Within the Department of Defense emotion overcame logic

on discussions of the role and importance of air power and the specific missions of air power in Vietnam. Somehow the bombing of North Vietnam became the symbol of the importance of air power, which was both tragic and illogical. Advocates of air power should have been the first to point out fallacies in this line of reasoning, but instead were, in many cases, the persons espousing it most vehemently. Air power was playing a vital role in the war—in transport between theaters and within the theater, in search-and-rescue, in reconnaissance and intelligence gathering and in close air support of ground forces. Air power enthusiasts strangely said little of these impressive military achievements. The fight over the effectiveness of air power centered, almost always, on the activity over North Vietnam, where the issue was one of strategic versus tactical applications—that is, whether the bombing was designed to disorganize the enemy's economy and destroy his morale or whether it was merely to support military operations in the South. Admiral Sharp in Honolulu and many others seemed never to retreat from the position that bombing "strategic" targets would cause the North Vietnamese to buckle, but McNamara never accepted this view.)

As the summer wore on, McNamara saw the country being ripped in two over the bombing issue. By August he was no longer pushing his 20th Parallel proposal, because on one flank the pressures of the Hawks were by then too great and on the other one could see more and more of the individual explosions of disenchantment which were to coalesce into a national frustration after the Communist Tet offensive the next year. The people were too torn and the debate too shrill at that time for a course which would satisfy neither Hawk nor Dove. Still seeking a way to stop the bombing under the right circumstances and bring the North Vietnamese to the conference table, however, he was working internally in the Pentagon on what was to become the San Antonio formula, announced by the President in a Texas speech on September 29, 1967.

But standing between formulation of a new peace conference formula and acceptance of it even within our own government was that powerful force of opinion demanding expanded bomb-

ing—however much in later years we may, consciously or sub-
consciously, try to pretend that it did not exist or could not
have existed.

To convince opinion leaders within the Executive Branch, the
Congress and the press that escalation could be ruinous, and to
provide a basis for the de-escalation offered in the San Antonio
formula, McNamara decided to analyze the tactical air war in
North Vietnam as it had not been analyzed publicly before.

For him, this was to be a unique experience. While he was
not to disclose his own previous de-escalatory recommendations
or attack current policy, he so assiduously outlined those objectives which bombing could never achieve that he came hazard-
ously close to boxing in the President for the future. I know of
no other such occasion during his seven years in office. His
cardinal rule had been that the Secretary of Defense should do
nothing, under any circumstances, which might limit the future
options of the President.

Attention was given in the Pentagon to the type of forum best
suited for the Secretary's deep bombing analysis. One possibility
was a major public address, but this was not considered feasible,
for no matter how the speech was written the press would have
regarded it as a one-man rebellion against the administration's
policy. A second choice was a formal news conference. The detailed statement he wanted to give, however, was too lengthy to
be presented at a meeting with the press. Beyond that, a news
conference is a risky venture for an official trying to inform or
educate the people on a specific issue. His side comment on another matter fresh in the news that day can capture the attention
of the press, and the important point he wants to make can
be lost.

In the midst of this, and as further evidence of the pressures
building for expansion, Clark M. Clifford returned from a two-
week trip to Southeast Asia on which the President had sent
him, and reported to the public: "There was unanimous agreement among all the allies that the bombing should be carried on
at its present level, or possibly an increased level."

At this time the Hawk opposition created two fortuitous openings which gave McNamara the opportunity to make his presentation under the best possible circumstances and to launch it with a ringing defense of President Johnson.

The first was the timely announcement by Senator John Stennis of Mississippi, chairman of the Senate Preparedness Subcommittee, that he would conduct a thorough probe into the "conduct and effectiveness of the air war in North Vietnam."

No platform could have been more ideal for a detailed analysis of what McNamara was trying to accomplish with the bombing and what tactical bombing could never achieve. He could support the President's basic bombing policy, state his own honest view that the objectives he and the President sought were conceived soundly and yet puncture arguments for an expanded campaign. Committee members, nearly all of whom were Hawkish, would interrogate him at length—which also was desirable for producing a worthwhile public record. Since the confrontation would be in the closed session of a Congressional committee, the press would be writing first from our prepared statement and later at leisure from a transcript of the proceedings instead of dashing in and out of an open committee room during the testimony to report each "hot exchange."

Testifying before any Congressional committee is an arduous experience, since the deck is so loaded in favor of the interrogators. It can also be humiliating, because in both House and Senate are petty, arrogant men who see sport in cowing officials of the Executive Branch. While I was treated with absolute courtesy by both Senators and members of the House in my own few appearances on Capitol Hill, in years spent covering Congress I witnessed many outrageous performances by fifth-rate bullies, and my associates in the Pentagon were subjected to some despicable treatment. It is all part of our system, and anyone not willing to accept it should stay out of the Executive Branch of the federal government, but one does not also have to like it.

Members of the Defense Department who had done their homework were never apprehensive, however, over appearing before Senator Stennis, a gracious gentleman committed to his

Senate responsibilities. Although he and McNamara disagreed on many issues, the Secretary respected him greatly for his intelligence, dedication and integrity. The Senator, I believe, returned that respect.

On this issue, of course, Stennis was a Hawk and wanted more bombing. His staff, which had conducted a two-man investigation to set the stage for the hearing, wanted more bombing; most members of his committee wanted more bombing; and the military witnesses who testified before them wanted more bombing. Nonetheless, the platform was excellent for our purposes.

The second break came as the hearings began, but two weeks before McNamara was to testify. Representative Gerald R. Ford of Michigan, Republican leader of the House of Representatives, stepped to the House floor to make a blistering attack on President Johnson and the entire administration for "handcuffing" U.S. airmen in North Vietnam. His speech included such statements as:

"Would the American people believe that in mid-1967, after two and one-half years of United States bombing of North Vietnam—an area about the size of Michigan—only three out of every ten significant military targets had ever been struck by U.S. air power?"

And:

"Must we accept as inevitable that the only way to fight this war is within the territory of South Vietnam, matching the enemy body for body, bayonet for bayonet, grenade for grenade?"

The Republican leader spoke of the "secret restraints" from Washington, and of an administration that had "pulled" its air punches. He criticized the leadership for having prevented American air power from hitting "hard enough and convincingly enough" to bring North Vietnam to its knees. He said there was "no justification for sending one more American" soldier until President Johnson removed the restrictions on bombing.

Ford's theme reflected the dominant pressures we felt, and his speech—a major political address—afforded us an outstanding opportunity to lay the groundwork for the lengthy statement which McNamara would be reading to the committee. In a short response to him, we could counter in advance some of the Hawkish military testimony which the committee and the public would be receiving prior to McNamara's appearance and, of immeasurable importance to help compensate for the antibombing tone of the Secretary's testimony, could simultaneously defend President Johnson against a rough political attack by one of the nation's top Republicans.

In order to command good newspaper and television play for his speech, Ford had used colorful, hard-hitting language. No matter how important the message, seldom does anyone in government say it in a monotone if he wants to see it in headlines or hear it on the Huntley-Brinkley show. From a professional standpoint, I thought Jerry Ford overplayed his charges. So strong was his attack that newsmen were driven immediately to the Pentagon for our response. We dropped everything to oblige them, with McNamara walking to my office to help expedite a statement so that we could have it in the first editions of the morning newspapers along with Ford's charges. We succeeded, although Ford had timed his release late enough so that he could make the network television shows that first night and we could not. Had his speech been a little milder, the newsmen would not have flocked to the Pentagon so quickly that day for our rebuttal and he might have had the morning papers also to himself.

In these charge-countercharge Congressional and political situations, we could not dilly-dally with polished language. Our initial objective was solely to insert something of our side into the same news stories which carried the blasts against us—which required that we keep our statement short enough (two or three brief paragraphs) so that newsmen might quote all of it and that we get it out rapidly. There would be time later in the week to draft a full reply to each of Ford's specific allegations, with paragraph-by-paragraph rebuttal, perhaps written as a response to a friendly Senator, who would insert it in the *Congressional Record* to keep the record straight and to try to prevent others from repeating Ford's erroneous charges.

We did not want the faceless Department of Defense or Assistant Secretary Goulding answering the prestigious Republican leader of the House. Within minutes after we had a copy of Ford's full text (it was folly to respond to a reporter's version of an attack upon you if the text of what actually was said was available) this statement was released over McNamara's name:

Mr. Ford's speech completely ignores the basic objectives of the air campaign against North Vietnam. The United States objective is not to invade, conquer or destroy North Vietnam, not to take actions which would broaden the war to bring in additional combatants at the cost of countless American lives and not to waste American lives needlessly on targets that do not contribute significantly to the North Vietnamese war effort.

As has been repeatedly stated publicly, the primary objective of the air campaign in the North is to reduce the flow of men and supplies from North Vietnam into South Vietnam or to increase the cost to North Vietnam of continuing that flow. This requires that the air attacks be directed primarily against the military lines of communication. They are.

It is true that there are restraints on the bombing, but they are restraints designed to save American lives, to avoid unnecessary devastation and civilian casualties in North Vietnam, and to avoid action which carries with it the high risk of widening the war with all that that implies. We believe the American public supports these restraints.

While members of the Joint Staff, associates of Paul Warnke —now Assistant Secretary for International Security Affairs— and people from my office were developing a point-by-point refutation of Ford, work continued on the major statement McNamara was to use before the Stennis subcommittee. That statement was to have this basic message for the Hawks: Stop kidding yourselves. There is no easy way out; no magic formula. Bombing North Vietnam is not going to "win the war" in the South. That is a snare and a delusion.

Warnke was the chief architect of the longer McNamara statement—as much as anyone other than the Secretary himself was ever chief architect of a McNamara statement. McNamara called in Warnke, ticked off the points he wanted to make and the order in which he wanted to make them, tossed across the desk some notes in his own left-handed scrawl and asked Paul to come up with a first draft. Warnke worked up a draft and turned it in to McNamara, who tinkered with it considerably and gave it to me for comment on how it would stand up in the public and political arena.

Sections of it did not, I felt, come across clearly enough for the average Congressman or the non-Pentagon reporter. Aware that it was largely a futile exercise since the Secretary already had approved a final version in his own mind and was about to testify, I spent a day and a night until 4 A.M. rewriting and reorganizing much of it, with the help of Dan, Dick and a battery of secretaries. McNamara kept most of his original language but accepted several of our structural changes.

His major goals were to make a convincing case against a less discriminating bombing campaign that would not end the war and might widen it, and, without opposing the President's policy, to build a foundation for partial or total cessation. As a backdrop, he wanted to try once again to implant his bombing objectives into the minds of the Congress, the press and the public; to assess the campaign against those objectives and to spell out differences and similarities between his views and those of the Joint Chiefs of Staff.

The Secretary of Defense began his testimony before the Preparedness Investigating Subcommittee of the Committee on Armed Services of the United States Senate at 10:10 on the morning of August 25, 1967. A copy of his prepared statement, from which we had deleted only a few lines for security reasons, was given newsmen by the committee. (The transcript was to be made available by the committee to the press later, again after relatively few deletions.)

The prepared statement began with a restatement of the three objectives of the air war against North Vietnam:

Our primary objective was to reduce the flow and/or increase the cost of the continued infiltration of men and supplies from North to South Vietnam.

It was also anticipated that these air operations would raise the morale of the South Vietnamese people who, at the time the bombing started, were under severe military pressure.

Finally, we hoped to make clear to the North Vietnamese leadership that so long as they continued their aggression against the South they would have to pay a price in the North.

All those who looked upon the stated objectives as something to skim over before getting to the meat of the debate never understood the air war in North Vietnam or Robert McNamara's position on it. Most of the hearing—most of the national debate—revolved around what the attacks were designed to accomplish.

"The bombing of North Vietnam," McNamara said, "has always been considered a supplement to and not a substitute for an effective counterinsurgency land and air campaign in South Vietnam."

It was vital to future policy decisions on the bombing to get across to the Congress and the people those objectives and that point. Whether 173,000 sorties north could be defended, or whether the campaign as mounted was the most effective one to achieve those objectives, or whether concentration on the Panhandle south of the 20th Parallel would be wiser militarily as well as politically and economically, were separate issues. But a case could be made for air attacks against North Vietnam if one weighed them against the objectives cited by McNamara. Weighed against other objectives, the bombing made less sense or no sense at all. What was frustrating so many of the military, so many members of the Senate committee, so many Hawkish editorial writers and columnists, so many parents of United States soldiers and so many other Americans who were urging a different kind of bombing was that they contemplated a different set of objectives—ones McNamara considered unachievable.

One of the frustrated men was Admiral Sharp in Honolulu,

the officer in nominal charge of the bombing of the North, who believed that the United States should apply steadily increasing pressure against the North in order to force Hanoi to cease its aggression in South Vietnam and to make Hanoi's continued support of the Vietcong insurgency as costly as possible. The Senate committee stated its concept of the objective in almost identical terms: "To cause North Vietnam to pay an unacceptable price for its aggression."

If we were trying to bomb hard enough to cause Hanoi to cease its aggression, or if we were trying to cause her to pay an unacceptable price, obviously we were trying to "bomb her out of the war," or "to her knees" or "to the conference table." These were simply other ways of saying that the Air War North could be a substitute for the Land War South.

Most of those who wanted to hit harder were looking for this substitute—the easy way out. They believed, as the Republican leader of the House had intimated, that if the administration would only unleash the Air Force and the Navy, we could smash North Vietnam's "industry" and make it impossible for Hanoi to continue to fight, or we could so disrupt their society that we would break their will and force them to the conference table, or we could stop the flow of men and supplies into the South and impose logistical starvation on the enemy there, or we could isolate North Vietnam from the rest of the world and prevent her from importing what was needed to support the war.

If bombing had been able to accomplish a single one of those things, the air war could have been a substitute for the ground war, and risks of widening the conflict could have been more acceptable. But McNamara was convinced that none of these could be achieved (without the use of nuclear weapons, which no official recommended), and he wanted to communicate that message to the people.

The Secretary told the Senators unequivocally that the bombing had met its stated objectives: undoubtedly it had sustained the morale of the South Vietnamese when they were in fear of military defeat; unquestionably it was forcing Hanoi to pay a price at home; and certainly it was making infiltration more difficult and costly. (The added cost was, for the most part, simply passed on to the Soviet Union—which could stand such a cost interminably.)

Partly to meet charges that we were engaged in a halfhearted effort, McNamara spewed figures at the committee, informing the Senators that the strikes were reported to have destroyed 4,100 vehicles, 7,400 watercraft and 1,400 pieces of railroad rolling stock.

"In addition," he said, "we have struck approximately 1,900 fixed targets in North Vietnam, including 57 significant bridges, 50 major rail yards, troop barracks, POL storage tanks and power plants. North Vietnam has been forced to divert an estimated 300,000 full-time, and at least an equal number of part-time, workers and troops, to the repair, dispersal and defense of the lines of communications and other targets which have been damaged. This diversion of some 500,000 people in a society already strained to maintain a marginal subsistence is a severe penalty."

The disadvantages of citing the bomb-damage figures were clear to us, since obviously they were ammunition for those who protested the David-and-Goliath aspects of the war and those who considered our effort in Southeast Asia a futile and/or immoral one. This was the public problem faced by the administration almost from the outset: those arguments which pacified the Hawks enraged the Doves. But the figures were accurate ones, politically helpful to the President in countering the opposition allegations that he was not doing enough in North Vietnam and psychologically helpful to McNamara in countering the approach that we could "win" if only we would "hit hard enough." They helped build the case against expansion, and expansion was the primary concern in 1967.

McNamara was, therefore, attempting, simultaneously, to convince the Hawks that the effort was not a feeble one and the Doves that it was not a futile one. As part of the first goal, and to further stifle the demands for unrestricted bombing, which had such dangerous potential for bringing in Red China or causing a Soviet military reaction in Southeast Asia or elsewhere, he deliberately emphasized all the points on which he and the Joint Chiefs of Staff were in agreeement.

Our air attacks in the North were of two different types. At the time of the hearing we had run approximately 173,000 sorties against North Vietnam. What we had been unable to get across to much of the press, the public and the Congress was that more than 90 percent of these were directed against lines of communication and the objects moving over them—roads, railroads and waterways, and trucks, locomotives, barges and other vehicles and vessels. While McNamara privately thought we were wasting an enormous amount of ordnance and would have preferred fewer attacks, the Chiefs were getting as many of these so-called "armed reconnaissance" (see-it-and-shoot-at-it) sorties as they wanted.

The remaining 10 percent of the sorties were flown against fixed targets—bridges, rail yards, vehicle depots, power plants and such feeble war industry as North Vietnam possessed. The Joint Chiefs had prepared a list of all the fixed targets in North Vietnam which they considered of military value. At the time of the hearing, 427 targets were on their list, 68 of which they did not themselves recommend attacking. Of the remaining 359, McNamara and the President had authorized strikes against 302—85 percent of the requests.

"There are only fifty-seven targets recommended by the Joint Chiefs of Staff against which strikes have not yet been authorized," McNamara summarized. "Whatever the merits of striking these fifty-seven targets may be, I believe it is clear that strikes against them will not materially shorten the war."

Not all of McNamara's critics among the air enthusiasts were impressed by his percentages. Granted, they said to him, that 90 percent of the effort is armed reconnaissance and only 10 percent is attack against fixed targets. Granted that the Chiefs are satisfied on the 90 percent and that there is no difference between you and them on 85 percent of the remaining 10 percent. But within that small percentage left, within those remaining fifty-seven targets you have not authorized, could be some so important that they would turn around the entire war.

Some could have been that important, but, with one exception, they were not, as the Chiefs themselves would have agreed. To convince the Senators, McNamara went down the entire list, target by target.

Five—three bridges and two railroad sidings—were adjacent to the Red Chinese border in the narrow buffer zone created to avoid accidental attack on that country.

Seven, in the heavily populated, heavily defended Hanoi-Haiphong area, were characterized by the Chiefs themselves as being of small value. These included two small concrete plants, a tiny machine shop, two rinky-dink battery shops and a ten-cent tire plant.

Twenty-five others in the Hanoi-Haiphong area were classified by the Joint Staff as being somewhat more important than those but still not of "significant" importance. McNamara listed them one by one, with his own comments. *Examples:*

A motor pool of 39,000 square feet—"You probably have on your farms barns bigger than that."

A vehicle repair shop of 48,000 square feet—"Any garage on any one of the side streets of Alexandria [Virginia] has more than that."

Vehicle depots of 64,000 square feet, 24,000 square feet and 27,000 square feet and a warehouse of 94,000 square feet—"[They] wouldn't fill in the corner of a Sears, Roebuck district warehouse."

Another storage area half that size . . . a transformer to an inoperative power plant.

"I submit to you," McNamara said, "I am Secretary of Defense and I am responsible for lives and I am not about to recommend the loss of American lives in relation to those targets."

Another batch consisted of nine petroleum targets, also in the heavily defended Hanoi-Haiphong area—lucrative targets, on superficial examination. But all nine comprised only 6 percent of the existing petroleum capacity of North Vietnam.

"I myself don't recommend we send pilots into Hanoi and Haiphong areas to take out targets as insignificant as that," said McNamara.

Four were more important targets in Hanoi and Haiphong— a railroad yard, a supply depot with 7 percent of the national storage capacity, another with 3 percent and a very heavily defended railroad bridge. McNamara thought we should keep an eye on the railroad yard and attack it when we could get in with reasonable losses, described the larger depot as a borderline case, recommended against the smaller one and regarded the bridge as not worth risking lives on.

The committee asked whether he could explain why military men such as General Wheeler and Admiral Sharp, who had access to all the same information, came to such different conclusions on them.

"Yes, I think so," he answered.

We come from different backgrounds and different experiences. . . . I am not at all impressed by a tire plant that produces 30 tires a day. I am not at all impressed by a national so-called steel capacity which doesn't produce any steel at all and produces only something on the order of 5,000 tons of pig iron a month. [He noted in his statement this was 1/20 of one percent of the U.S. output.] I would have lost that in the backroom of what I considered a relatively small pig iron production capacity in River Rouge.

So this different experience brings different judgments. I am not impressed by battery plants that turn out 300 tons of wet cells per year. I am not impressed by vehicle repair shops that have 20,000 square feet or 40,000 square feet. The smallest assembly plant I had [at Ford] had one million square feet.

So these are negligible industrial facilities, and frankly I am not prepared to recommend that we lose American lives in taking them out. Maybe some others are. They have the authority to make the judgment. If they do, I will follow it without question, but I am not prepared to recommend it.

North Vietnam had no real "warmaking industrial base," he summarized, and hence no amount of bombing, no unleashing of the Air Force, no change in bombing policy could "destroy" her "warmaking industrial base."

While the Secretary and we in OASD (PA) kept saying this, however, people could not and would not accept it. So many related the country of North Vietnam to our own. Everyone knew that it was not our kind of industrial nation, but even so it appeared natural that certain types of air attacks would have a crippling effect if only we executed them well enough and kept at them long enough. For example, all Americans are familiar with the incredible difficulties we suffer in any part of this country when there is a power blackout. Eliminating North Vietnam's power supply might not knock her out of the war, but surely it would have a tremendous impact on her economy and her ability to function as a nation.

Not at all. Among the charges by Representative Ford was that one-third of North Vietnam's total power targets and all her hydroelectric generating facilities were forbidden targets by "orders from on high." Small wonder that the public sought expansion of the bombing; what possible reason could the administration have for not hitting the hydroelectric plants? But the sweeping charge obscured the facts, and such allegations as this could be answered only by reciting the statistics and putting the accusation into perspective. The fact was that of twenty-two power plant sites in North Vietnam, strikes had been authorized and carried out against fourteen (including one hydroelectric plant), and that these fourteen represented 86 percent of the total national capacity. True, no attacks had been authorized against five of the six hydroelectric plants. But one essential point was that all six represented less than 5 percent of North Vietnam's entire national power capacity. And the other essential point was that the entire power produced by all plants in North Vietnam was less than one-fifth the amount generated by the Potomac Electric Power Company in Alexandria, Virginia.

One of the plants which we had knocked out was at the port

of Haiphong. While Americans picture how the port of New York would be tied up without power, the economy of North Vietnam was not dependent upon power systems. After activating some portable generators in Haiphong, the Communists continued off-loading ships at a steady pace, actually increasing their level of imports 45 percent the year after the power plant was out.

Sufficient electricity for war-related activities and essential services throughout the country was provided by the two thousand diesel-driven generating sets which were in operation. In regard to power, as in all other modern industrial respects, Vietnam was a primitive country. The Red River Valley is not the Ruhr Valley; Hanoi, even if targeted, is not Hamburg. Haiphong and Cam Pha are not Bremen and Düsseldorf. Most Americans were aware of this, but their minds rejected the unfamiliar. It is my belief that the Congress of the United States did not begin to comprehend this fact until Robert McNamara cited the facts and figures, and gave them meaning by making concrete comparisons in terms of American equivalents—and even then many members refused to accept it.

Having gone over fifty of the fifty-seven fixed targets in detail, McNamara turned to the other seven. It was important to deal with each. The case for expanded bombing was an emotional one; McNamara was determined to destroy it with point-by-point logic. Four of the remaining seven targets were airfields: a jet-capable field at Cat Bi, a strip able to handle transports at Bac Mai, the international airport in Hanoi, called Gia Lam, and North Vietnam's major MIG base at Phuc Yen.

The other seven of North Vietnam's eleven air bases had been attacked. No one considered Cat Bi or Bac Mai of enough military value to quarrel about. Phuc Yen was more controversial. The Joint Chiefs of Staff wanted to strike it; McNamara regarded it as a marginal target. His reasoning was simple: he thought we might lose more United States pilots to ground defenses by attacking it consistently and keeping it inoperable than we would lose to MIGs based there if we did not attack it. His primary consideration was which course was safest for American pilots. Our losses to MIGs that far in 1967 had been twelve aircraft. At Phuc Yen the Communists had only eleven planes, protected by heavy antiaircraft fire. Ten miles away at Gia Lam were another nine MIGs, although its capacity was forty. Even if he were wrong, the Secretary added, and if we could keep Phuc Yen inoperable without undue losses, the MIGs could then move to Gia Lam, and bombing Hanoi's international airport carried a host of political problems and a severe danger of heavy civilian casualties. Aware of White House views, he acknowledged that this was a marginal decision and indicated Phuc Yen might soon be added to the list. (It was added shortly, and the results proved McNamara's earlier position correct.)

The other three targets on the list recommended by the Chiefs were the three deep-water ports of North Vietnam: Cam Pha, Hon Gai and Haiphong. The first two, in General Wheeler's own words, were "peanuts." The third, Haiphong, was not.

This was one of the two real bombing issues between the members of the Joint Chiefs of Staff and the Secretary of Defense. It was one of the primary reasons for his testimony, for Haiphong was the key to an expanded bombing campaign—a campaign involving not only the port but many additional targets.

(As already indicated, the other major issue between McNamara and the military on the air attacks was his desire to halt them.)

The immediate Haiphong question was whether we should bomb the port facilities there, attempting to prevent ships of the Soviet Union, Communist China and other nations from unloading in the harbor. Joined with it was the companion issue of mining the harbor.

Potential advantages of closing sea importation routes into North Vietnam were obvious. Without imports Hanoi could not continue the war. That was certain. Inasmuch as the great bulk of material came into the country through the port of Haiphong, it appeared sensible for the United States to bomb and/or mine that port, thus keeping out such material. Proponents of this course seized upon estimates from the intelligence experts to support their case—North Vietnam imported 5,800 tons a day for all purposes, of which 4,700 tons came through Haiphong.

Pressures within the administration and within the Congress were strong for ordering the Navy and the Air Force to cut off those 4,700 tons.

But Ho Chi Minh's reliance on Haiphong was for convenience, not by necessity. North Vietnam's 5,800 tons of total imports, by land and sea, did not begin to equal her importing capacity. The three ports, together with roads and railroads from Red China, were capable of handling 14,000 tons a day—two and one-half times the actual flow.

McNamara took the Senators over the Haiphong hurdles one at a time. The first was whether it was possible, by mining and bombing, to close the three ports tightly. No evidence had been produced by military witnesses that this could be done. But even if they could be shut down, North Vietnam still would be able to import more than 8,400 tons per day by rail, road and water-way—a significantly higher figure than she actually was import-ing. And even if we then mounted such frequent and successful air strikes against those lines of communication as to cut that figure in half—and no proof was presented that this could be done—that still would leave North Vietnam with 4,200 tons a day for all purposes, or more than two-thirds of her current total imports.

War-supporting material was, of course, only a small percent-age of her total imports, and actual military equipment was only about 550 tons a day. McNamara went on to testify:

> Since the daily importation of military and war-supporting material totals far less than this [4,200 tons a day], it seems obvious that cutting off sea imports would not prevent North Vietnam from con-tinuing its present level of military operations in the south . . . elimina-tion of Haiphong and the two other ports as a source of supply would not, in fact, eliminate seaborne imports. . . . The North Vietnamese seacoast runs for 400 miles. Many locations are suitable for over-the-beach operations. The mining of Haiphong or the total destruction

of Haiphong port facilities would not prevent offshore unloading of foreign shipping.

McNamara told the Senators how the North Vietnamese had successfully overcome our destruction of petroleum-unloading facilities at Haiphong by off-loading petroleum and oil drums into lighters and barges and bringing them ashore at night. They could do exactly the same thing with other material. And if they could not, we still would not have isolated them.

"Effective interdiction of this lighterage, even if the inevitable damage to foreign shipping were to be accepted, would only lead to total reliance on land importation through Communist China," the Secretary testified. "The common border between the two countries is about 500 miles long."

Not a single person who advocated bombing the port facilities, mining the harbors or both produced a plan showing that these actions would prevent North Vietnam from importing sufficiently to continue to support the war. Not a shred of evidence was produced to indicate that this would be the case.

"It certainly would reduce the imports," McNamara said. "It would certainly increase the cost of importing by sea. But it is quite clear, I think, that they could continue to do so over the beach or by other means."

While some proponents of expanded bombing grudgingly accepted McNamara's logic on the Haiphong issue, they turned immediately to other unattacked targets to plead their case for additional effort. Again, the difficulties revolved around the lack of mutual understanding of the basic objectives. When Mc-Namara declared that bombing alone would not bring Hanoi to the conference table, Senator Stennis was asked on a television show whether he agreed.

"Well," replied the Senator, "I reject that conclusion."

By that rejection, one of the nation's most powerful Senators and unquestionably the most powerful on defense matters was saying that the war in the North could be a substitute for the one in the South. If bombing alone would bring Hanoi to the peace table, we did not need 525,000 troops fighting in the

South, nor an expenditure of $25 to $30 billion a year, nor all of the casualties. If bombing alone could do it, or might do it, then the Republican position taken by the GOP leader in the House and echoed by the Republican National Committee was right, and the expansionist position taken by the military was right, and the Democratic position taken by Senator Stennis and repeated by most (not all) of his party colleagues in the Senate was right, and McNamara was a timid, stubborn fool.

The President could, of course, have changed the selective-bombing campaign, abandoning the target-by-target analysis which balanced the military importance of the target against its probable cost in American lives and its risk of expanding the war to involve Red China or the Soviet Union. He could have launched an all-out effort to destroy Hanoi's will, bombing the cities as the cities of Europe were bombed in World War II. But no intelligence reports gave evidence that such a campaign would change the resolve of the North Vietnamese people. The economy was agrarian and simple. The people were accustomed to few comforts; they were not dependent upon great cities for their welfare; they could be fed without reliance on truck or rail transport; they were used to discipline.

McNamara believed that even all-out people-killing attacks upon Hanoi—which were recommended by none of the military—would only have caused the government to retreat to the hills and might have brought in Red China, while forfeiting the tenuous political support of Western allies along with that of Japan, Australia and New Zealand. The continued functioning of a North Vietnamese government was not tied to a viable city of Hanoi. Nothing in the past reaction of the leaders or the people provided any confidence that they could be bombed to the conference table.

If a different bombing campaign would not shut off imports or break the will of the North Vietnamese, would it reduce substantially the flow of men and supplies south? Again, McNamara thought not, chiefly because the capacity of the lines of communication to move supplies so exceeded the minimal flow necessary to support the level of military activity chosen by Hanoi in the South. McNamara told the committee we did not know exactly how much infiltrated material was needed to supply the North Vietnamese and the Vietcong, excluding food. Estimates from the intelligence community, however, were that the quantity was very small.

"The reported figure is 15 tons per day," McNamara testified. "But even if the quantity were five times that amount it could be transported by only a few trucks. This is the small flow of material which we are attempting to prevent from entering South Vietnam through a pipeline which has an outlet capacity of more than 200 tons per day."

We had warned McNamara that the Senators would challenge the fifteen-ton-per-day figure, and he had no confidence in it himself. After presenting it to the committee as the best intelligence estimate, because it was, he suggested that they consider a 500 percent increase in the base figure, or ninety tons per day. The amount was still too small to be stopped or sharply reduced.

One of the reasons for such a low figure, whether fifteen or ninety tons per day, was that it did not count food, which was estimated by different means. A second was that it excluded anything coming by sea into Cambodia and then across to South Vietnam. A third was that the enemy battalions in the South averaged only one combat day in thirty. McNamara believed that they could have raised that level of activity if they chose and still infiltrated enough to supply themselves. Some of the military thought that the Communists did want to raise it but were thwarted by the bombing from doing so, although no evidence to support that view was developed.

I saw no intelligence report, either from the military or the Central Intelligence Agency, which suggested that increased bombing could cut the flow south. If fifteen tons plus perhaps ten tons of food a day was correct, the North Vietnamese needed only eight to ten trucks a day to move it, and even if one accepted McNamara's arbitrary 500 percent increase, only forty to fifty trucks a day were required. No one in the military figured out a way to stop that number of trucks—or the porters and bicycles that could replace them—from moving across mountain trails by night and under dense jungle canopy by day.

From a public affairs standpoint, we who were supporting the Secretary faced the same type of problem with infiltration that we had with "industrial" bombing. Americans pictured the North Vietnamese supplying their troops with the massive shipping we pushed into South Vietnam, or they saw the great Allied truck convoys of World War II moving over the roads of Western Europe. The thought of a combat battalion fighting only one day a month, or of an army existing on supplies delivered by ten to fifty trucks every twenty-four hours—one truck every two hours or two trucks every hour—was not a thought at all; it was unthinkable.

Infiltration in the fall of 1967 was running perhaps five thousand men a month. Imagine a civil war in the United States, consider yourself a Southern general and ask whether Yankee invaders moving through the mountains of West Virginia every twenty-four hours—eight men an hour—could be stopped by your Southern Air Force. You would hit some. You would destroy some of their trucks, moving without headlights at night on winding dirt roads, beneath the tree canopy. You would make it more difficult for them. You could force them to send ten—or even fifteen—an hour to get eight through. You could make them fear each mile and yearn to ride safely all day in comfort on a railroad train. You could ensure that each man spent much more time in transit. But could you keep the rate beneath eight men per hour, or could you limit it to eight per hour?

Robert McNamara contended that the United States could not do so in Southeast Asia.

The Senators questioned the Secretary of Defense from 10:10 in the morning until 5:25 that afternoon. All day, in a dozen ways, he made and remade the same points. The air war had three objectives, and it was meeting those objectives, but it was not a substitute for the war in the South. No matter how we expanded it, or what targets were added or what actions were taken, we could not stop infiltration, we could not break the will of the people, we could not bomb Hanoi to the conference table, we could not seal off the country, we could not cripple this non-industrial nation.

Most of the resources of the North Vietnamese, other than manpower, were supplied from outside sources. The production bases, the new and finished materials, the transportation to North Vietnam, the equipment to transport from North Vietnam to Laos, Cambodia and South Vietnam, and even some of the man-power used in the North, came from other nations—mostly the U.S.S.R. and Red China. The ability to supply the necessary levels was well within the capabilities of these other nations—even if sustained over long periods and/or at higher levels. The North Vietnamese and their outside suppliers could substitute almost infinite ways of keeping supplies moving into and through North Vietnam. It was almost impossible in 1967 to persuade emotional air-power advocates to pay serious attention to the all-important principle of substitution—whether substituting portable generators for power plants, porters for trucks or light-erage for deep-sea ports. Most such substitutions required intensive manpower resources and the application of these re-sources. The North Vietnamese, the Chinese and the U.S.S.R. could supply both the manpower and the will.

Increased bombing could make life more difficult for North Vietnam, but at a combination of two costs. One, if we attacked some of the targets in the heavily defended areas of Hanoi and Haiphong, was a cost of additional American lives—with ques-tionable military gain. The other, if we bombed adjacent to the Chinese border, mined the ports or struck shipping and port facilities, was a cost of possibly bringing Red China into the war and possibly forcing a Soviet reaction in Vietnam, in Berlin or elsewhere. The Secretary of Defense was prepared to take those grim risks if the potential gains made them worth taking. In his view, expanded bombing of North Vietnam could not produce a result worthy of the risks.

While McNamara was to be overruled on Phuc Yen and some of the other targets in the weeks ahead, these reverses were of relatively minor importance. What was critical to the future of the war and essential for the bombing halt to come the next year was that the Secretary of Defense won his principal case. His arguments against mining or bombing the port of Haiphong were accepted by the President, and those dangerous actions, with their great potential of widening the war, were never taken by the Johnson administration.

McNamara's strong stand within the government against mining or bombing Haiphong and the other ports was the brake which prevented the air war in the North from slipping gradually into an expanded and disparate operation with chilling ramifications. Had the military and the more Hawkish civilians in the administration convinced the President on the Haiphong issue, they unquestionably would have pressed on for a more intensified attack in the North. Their program was developed and had been submitted. Some foreign shipping inevitably would have been hit as a deliberate campaign of "shouldering" ships out of the harbors was carried on. Restrictions against armed reconnaissance near "downtown" Hanoi and Haiphong would have been eased. All airfields, including the international airport at Gia Lam, would have been raided persistently. After the harbors had been mined and the ports bombed, special attention would have been given the rail lines coming down from Red China, and especially the northeast line, which could have become the major supply route. The buffer zone along the Chinese border would have been shrunk. And the irrigation dikes might have been targeted.

These actions, McNamara felt, would have complicated gravely the eventual chances of ending the war. It was his view that the Soviet Union eventually would be of assistance in bringing North Vietnam to the conference table—particularly if we de-escalated the bombing, but possibly in any event. (This proved to be the case in 1968.) He also felt, along with most others in government, that China would resist any settlement. (This also proved to be accurate in 1968.) But bombing the ports and moving in other ways to tighten sea imports obviously would force Hanoi to rely more upon Red China as a supplier, and China's control of the overland supply routes undoubtedly would put her in a position to exert additional pressure on Hanoi to keep fighting. As McNamara saw it, we would be driving North Vietnam away from the ally which might prefer a settlement and toward the ally which definitely preferred war.

No one could be certain how the Soviet Union would react to attacks against the port. She would certainly be angry and embarrassed; she would not suffer humiliation gladly; she would respond in some way if her ships were blown up by mines or forced out of a harbor by bombs. In Southeast Asia she might have escalated her material assistance by giving Hanoi Komar guided-missile patrol boats carrying Styx missiles of the type which the Arabs used to sink an Israeli desroyer—and which could constitute a threat to our ships in the Tonkin Gulf—or by providing medium jet bombers which could reach South Vietnam. She also might have reacted elsewhere in the world to regain prestige—Berlin was a major possibility; Korea and Turkey were others. Also, at any time she could involve herself additionally in Vietnam by sending "volunteer" pilots for duty in the North or the South.

China's reaction was another question mark. McNamara believed that North Vietnam had received guarantees of assistance from Red China before ever sending combat troops across the DMZ—guarantees against the loss of the country or the government. One of the unknowns was the point at which China would consider the survival of North Vietnam to be at stake. It was at least a possibility that she would look upon attacks against the port as a major step in a new United States campaign to force Hanoi to surrender, and would intervene in the South with her own volunteer troops or aircraft.

Neither McNamara nor anyone else knew whether mining or bombing the ports would lead to these particular sobering and ominous reactions by the Soviet Union or Communist China

—but no one knew that they would not. It is my belief that the escalation proposed in 1967 would have been catastrophic and would have foreclosed both the bombing limitation the following March and the bombing halt the following October.

Whether McNamara's internal effort would have sufficed against the pressures from the military, the Congress, the public and the administration Hawks had it not been for his additional public testimony is doubtful. Clearly the Secretary's logic had an impact on Congress, and certainly the headlines across the country indicating that he was opposed to the bombing caused some of the Hawks and the fence-sitters to review their own thinking. While he actually had not voiced opposition publicly to the current bombing, that was the tone of the headlines and news stories.

"Bombing Curb Is Explained By McNamara," said the Washington *Post*.

"McNamara Doubts Bombing In North Can End The War," said the *New York Times*. "Differs With Military Chiefs on Escalation In Testimony Before Panel Of Senate"; "Opposes New Targets."

"McNamara Emphasizes Ground War," said the Baltimore *Sun*.

The Secretary did not win over the Hawks on the Senate Armed Services Committee. Senator Strom Thurmond, the South Carolina Republican, described McNamara's assessment as a policy of "stalemate, appeasement and no-win." Senator Stuart Symington of Missouri, former Secretary of the Air Force, was visibly disgusted with what he considered to be McNamara's lack of faith in air power and told newsmen that if McNamara was right we should get out of Vietnam without delay.

The astonishing paradox of the air war in the North is that the two Secretaries of Defense played such immense parts in restraining and stopping it. The McNamara triumph of 1967 was to prevent the bombing from going any further. The triumph of Clark Clifford in 1968 was to help convince the President that the bombing should be turned down—and then off.

In one way McNamara had the more difficult job. He was fighting not only strong forces within the government but the largest share of public opinion, however difficult it became later to recall the Hawkish pressures and the temper of the country then. In another way, Clifford's task was more difficult. While he was riding with public opinion and using it as his ally in his internal struggle, publicly he was considerably out in front of the President most of the time—a dangerous location and one not occupied with permanence.

The rear-guard action of McNamara unquestionably was more responsible than anything else for holding down the bombing; within the councils of the men who counted with the President, his was the strongest voice for restraint. The vanguard action of Clifford was more responsible than anything else for stopping the bombing; within the councils of the men who saw the President daily, his was the strongest voice for de-escalation and patience.

Each of the four McNamara moves against widening and for reducing U.S. air activity in North Vietnam in 1967 was of the greatest importance to the future. All dovetailed together: his attempt in the spring to cut back the bombing to the 20th Parallel, his internal fight all summer against mining and/or bombing the port at Haiphong, his public analysis of the operations in the fall to show the futility of expanding the attacks as so many were urging and, finally, his role in developing the San Antonio formula.

I think it likely that the President would not have accepted the San Antonio formula had McNamara not laid the groundwork for a possible bombing cessation by his public testimony. And without presidential acceptance of that formula in the fall of 1967, the transition within the administration to the bombing limitation in the spring of 1968 would have been a thousandfold more difficult—if not impossible.

Politically, the President could not conceivably have decreased the air operations if McNamara had permitted to stand unchallenged the military view that a limitation would increase, even temporarily, U.S. casualties in the South. Through his August, 1967, testimony, McNamara put into perspective that casualty allegation and many other freewheeling statements being made. Some he disproved categorically; others he weakened by pointing out the absence of facts supporting them. McNamara insisted that the Senators—and the public—demand factual answers to all the questions raised by proponents of increased operations and opponents of a limitation or cessation. How would a reduction cause more casualties? Was the bombing stopping or slowing infiltration of men or supplies or merely making it more difficult? If the latter, in what manner could it influence casualties in the South? By what percentage would mining Haiphong cut down total imports? How? How much of the tonnage entering through Haiphong would enter in other ways? What other ways? How much of a total import decrease was needed to influence the flow south? Could this be achieved? How?

Admiral Sharp had testified, for example, that stopping the bombing "generally would be a disaster for the United States," and that it would prolong the war, require more American troops and result in more American casualties. Stopping the bombing under what conditions? Stopping if the North Vietnamese agreed to stop infiltration, and starting again if they continued to infiltrate? Would that be a disaster? Stopping if the North Vietnamese observed the Demilitarized Zone? The Secretary of Defense was not advocating stopping the bombing without ever getting anything in return. But he was arguing internally, and his testimony was designed to leave the impression publicly, that he was willing to stop it instantly and permanently if such a move would be a step toward peace. He sought, through logic, analysis and fact, to force the Congress and the people to keep their minds open; it was essential that they do so if we were to extricate ourselves satisfactorily from this involvement.

On many points we never could catch up with all the headlines, which was not the fault of the news media but rather inherent in the system. The Secretary of Defense testified subsequent to the generals and admirals, each of whom appeared individually

and each of whom earned a headline the day after his testimony.
The result was that there were many days of news stories on the
military view for escalation, but McNamara's position for restraint was reported, in the daily press, principally on one day
alone. On that day he attempted to respond both to the points
made by other witnesses and to statements being circulated by
retired military personnel and others in the outside world.

One allegation was that if we decreased the bombing, additional free world combat troops would be needed in the South.
McNamara testified that there was no evidence to support this
view—and pointed out that the testimony of the military also
failed to support the conclusion that there was a direct relationship between the level of bombing of the North and the U.S.
forces required in the South.

Some officers had contended that casualties would have been
reduced had we mounted the campaign less gradually, without
all the limitations and restrictions. Again, McNamara cited the
lack of data, stressing that he had seen no evidence to back up
that contention from any of the agencies involved in analysis
of our North and South operations.

Another statement was that infiltration would have been reduced by earlier acceptance of the Chiefs' recommendations for
more severe bombings. McNamara called for corroboration and
still again noted the absence of evidence.

Some critics were saying that we could have forced the Vietnamese to pay a stiffer price by expanding the bombing sooner.
McNamara commented:

I certainly don't want to argue the point that if more attacks had
been made a year ago the price would have been higher. I think
that is clear. There also might have been other side effects that would
have more than offset that. That is what we were concerned about.

But I do want to emphasize to you that the difference in the
price, if you want to call it that, from the campaign that was carried
out compared to the campaign that was recommended, was very
small indeed. If you want to measure it in dollars, you can just look
at the industrial capacity that has been destroyed and the value of it.
A year ago there either was none or a very small percentage of the

power capacity that had been destroyed; none of the steel capacity, the so-called steel capacity, or the cement capacity, or the explosives plant capacity had been destroyed. Today it has all been destroyed.

What is the difference in cost? $44 million. Now I submit to you that is not a very large difference.

The Senators quoted the Chiefs on mining Haiphong. Mc-Namara pointed out what the Chiefs had left unsaid:

May I just go further to say that I know of no Chief who has said that . . . mining the port of Haiphong would stop in any significant degree the importation of military equipment. . . . Now that isn't to say that they don't recommend mining. They do. But they don't go to the next step and say "We recommend mining it because we believe this will stop the importation of military equipment and war-related matériel."

. . . not only have the Chiefs not said that mining it would stop the importation of the goods that presently come through it, but I haven't seen them make any statement at all of how much of a reduction would occur, and I think it is quite reasonable to understand why they haven't, because all the evidence indicates that there would be no significant reduction. . . .

There is no statement by a Chief that I am aware of that says the elimination of Haiphong would shorten the war by x period or by a significant period, and no statement by a Chief that I know of that says the elimination of Haiphong would reduce the imports of military equipment and war-related matériel by a specified percentage amount or anything approaching such an estimate. . . . I am not in any way trying to minimize the strength of their [the Chiefs'] feelings on it. I am simply saying that they have not translated the destruction of that port in terms of time or effect or in terms of quantities of material imported into or distributed out of North Vietnam.

(I had been present a few weeks earlier at a colloquy between the Secretary and one of the nation's highest-ranking military officers, who was arguing the case for mining Haiphong Harbor. McNamara asked him whether he would still press for that option if he were given the intelligence judgment that such an act would bring serious retaliatory action from the U.S.S.R. The officer declined to answer. He would only say that he did not think the U.S.S.R. would respond in any such way. McNamara pursued the point: "*If* that were the intelligence estimate," he asked again, "would you nonetheless recommend mining the harbor?" Again the officer responded only by stating his opinion that the Soviet would not react in that fashion. He refused to meet head on this most critical question.)

The Senators, looking for the fastest satisfactory way out of the entire commitment, wanted to believe that destruction of the fifty-seven targets left on the list—including the ports— would end the war sooner. McNamara came back to this issue over and over again, noting what the Chiefs had said and what they had not said:

Mr. Chairman, may I say this is such an important point that I do not want to belabor it, but I want to tell you I think there is some misunderstanding here on this particular point of whether these 57 targets, if destroyed, would materially shorten the war. I do not believe the Chiefs would say that. That is not the basis for their recommendation. And I am not prepared to say their recommendation is wrong, gentlemen. All I can tell you is that as of the moment I would not support it. But I may be wrong and they may be right. It would not be the first time that I am wrong and they are right. But the point I want to leave with you and the important point is that they do not say that the destruction of these 57 targets will materially shorten the war.

McNamara was asked whether decreasing the air effort in the North would increase casualties in the South. Generals Wheeler and McConnell both had testified to that effect.

"Yes, I read that testimony, but I do not know what evidence they had to support that opinion," McNamara said.

"But in any event, you do not agree with them?" he was asked.

"I do not agree; I do not," said the Secretary.

One argument being made was that we could decrease infiltration by conducting even more of a campaign against bridges. McNamara pointed out two recent examples: in one, the North Vietnamese had constructed a bypass even before the main span was knocked out; in the other, they were ferrying across the river without difficulty. Bombing bridges, he insisted, did not stop

AUGUST, 1967   209

the flow of traffic, although it increased the cost and the burden.

We could and did bomb trucks. The intelligence reports indicated that North Vietnam had an inventory of 9,000 trucks in February, 1965; that we had destroyed 4,100 and damaged another 4,000, and that their current inventory was between 10,000 and 12,000. The new trucks came, of course, from imports. To those who expected that bombing would stop infiltration, attacking trucks was disappointing. To those who expected that bombing would make infiltration more costly and difficult, attacking trucks did help. McNamara kept bringing the Senators back to the objectives of the campaign.

This was Hawk country. Senator Jack Miller, Iowa Republican, told McNamara he thought it would be easier to tell the people that they were faced with a long war if the people were satisfied that all military targets had been knocked out. The people, Miller declared, were saying that if we were not willing to assume greater risks, then we should get out.

McNamara responded that he did not believe we should assume risks simply because the people were unaware of the magnitude of those risks.

"We as a government can't function without the support of our people," he said. "I realize that. And it is my responsibility and it is yours to face these problems with our people and attempt to explain them. But I think each of us would agree that whether we explain them to their satisfaction or whether we don't explain them to their satisfaction, we then must make our own judgments as to how we would recommend that our nation behave, and I am not about to recommend that it behave in a way that endangers the security of this nation."

McNamara made it unmistakably clear that he believed the expanded bombing, with the mining of Haiphong, would endanger seriously the security of the nation.

Believing it mandatory that the North Vietnamese be brought to the conference table, and convinced that bombing would not and could not drive them there, McNamara considered it critical to find another way to achieve that result. He had hoped in late

1966 and early 1967 that the thirty-seven-day pause would do the trick, but he was wrong. He had hoped in the spring of 1967 that the 20th Parallel limitation would be a step in the right direction, but that recommendation was disapproved. Now he was seeking a new way. He had established a foundation for it by preventing the bombing from being oversold.

A major problem in working out a new approach then was the same problem that had confronted him before and that we were to face in 1968. The administration was not prepared to stop the bombing until and unless the United States received something in return, and the North Vietnamese would have no part of a "conditional" cessation. From their viewpoint, or at least from the one they adopted publicly, we were committing an act of war against their homeland and we had no right to ask for "conditions" under which the bombing would be stopped. But the official U.S. position was that it was as legitimate for us to bomb the North as it was for the North to make war on the South.

The San Antonio formula was developed in late summer by McNamara, Nitze and Warnke in the Pentagon, with outside assistance from Under Secretary of State Nicholas deB. Katzenbach and Henry Kissinger, as a means around this impasse and in response to direct indications through nonofficial sources that Hanoi was interested in talks. An early draft was worked on in August. In final form, with one major McNamara change in language, it surfaced in San Antonio on September 29, when the President said:

"As we have told Hanoi time and time and time again, the heart of the matter is this: The United States is willing immediately to stop all aerial and naval bombardment of North Vietnam when this will lead promptly to productive discussion. We would, of course, assume that, while discussions proceed, North Vietnam would not take advantage of the bombing cessation or limitation."

The original draft had used the words "will lead to negotiations," which McNamara changed to "will lead promptly to productive discussion."

Possibly because they were unaware of how deeply the North Vietnamese felt about prior "conditions" and thus of the importance of this offer, the editorial writers and columnists did not pay a great deal of attention to it. While stories were carried on the front pages of the newspapers, as they would be on any presidential speech on Vietnam, for the most part newsmen and the public missed the significance of the new formula.

McNamara was astonished by this general lack of reaction to the proposal, which constituted a tremendous change in the United States position. Until now we had insisted that we would brook absolutely no infiltration if we were to stop the bombing. The San Antonio speech clearly permitted infiltration at the present rate, although it did not allow for an increase. Beyond that, and perhaps of even greater importance to the North Vietnamese, this formula for stopping the bombing demanded no advance "conditions." It did not say that we would stop the bombing *if* Hanoi promised not to take advantage of it, but rather that we would stop the bombing and *assume* that Hanoi would not take advantage of it. We were protected because if our assumption turned out to be incorrect we could resume the bombing. Having stopped without condition, we could begin again without condition. The North Vietnamese, in McNamara's view, could accept the proposal if they wanted negotiations because they were being given their major demand that we stop the attacks unconditionally.

Instead, the Communists immediately denounced the San Antonio formula as a further attempt to impose conditions. Again, our understanding and predictions about Hanoi proved incomplete and faulty. Significantly, however, the eventual bombing halt a year and a month after the San Antonio speech was predicated on just such an assumption and a solid indication from the North Vietnamese that they understood the basis on which we were acting.

Robert S. McNamara never attempted to avoid responsibility for the bombing of North Vietnam, which began under his stewardship on August 5, 1964, nor do I mean in this discussion of his 1967 de-escalatory efforts to disassociate him from the earlier air campaign. By the date of the hearing we had flown more than 173,000 sorties, as mentioned earlier, all under McNamara's regime as Secretary of Defense.

Even though from the beginning the restraints put upon the pilots were the tightest in air warfare, the target list nonetheless grew larger and larger as the years passed, and the total ordnance expended on North Vietnam was incredible. The Chiefs obtained a great deal of what they wanted—but not the way they wanted it, and not Haiphong Harbor and the additional expansion sought by the military in 1967. They objected to the very concept McNamara insisted upon: the gradual application of force in this nuclear age. I do not know the answer to the basic questions of whether heavy nationwide attacks at the outset would have bombed Hanoi out of the war or bombed Red Chinese or Soviet volunteers into it, although I consider the latter much more likely.

Whether McNamara could have exerted even greater influence and kept the air war more restrained is doubtful. Politically, it would have been impossible to deploy more than a half-million troops to South Vietnam without attacking North Vietnam by air. Certainly the United States tried as no attacking nation had ever tried to spare civilians in the North. Of course it did not succeed perfectly or even well enough; sparing all civilians was never an achievable goal. But if the responsibility for failing to bring about internal agreement on the objectives of the air campaign against North Vietnam was largely Robert McNamara's, and it was, so was the credit for restraint largely his—humanitarian local restraint in the selection of targets and in the limitations clamped upon our pilots; wise international restraint in his obdurate position against the moves which might have widened the war, brought about a military confrontation with Communist China or the Soviet Union and turned a nightmare into a catastrophe.

McNamara did not give up at the rejection of the San Antonio formula. Within the administration, he continued to fight for unilateral de-escalation. Until he left office February 29, 1968, he was convinced that we could not bomb Hanoi out of the war and that a continuation of our present course would not effect a satisfactory termination within a satisfactory period of time. He believed also that there would be no visible signs of progress and that pressures would rise to expand both northern air operations and southern ground operations, the latter into sanctuary areas across foreign borders. To forestall these escalatory acts, he favored stopping the bombing unilaterally, announcing publicly that we would send no additional troops and gradually transferring the burden of fighting to the South Vietnamese. This course, he thought, stood a good chance of bringing Hanoi to the peace table and another good chance of reciprocal de-escalation on her part—most likely cessation of activity across the DMZ.

Again, these final recommendations for reducing the fires under the war were rejected, despite the success of his efforts of greater long-term importance to prevent those fires from increasing.

"Baby murderer," read the signs of the Communists when Robert McNamara traveled to India eighteen months later as President of the World Bank, and his involvement in the war was major and indisputable. But it was McNamara who tried futilely to set the peace table with a thirty-seven-day pause over Christmas of 1965; McNamara who sought to cut back the bombing to the 20th Parallel in the spring of 1967; McNamara who stood against the mining and expanded attacks sought by the Joint Chiefs that summer; McNamara who analyzed the air war for the Congress and the people to keep American emotions in tow that August; McNamara who produced the San Antonio formula that fall; McNamara who fought still again to stabilize and de-escalate before the President nominated him to the World Bank. The first giant United States actions toward uncoupling the war were not to come until March and October of the next year, but neither the skills nor the prayers of Clark Clifford, Averell Harriman and Cyrus Vance would have then prevailed had there not been the work, the study, the analysis, the prescience and the courage of Robert McNamara before them.

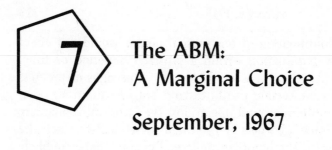

The ABM:
A Marginal Choice
September, 1967

The air war in the North was the first major issue in the fall of 1967 on which Robert McNamara was out of step with most of the military and, of greater significance, at variance with his President. The antiballistic missile was the second.

In one major way, the two cases were not comparable. On the air war, the Secretary of Defense had moved forward on his own, knowing that between the lines of his public testimony were conclusions and proposals which had been rejected or ignored by the President of the United States. To do so was, as has been indicated, a form of heresy for him. But on the issue of whether the nation should deploy a system designed to intercept incoming enemy ballistic missiles launched from six thousand miles away, or what kind of a system to deploy, McNamara did not speak out publicly until every word that he wanted to say had been approved in full both by the Department of State and by the White House.

This was not a routine achievement, for nearly everyone outside our immediate family was opposed to the deployment decision he announced, to the strategic nuclear lecture which came with the announcement or to both. The Doves were shocked because he went much too far and the Hawks because he did not go nearly far enough. While the outside Doves were the most shrill in their protests, the inside Hawks had posed much more of a problem, and the victory over them was the significant one.

From the standpoint of my office, McNamara's performance on the ABM was something of a triumph. I considered it the noncrisis issue on which was achieved the greatest temporary success in communicating with a few selected newsmen on a most discriminatory basis. Not all of those newsmen agreed with his conclusions, but that is a separate issue. My office had, in my concept of the job, no responsibility to try to convince the people that the government's course was correct. Our function was not to propagandize, but to get the facts before the citizens. Obviously we desired public acceptance, for the sake of the President, but we did not campaign to achieve it.

The speech in which the Secretary announced the decision was given to the annual conference of the United Press International Editors and Publishers in San Francisco on September 18, 1967. The hard news in it was that he was instructing the Army to proceed with the development and deployment of a thin antiballistic missile system oriented against the type of rocket attack Red China might be able to launch against our cities in the mid-1970s. The important news in it, however, was that he was unchanged in his opposition to building a large antiballistic missile net designed to try to protect the people of the United States against the kind of massive, sophisticated attack which the Soviet Union could launch at our cities.

And his reason for giving the speech, rather than making either announcement in a Pentagon press release, was to explain in the most meticulous fashion possible the entire strategic nuclear offense-defensive posture of the United States vis-à-vis the Soviet Union, reviewing as rationally as he was able the reasons why it would not make military, diplomatic or economic sense for us to build a bigger ABM defense net on the basis of current technical knowledge, no matter whether the Soviets were building one or not.

Because no subject was so important to him as nuclear strategy, the Secretary exerted more personal effort to explain this speech to the press (and thus to the people) than any other he made while in the government. For that reason alone, the ABM speech merits a place in a book on public affairs issues and controversies during the last half of the Kennedy-Johnson years. It merits attention, too, as an example of how easy it is to communicate with a few individuals among the responsible press when a Cabinet officer personally takes the time to do so. Unfortunately, the ABM issue is also an example of how the people can be misinformed by well-meaning newsmen—particularly editorial writers—who are nonexpert in military matters and still do not take time to study the public record.

As this is written, President Nixon's administration still is involved deeply in ABM controversy, and television commentators still are noting that this multibillion-dollar subject is so complex that the public will never understand it. This is nonsense. No major issues in the strategic nuclear area are too complex for the American citizen to understand, and not a grain of technical, scientific or engineering knowledge is required to comprehend the main points of the debate.

Nor is it government secrecy or government reluctance— neither the Johnson government nor the Nixon government—to release information which precludes understanding. Any United States newspaper which spent as much time, space and effort analyzing strategic nuclear warfare as it does reporting its city's professional football team could put all necessary information before the people rapidly, and any reader who spent one-quarter as much time reading that information as he does following that football team could form an educated and intelligent opinion.

Having spent eighteen years in the business, I am not unaware of the economics of newspapering, and I am cognizant also of the fact that more persons will watch the Baltimore Colts play the Cleveland Browns on television than will tune in a documentary on the antiballistic missile. It is also true that newspapers and television news organizations do not want to expend the money and effort required to develop within themselves the kind of experience in military fields that they have in the fields of local, state and national politics. Only a handful of newspapers consider defense issues important enough to merit coverage by their own expert correspondents, which is their business, not the business of the government. But all the news organizations which choose not to allocate their resources so as to gain for themselves the knowledge in defense matters that they have in politics, professional basketball, local criminal courts, the police beat and nightclub gossip columns should not blindly condemn the government for failing to put the information before the people and should not seek refuge in protesting that the issues are too complex to understand. The public record is replete with available information on all sides of the ABM; my seventeen-year-old son, Kent, used it in the spring of 1969 to debate the issue in his public high school. He found the facts and so could any other seventeen-year-old, or any editorial writer or television commentator.

The major thrust of McNamara's short ABM information campaign in 1967 was to review the public record for selected newsmen so that they could keep his speech in proper perspective. The most remarkable day in that campaign was Saturday, September 16—two days before the speech. At half-hour intervals, some of the most prestigious members of the Washington press corps were shuttled in and out of the Secretary's office to receive a personal advance copy of the address, listen to McNamara's review of the background and ask any questions they could conjure up—so long as they were out of one door before the next man came in the other.

Included were a few of the nation's leading columnists and representatives of some of the news organizations we considered particularly influential—the Washington *Post*, the *New York Times*, the Los Angeles *Times*, *Life*, NBC and CBS.

Managing Editor Benjamin Bradlee and Editorial Writer Philip Geyelin of the Washington *Post* began the parade at

11 A.M. Richard B. Stolley, *Life* Washington Bureau Chief, and
a team working with him on a lengthy ABM interview due to
appear the week after the speech, were in at 11:30. Just before
lunch Robert Donovan, head of the Washington Bureau of the
Los Angeles *Times* and one of the most professional and responsible newspapermen in the city, saw the Secretary for his half-hour.
McNamara and I then had lunch with Columnist William S.
White at 1:00 in the Secretary's dining room. (The dining room
is actually a large conference room just off the Secretary's main
office. The conference table in the center normally was not used
for lunch, but a small table was set in one corner each day for the
Secretary and the Deputy Secretary. Sometimes they ate alone;
sometimes a Service Secretary, an Assistant Secretary of Defense
or an outside guest would join them. Under both McNamara
and Clifford, the Chairman of the Joint Chiefs of Staff was invited for lunch each Monday, prior to the meeting of the Joint
Chiefs which they all attended. The room also served as a handy
inner route between the Secretary's office and the private office
of the Deputy Secretary, permitting either to visit the other
without going into the outer corridor or through visitors' reception rooms. Robert McNamara raced several times a day into
Cyrus Vance's office—always in shirt sleeves—when Vance was
Deputy Secretary.)

After lunch, we went back on the assembly line. Eric Sevareid
of CBS came in at 2:00; Tom Wicker of the *New York Times* at
2:30; Roscoe Drummond and his son and associate, Geoffrey,
at 3:00 and Columnist Marquis Childs at 3:30. (We had jumped
the gun with John Chancellor of NBC, who was out of town
over the weekend and had seen the Secretary Friday afternoon.)
In most cases, the men went first to my office in Room 2E 800 on
the floor below. Not until one was escorted out the front door of
the Pentagon were my secretaries buzzed to send up the next
candidate.

We engaged in this secretive, rather unseemly exercise because
McNamara was passionately concerned that the people be ex-

posed to his reasoning on strategic nuclear matters. It was never of particular importance to him whether the public understood his position on the TFX aircraft or the M16 rifle, and he expressed few personal opinions publicly on the war the last two years (except on the bombing of the North), but this antiballistic missile speech was the most carefully reasoned and drafted address of his seven years.

Not one of our news visitors was an expert on nuclear strategy, but all were news professionals, with broad Washington experience, particularly in international affairs and/or national politics.

As suggested earlier, this was one of the problems which confronted our office. Aside from the Pentagon regulars—the newspaper and television men who make their living covering military affairs—few members of the huge Washington press corps are familiar with defense issues. And yet the matters in which the Pentagon is involved are sometimes so important that the non-expert generalists among Washington newsmen flow across the bridges from downtown to handle the stories. They then disappear for weeks or months until the next crisis, which they greet with equal inexperience.

This approach to covering Pentagon news cannot succeed. For several years as a reporter I tried it before finally moving to my own desk in the Pentagon press room and working there on a full-time basis, except when handling manned-spacecraft stories and presidential election campaigns. Often while covering the Pentagon on a 20 percent basis I fooled my editors and readers into thinking I was an expert, but I did not fool my colleagues who were full-time military specialists nor the official sources with whom I had to work. Members of the Washington press corps who attempt to dip in and out of the Pentagon on crisis stories or major issues cannot compete with a specialist in military affairs who is spending all his time, year after year, on these matters—working in the Pentagon, covering defense hearings on Capitol Hill, visiting military commands in the United States and overseas, participating in seminars at war colleges and independent institutes, reading the latest output from the academicians. The city editor in Chicago does not permit the reporter covering the business beat to handle a crisis story in City Hall, and the managing editor should not expect expert coverage of a military crisis or major defense story from a generalist in his Washington bureau.

But our guests that Saturday were important and influential, if not knowledgeable in military affairs, and all but two spent more time trying to learn from the Secretary than to teach him. In my four years in the government I was astounded by the number of newsmen who, after waiting days or weeks for an appointment with a Secretary of Defense, then consumed a good share of their visit by instructing him on the performance of his job or in telling him what other high officials of the government had told them. It was truly remarkable.

On this occasion, we had chosen each participant with a specific purpose in mind. Through Bradlee and Geyelin we hoped to achieve a reasonably rational editorial in the *Post* and, more importantly to us, to spark their interest in the speech so that the *Post* might run a full text. From Wicker we sought an intelligent column, input into his New Work office for an editorial, and a recommendation to the *Times* in New York that consideration be given to printing the text.

Columnists were included that Saturday because they usually will take time to think before they write, because of their potential influence on editorial writers as well as ordinary readers and because they were apt to pass up the speech completely unless we gave them advance lead time, since most of them wrote several days before publication.

Robert Donovan was important to us because the Los Angeles *Times* is the most influential newspaper on the West Coast and because he can be counted upon always for an honest, intelligent, balanced effort. He is an outstanding newspaperman—an analyst of merited prestige who has remained a crackerjack reporter. John Chancellor and Eric Sevareid enjoyed sufficient status on their own networks so that they would be able to insert their comments on the speech into the Monday night NBC Huntley-Brinkley and CBS Walter Cronkite shows.

Each man was given a copy of the speech, although it was not to be delivered until 6 P.M. Monday Washington time and would not be available to the rest of the press corps until Monday morning. While the pursuit of this dual-standard course was not calculated to increase the popularity of the Assistant Secretary, since it was admittedly unfair, we had decided that it was not feasible to pass out two thousand copies of the speech to the Washington press corps as early as Saturday, or even to limit distribution to the fifty names on our "Pentagon regular" list. The risk of the ABM decision's leaking out, possibly in a garbled version, was too great. So our Saturday decision to set up the interviews with the Secretary was a clear compromise. The arrangement helped the newsmen who had been invited to come in, gave the composing rooms of the *Post* and *Times* forty-eight extra hours to handle the text, permitted the network correspondents to convince their New York producers that they had inside information from Mc-Namara for the Monday night shows and provided several columnists with extra time to write.

Despite the unfairness, an issue of grave importance to our country was presented to the people in a more orderly, thoughtful, logical fashion because of Robert McNamara's long Saturday of individual interviews. Yet the compromise was not so much an acceptable solution as an emergency measure. No Secretary of Defense really has time to see nine separate newsmen on one day. Nor would the press tolerate this unfair early dissemination of the speeches, even though everyone was bound by the same publication time Monday night.

The major ABM issues before the country in the fall of 1967 were what the Soviet Union was doing about building an anti-ballistic missile system and what our proper response should be. Generally speaking, the more conservative Republicans, the Southern Democrats, the retired military, most of the active military (particularly the Army) and the rest of those usually identified as Hawkish favored production and deployment of the biggest

ABM we could build—because they wanted as much protection against nuclear attack as they could buy at any price, because they feared that any Soviet ABM deployment would tip the nuclear balance toward Russia, because they believed that the experience we would gain in producing the best system today would lead to a better system tomorrow. The more liberal Republicans, the Northern Democrats, the most vocal academicians and others usually identified as Dovish opposed the deployment —because they wanted to spend the money on urban problems, because they were against continuation of the arms race, because they had faith in an eventual accommodation (not trust or friendship) with the Soviet Union, because they considered the defense budget too high, because they doubted the effectiveness of any ABM system.

Both within and outside the administration, the pressures for deployment of a huge multibillion-dollar system were far heavier than those against deployment. It was obvious in 1967 to any of us who had been involved in national political campaigns that the failure of the President to approve an ABM while the Russians were proceeding with one would be a definite political issue in 1968.

One other part of the equation was the gradual development by Red China of its offensive capabilities. It was learning how to make nuclear explosives and missiles to carry them. To the Congress, the press and the public, however, the Chinese offensive progress was not nearly so much of an argument for an ABM as the Soviet defensive actions. The notion that the Russians were building an atomic shield for their people while we were not was the strongest public argument of the Hawks.

To achieve his review of the record, McNamara began his Saturday sessions by referring the newsmen to the lengthy statement he had made to Congress in January—called his annual "Posture Statement" by everyone except the Secretary, who did not like the term and would not use it. The unclassified version of the 1967 (Fiscal 1968) statement was 207 pages long. Within the section on "Strategic Forces"—a section presented each year in laborious detail—he had said this:

We have been aware for many years that the Soviets have been working on an anti-ballistic missile defense system, just as we have been. After a series of abortive starts, it now appears that the Soviets are deploying such a system (using the "GALOSH" missile, publicly displayed in 1964 around Moscow). They are also deploying another type of defensive system elsewhere in the Soviet Union, but the weight of the evidence at this time suggests that this system is not intended primarily for anti-ballistic missile defense. However, knowing what we do about past Soviet predilections for defense systems, we must, for the time being, plan our forces on the assumption that that they will have deployed some sort of an ABM system around their major cities by the early 1970s . . . [to] cost the Soviet Union at least $20 to $25 billion.

That summarized our best intelligence on Russia. We had always assumed that the Russians would deploy an ABM and long had planned our offensive forces on that assumption. There was no other intelligent way to plan.

McNamara then showed the newsmen what he had said about Red China's atomic developments back in January. He had written that a significant Red Chinese nuclear threat to the continental United States would not develop before the mid-1970s and that an "austere" ABM defense oriented against an attack on our cities by Red China "might" offer a high degree of protection through the 1970s. But, he had added, it was "not clear" that we needed such a defense—and in any case the decision did not have to be made then in January since it would still take us less time to build the shield than it would the Chinese to develop the nuclear warheads and the missiles.

In his Posture Statement, McNamara had also discussed the third possible type of antiballistic missile net, in addition to one designed to try to protect our cities against a Soviet attack and a second which might protect them against the smaller, simpler Chinese attack. That was a system to defend some or all of our land-based missiles against a strike aimed at crippling them.

On the major issue of why the United States should not respond to a Soviet antiballistic missile system with a massive system of its own, the Secretary's speech was self-explanatory. He had written in 1965 that the proper U.S. response to a Soviet ABM was an improved offense of our own, not a futile effort to protect our cities with a leaky sieve. That was his position in 1966, in January of 1967, in September of 1967 when he made the speech, and in March of 1968 when he left the Pentagon. What we feared most that September were uninformed and oversimplified news stories, columns, editorials and television commentary that McNamara, long an opponent of the ABM, had reversed his course and now was proposing an ABM. Such an interpretation would defeat the main purpose of the address, which was to set out rationally his opposition to a large-scale system designed to attempt to protect our cities against Soviet attack. Our objective with the uninitiated newsmen on Saturday was to show them that the possibility of deploying a system against a possible Red Chinese attack was not a new idea, that McNamara had examined it months earlier, that he had discussed it publicly, that he had noted its possible merit, that he had pointed out the number of lives it might save and that his public conclusion had been in January (or December, when the statement was actually written) that it was not yet necessary to make a decision on it.

The practice of putting off a decision until the calendar of events indicated that the time had come when it was absolutely necessary to make it was typical of McNamara. To delay beyond the time when the decision should be made was unwise, resulted from weakness and was costly in terms of money or effectiveness. But he always resisted all pressures for a premature decision, insisting on keeping open all options, seeing all the latest developments and examining the situation at the last practical moment. In decisions on major weapons systems, he assumed that the opposition would build a better weapon faster than the most cautious intelligence estimates, and then assumed that the United States would encounter more obstacles than the most pessimistic adviser foresaw. Within that framework, he would postpone the decision as long as possible in order to have before him the maximum information on which to base it. This McNamara technique infuriated members of Congress, officers of the military services and individuals on his own staff who were pressing for early decisions, but he considered it essential to sound management.

Before the newsmen arrived on Saturday we had made duplicate copies of the two most relevant pages of the January Posture Statement and one page from the statement McNamara had read Congress a year earlier. The Secretary handed each man a set from a desk drawer as he talked. In simple language, written for the nonexpert in Congress, these pages summarized the past McNamara position. He had kept open the decision on deploying interceptor missiles to protect our cities against a future Red Chinese attack, kept open the decision on installing some defense of our own land-based offensive intercontinental missiles, asked Congress for several hundred millions more to continue research toward an impenetrable ABM wall which would safeguard our people against attack by anyone, remained enthusiastic about arms limitation talks with the Soviet, spent billions of dollars improving our offensive weapons so that they could overwhelm a Soviet defense and, from the outset, opposed production of a massive ABM of our own.

From a fiscal standpoint at home and an arms race standpoint, McNamara thought almost nothing would be so disastrous for the nation as to embark on all or any part of the $40 billion anti-Soviet system. It was all-important to him that proponents of that system not be misled into thinking that he supported it and not be given the chance to claim his support. Therefore, it was essential that the newsmen understand perfectly what the announcement was and what it was not. It was essential that they understand that the Chinese-oriented deployment (and the piggyback protection which would come with it for a few land-based Minuteman missiles) was not inconsistent with his former position. The record was clear, and we wanted to saturate the newsmen with that record.

Walking with the newsmen to the Pentagon door, I made one additional new point. It had often been written and was said frequently on Capitol Hill that the Joint Chiefs of Staff were strongly and unanimously in favor of deploying the full-scale $40 billion ABM. The fact was that the Air Force was not an enthusiastic proponent of such a system. The ABM is an Army project and has been supported traditionally more by the Army than by the other services. While the Air Force was willing to concur on a Joint Chiefs paper recommending the ABM to the Secretary of Defense, it would far rather have put $40 billion into its own new offensive missiles, a new manned bomber and other Air Force projects than into an Army defensive net. As the newsmen left the building, I gave each a copy of one page of unclassified testimony presented to the Senate Armed Services Committee in February, 1967, by General J. P. McConnell, Air Force Chief of Staff. In that hearing, General McConnell had said:

My opinion was, and is, that we should commence deployment of about a $3.5 to $4 billion anti-ballistic missile defense capability. In my opinion, that will do everything that we can anticipate a reasonable missile defense can do. We cannot possibly defend against a full-scale ballistic attack with anti-ballistic missiles, even as they can't defend against us.

The McConnell statement, overlooked by nearly all of the press except two or three Pentagon regulars, was important because it supported the position McNamara was announcing in his speech. It was interesting, also, because it was indicative of a problem which faces a Secretary of Defense—or an Assistant Secretary for Public Affairs. The Chiefs of Staff are a chummy group who work well together, backing each other's projects in a logrolling fashion. All will certify that the new aircraft carrier proposed by the Navy is necessary and worthwhile. All will agree that it fills a gap in our defense structure. And they mean it— and perhaps it does. Their recommendation to the Secretary of Defense or the Congress for a new carrier will be unanimous. If the Secretary does not go along, outside critics will make speeches and newsmen will write stories that the civilian Secretary of Defense is blocking a unanimous recommendation of the Joint Chiefs of Staff and imposing his civilian judgment upon their vast military know-how.

But sit across the table from the Chiefs and put to them these questions: "The President will not accept our budget and insists that we reduce it. What are your priorities? Is the new carrier essential this year?" From services other than the Navy, the answer will be "no." Unanimity disappears. The carrier is now less important than the new Air Force fighter plane or the new Army division. We need it someday, but it can be postponed.

After reviewing the past record, McNamara took the newsmen through his speech on a point-by-point basis:

1. The cornerstone of our strategic policy is to deter an enemy from attacking us by being able at all times, even after a surprise attack, to destroy his military forces and his society. Not only must we have this power; he must believe that we have it. Otherwise, it might not deter.

2. To be certain we have it, in estimating his forces and his plans, we must always prepare for the worst plausible case. We have done so. Our strategic alert forces alone carry more than 2,200 weapons, averaging one megaton each. And four hundred one-megaton weapons delivered on the Soviet would destroy more than one-third her population and one-half her industry.

3. The Soviet Union today cannot strike us a blow hard enough to prohibit us from hitting back with enough force to destroy it as a modern society—and we cannot strike such a blow against her. Nor, in the foreseeable future, can either country achieve such strength.

4. Whether measured in gross megatonnage or missile launchers, we possess nuclear superiority over the Soviet Union today. But both yardsticks are misleading. The most meaningful and realistic measurement is the number of separate warheads that can be delivered with accuracy on individual enemy targets. By

that yardstick, our numerical superiority is three or four to one. We will maintain a numerical superiority as far ahead as we can realistically plan.

5. That numerical superiority is, however, of limited significance. It cannot keep the Soviets from destroying us. Neither, for the first time in history, does it translate effectively into political control or diplomatic leverage. Our numerical superiority does not prevent Soviet support of the North Vietnamese; our monopoly did not prevent Soviet support of the North Koreans. We must, therefore, maintain substantial non-nuclear forces as well.

6. The arms race is fueled by action-reaction phenomena—or, more precisely, by action and/or potential action-reaction phenomena. Both the United States and the Soviet Union have overbuilt over the last decade because both felt their survival rested on their ability to destroy the attacker, even after absorbing a surprise attack—and neither knew precisely how far the other was going.

7. We have the resources, technology and will to do whatever is required to keep that retaliatory strength. But since both sides now have a deterrent in excess of individual needs, both nations would benefit from a properly safeguarded agreement to limit—and later to reduce—our offensive and defensive strategic nuclear forces.

8. The Soviet Union is now deploying an ABM system. We have already taken the offensive steps necessary to assure penetration by our missiles, and the Soviet ABM does not, therefore, impose a threat on our ability to inflict unacceptable damage on her country and people.

9. If we could build an impenetrable shield against a Soviet attack, we would do so, at a cost of $40 billion or several times that amount. We cannot, because any system now feasible involves firing defensive missiles at incoming offensive warheads and such a defense can be defeated if the attacker sends more warheads (and dummy warheads) than there are defensive missiles. If we sought to achieve a defensive advantage by building

a heavy ABM system, the Soviets would be motivated strongly to cancel that advantage by building more and/or better offensive missiles—which is exactly what we have done to offset their limited ABM net.

10. If the evidence indicates that the Soviets intend to turn their modest ABM into a massive one, we have the time and the technology to increase both the quality and quantity of our offensive forces so as to deny them an edge in the nuclear balance. We much prefer that we and the Soviets begin talks that will lead to a realistic strategic-arms-limitation agreement. But if the talks fail, and if the Soviets do increase their defense, we have taken all necessary steps to permit us to increase further our offense so that we can always respond to an attack by penetrating and destroying the Soviet Union as a twentieth-century society. This action-reaction course would be a foolish and feckless one, providing neither nation with greater nuclear capability.

11. There are other uses for an ABM than to protect against a Soviet attack on our cities. One is to safeguard our own offensive missiles from their attack. A second is in relation to a future attack from Red China, which may have a first ICBM in the early 1970s and a modest force in the mid-seventies. Until now, it has not been necessary to decide whether a light ABM might be advantageous as a counter to Red China's nuclear development. But if we do want such a system, the time for decision has come.

12. We have the power to destroy Communist China completely—her weapons and her society. That should deter China as it deters the Soviet. But is there any possibility (not a likelihood, but a possibility) that by the mid-1970s China might miscalculate and attempt a suicidal, insane nuclear attack upon us? Since there is at least a possibility, there are marginal grounds for concluding that it would be prudent to deploy a light system.

13. Such a system also would indicate to Asians that we intended to deter Red China from nuclear blackmail and thus discourage nuclear proliferation among non-nuclear countries.

It would enable us to defend further our Minuteman sites against Soviet attack. And it would add protection to our population against the improbable accidental launch of an ICBM by any nuclear power.

14. We have, therefore, decided to begin production later this year of a thin, Chinese-oriented ABM system. Preliminary cost estimates are $5 billion. We recognize two dangers in this decision. One is that independent Asian nations might think that this is a substitute for their maintaining their own conventional forces. The second is that temptation to expand this into a heavy, Soviet-oriented system will be substantial.

15. Every future age of man is going to be an atomic age. We must face the danger of thermonuclear holocaust rationally and realistically. Unlimited war is no longer foolish, but suicidal. The root of man's security lies in his mind. The world requires a new race toward reasonableness. We had better all run that race.

Sunday was a day off for us. The Secretary and I flew to San Francisco in one of the four-engine Jet Stars which he—and we other presidential appointees in the Department—used for business travel within the United States. There was little for me to do out there unless an emergency developed. Orville Splitt, a talented high-level civil servant who was my Special Assistant, had flown out several days earlier to oversee arrangements.

Back in Washington on Monday, preparations continued in high gear. Dan Henkin, Dick Fryklund and I had made a list of the members of the Pentagon press corps who were to get special treatment. This group included, but was not limited to, all Pentagon regulars who were employed by such general news organizations as the Associated Press and United Press International, the Washington *Post* and the *Evening Star*, the Baltimore *Sun*, the *New York Times*, the *Wall Street Journal*, the *Christian Science Monitor*, *Time* and *Newsweek*, and the four networks— ABC, CBS, NBC and the Mutual Broadcasting System. In most cases the Pentagon reporters would handle the story of the speech, even though they had not gone west, writing from Washington with a San Francisco dateline.

In the Pentagon on Monday morning, Dan Henkin gathered up Fred Hoffman of AP and Don May of UPI and took them to Deputy Secretary Nitze's office for a rerun of McNamara's Saturday sessions. I had dictated lengthy notes of those interviews for Henkin, Fryklund and Nitze, so that they could provide the Pentagon regulars with everything McNamara had given the other men on Saturday. Henkin and Fryklund then systematically and separately called in each of the others on their lists. While these men did not have the thirty minutes with the Secretary, they actually received as much background information and Mc-Namara rationale as the Saturday guests. Several times Henkin telephoned me in San Francisco for additional guidance from McNamara. By day's end, Nitze, Henkin and Fryklund had briefed twenty-seven more newsmen in Washington, so that nearly forty persons had received individual, authoritative briefings on the contents of the speech and its background before any major stories were written.

We succeeded in one major objective and failed in another as a result of the work done Saturday, Monday and in the days to follow. I cannot think of another occasion on which we came out that well.

Reviewing newspaper and television reaction to the speech, we felt that most newsmen understood and wrote accurately that McNamara was as opposed as ever to deploying a massive ABM designed to try to protect American cities against the kind of attack the Soviet could launch. We were gratified by that reaction.

Many newsmen, however, wrote that McNamara had reversed his earlier public position on the Chinese-oriented system. Although not surprised, we were disappointed by the accent on "reversal," which is what we had sought to avoid.

It was clear that many non-Pentagon newsmen who interpreted the speech publicly had not read the record—a failing which challenges my charitable instincts. Every reporter, columnist, editorial writer or television commentator who wrote or spoke seriously on national defense issues during the year should have routinely analyzed each of McNamara's Posture Statements, studied his public news conferences and kept up with the hundreds of pages of unclassified Congressional testimony of McNamara and other top officials before the Armed Services Committees and Defense Appropriations Subcommittees of both House and Senate. In the defense field too much misleading information is put before the people by persons commenting on important military issues without adequate knowledge or study.

A few writers who had read the record in detail were aware that there had been no reversal and that the Secretary's speech was consistent with earlier public statements on Red China, but nonetheless had difficulty reconciling his all-out opposition to the $40 billion Soviet-oriented system with his defense of a $5 billion Chinese-oriented net. His logic disturbed them.

Perhaps the most important word in the "Chinese" section of the San Francisco address was "marginal," which McNamara used to describe the decision. By definition, a marginal decision is one close to the lower limit of acceptability. Had there been no outside elements in the equation in the fall of 1967 Robert McNamara would have found the administration decision to deploy the thin system unacceptable.

But outside elements were injected into the equation. In the first year of the next administration, the ABM battle was whether to deploy portions of a thin system (changed somewhat under Secretary of Defense Melvin Laird to put more emphasis on protecting our land-based missiles than on defending cities against possible future Chinese attack) or to deploy no system at all. The temper of the country had shifted significantly on all defense spending, including that for the ABM. It was forgotten that in 1966 Congress actually had appropriated $168 million for the production and deployment of a massive ABM system— an appropriation which McNamara refused to spend. Pressures in 1966 and 1967 were intense for the all-out $40 billion shield.

These came not only from Congress but from most of the military, nearly all of McNamara's own senior advisers in the research and engineering fields and much of the public. Initiation of production of the full-scale system was blocked through 1966 and 1967 only by the adamant personal opposition of McNamara and Cyrus Vance. And the pressures were almost certain to increase from the White House in 1968 as the Republicans trumpeted the Soviet deployment and bore in on the failure of President Johnson to protect his people as Premier Kosygin was protecting the Russians. Our choice in the Pentagon in the late summer and fall of 1967 was not a small ABM versus none at all, but rather a small ABM versus a big one.

Under those circumstances, McNamara was willing to accept the marginal decision and pay $5 billion for something marginally worthwhile but not mandatory rather than spend $40 billion for something he considered worthless in itself, certain to further escalate the arms race and likely to interfere seriously with possible arms-limitations talks with the Soviet Union.

The language in the Posture Statement on the possibility of a Chinese-oriented system had been written with great care in November and December of 1966 by two men—McNamara and Vance. I regarded it as escape-hatch language. Had the Chinese program slipped visibly in 1967, or the Soviets stopped their construction, domestic military and political pressures might have eased during 1967 (as they had by 1969). In that event, I believe McNamara would have won the battle against even the thin ABM. But the pressures had not eased, and the September announcement that we would move forward with the thin system staved off demands for the thick one until the temper of the country had changed.

Some of the Doves—among the press, the Congress and the people—who had regarded McNamara as their champion in their joint opposition to the large deployment looked upon him as an illogical traitor in September, 1967. Had it not been for McNamara, I believe that the administration would have recommended an anti-Soviet deployment and that Congress, in the election year of 1968, would have approved it.

As usual, the most accurate stories on McNamara's ABM rationale came from the responsible members of the Pentagon press corps—which is, incidentally, generally underestimated in the curious strata of Washington newspapermen.

Men covering the State Department, men interested chiefly in the "Big Issues," smoke their pipes, speak from the depths of their bellies as good diplomats should, use the word "pragmatic" in their stories and look down their noses at the hardware-happy Pentagon reporters who lack real understanding of the importance of sensitive international relations.

Men covering the White House sip a heady wine in the personal relationship they almost establish with a President—a far more distant one, with a few rare exceptions, than the copy and attitude of some would have us believe, but vicariously closer than the reader in Kokomo—and look down their noses at the international theorists assigned to State, who lack real understanding of practical political presidential realities.

Men covering Capitol Hill slip into a soft-shoe intimacy with Congressmen and Senators—who are wonderful for newsmen to work with because of the freedom they have to express their independent views—and, in their confidence that Congress is the true source of power and true manifestation of democracy, look down their noses at all reporters working in any part of the bureaucratic Executive Branch.

All three of these groups write news stories on major defense issues, most of them with an appalling lack of preparation—although in their own fields many of these reporters are excellent.

And the responsible members of the underrated press corps of the Pentagon sit in their grubby room on the second floor of the big building and pore over the statements of top Defense officials, checking them against the outstanding files many keep. Their dog-eared copies of the huge budget book, the Posture Statements and dozens of volumes of Congressional testimony are underlined and indexed by their own work, and the margins are annotated. While they do understand the hardware of weapons systems, the good ones also are experts on the NATO alliance or the Middle East tinderbox, and several of them know more about nuclear strategy than some of the academicians who write on the subject.

The Pentagon press, for example, was aware that McNamara had engaged in this exchange on May 18, four months before the San Francisco speech:

QUESTION: Mr. Secretary, if we deployed an ABM system for defense against a Chinese threat, do you think a country such as India would lay claim to the need for such a system?

SECRETARY MCNAMARA: Let me stop before answering the question to draw your attention to the need to distinguish very carefully between an anti-ballistic missile system deployed to protect our population against heavy strategic nuclear attacks of the kind that the Soviet Union is capable of . . . on the one hand, versus protection of population against light attacks, on the other. . . .

We are not capable, in my opinion, of protecting our population with ABM's against Soviet attacks, but we are capable of protecting our population against the type of attack that the Red Chinese might mount against us in the mid- or late-1970's.

I frequently read in the press discussions of anti-ballistic missile systems which fail to distinguish between these two types of systems and which, therefore, are quite misleading in indicating the capability that we have for protecting our people.

Whether or not India would or would not wish to deploy an anti-ballistic missile system to protect itself against a potential attack from Red China, assuming we did, I can't say. My guess is they would. . . .

I am not taking a position on whether we should or should not have a light defense against a capability such as the Red Chinese would have in the mid-1970's. We haven't had to face that decision as yet because the lead time that they have to develop their offensive system is greater than the lead time we would require to develop the light defense.

But outside the Pentagon press room, most newspapermen in the nation who comment on these matters are not up to the task, and so an editorial appearing in the Newport News *Daily Press* only four days after that May news conference said this, in part:

> Since the Secretary of Defense has changed his mind about the Chinese threat and the proper response thereto, there is reason to wonder whether he might later undergo a similar shift of viewpoint about the Soviets.

Many Washington officials would not be disturbed about the Newport News *Daily Press*, not as widely known or influential in this country and overseas as the *New York Times* or the *Washington Post*. I was not among these officials; the Newport Newses of this country are inhabited by a lot more Americans than live in Washington and New York.

To help keep the record straight, we wrote a short letter to the editor restating the case. It was typical of many others sent to other newspapers across the country, with the objective not of publication but of informing the editors in the hope of deterring future misstatements.

In the office of the Assistant Secretary of Defense (Public Affairs), we considered the ignorance of local editorial writers and local columnists even more of a problem than the general lack of defense expertise in the non-Pentagon Washington press corps. I do not know what the government can do to help alleviate this situation. Even most of our largest newspapers— there are two or three exceptions—cannot afford specialists on nuclear strategy in their home offices. But how is the reader to know how much faith to put in the unidentified author of the editorial he studies? Two editorials will appear side by side, one on the current political situation in the state and the other on the antiballistic missile. The first has been written by a man who has devoted twenty years of his life to covering state politics. Besides understanding the issues, he knows every county chairman, every important lobbyist, every influential legislator and nearly all of the inner machinations of the political parties. He is an expert. The author of the second is a rank amateur in the field he is examining, and most of the time he has done very little serious homework. The one editorial should be of great value to the reader; whether he agrees with the conclusions is unimportant. The second can only confuse the reader with its misinformation—which he cannot identify as misinformation. Consider this excerpt from the *National Observer* on August 7, 1967:

> Whether the United States builds or does not build an ABM network is a matter far too important to all Americans to be left to a small group of men in Washington—or the Kremlin. The people have a right to know what the real facts and alternatives are before they're saddled with a split decision or none at all.

In the Pentagon we were in total agreement. But the real facts *were* available. The alternatives *had* been spelled out. The record was there not only for a small group of men in Washington or the Kremlin, but for every literate individual. The government has no responsibility to spoon-feed each publication, nor would Congress support the budget this would require. How, then, does the *National Observer*, a publication of high repute, learn that the information is available?

Cognizant of the ignorance of his audience on nuclear matters, McNamara sprayed the language of his San Francisco speech with nuclearese. I wanted him to let my people go over it to turn the gobbledegook into English, but he refused. His purpose was to educate. He had a message to deliver—that a thick $40 billion ABM made no sense. Familiarity with the terms would help equip the editors listening to him in San Francisco—and the people—to consider intelligently the ABM battle that was still ahead. He insisted that the text include "first-strike capability," "second-strike capability," "survivability," "assured destruction," and "penetration aids," knowing that members of Congress and the professional Hawks would be using this language as they made their pitch for the full-scale system.

Later I reluctantly agreed that he had made some progress— not a great deal, but some, and much more than he would have achieved if his "ility" effort had been halfhearted. This also was typical McNamara. Never did he expect 100 percent success, but he always demanded—and exerted—maximum effort toward total success. He would ask his staff to produce by 7 P.M. the next day an amount of work which could not be done under any circumstances in four days. He would not get it all, but he would get much more of it than he would have by asking us simply to do as much as we could by the next night. He never asked for anything without establishing a time limitation, and he always asked for far more than he was entitled to within that time period. The system is an excellent one—if you have or can find persons willing to work. While the military establishment has many faults, among them are not laziness or an inclination to avoid responsibility.

Flying from San Francisco back to Washington, we discussed some of the risks which accompanied the speech and the ABM decision.

One was the effect of the announcement on the Soviet Union. Would it, as many Doves contended, lessen the chances of beginning negotiations on arms limitation? McNamara thought not. The Russians, he believed, would not be misled by this thin ABM. From their own sophistication and technical competence they would know that the system as described would not be capable of protecting the U.S. population against a Soviet attack.

Another danger was whether our people or others in the world would look upon the deployment decision as a step away from the nonproliferation treaty, a draft of which was being negotiated between representatives of the Soviet Union and the United States. McNamara did not regard it as a block to the treaty. On the contrary, he believed it would help deter Asian nations from building their own nuclear forces, since they should feel that our ability to neutralize a Chinese attack would make us more likely to support them against Red Chinese nuclear blackmail. Under these circumstances it became more illogical for an Asian nation to attempt to create its own national nuclear arsenal.

A third concern was the violence of the reaction of our NATO partners. This one had personal implications, inasmuch as we were going to Ankara the next week for a meeting of the NATO Nuclear Planning Group. Knowing that many of the NPG delegates would misunderstand the deployment announcement, McNamara expected considerable sulking from them. He was prepared to argue that the Chinese-oriented system had nothing to do with NATO, but he did not expect them to believe that until he had a chance to convince them personally. To help in this effort, we took along several dozen copies of the speech and several dozen reprints of an excellent question-and-answer interview with McNamara in the new *Life* Magazine, an interview on which Dick Stolley of *Life* had spent weeks. Its publication had been timed to coincide with the delivery of the speech.

The gravest danger, demanding the most attention, was the attempt that would be made to use the thin ABM as a wedge toward deployment of a full-scale Soviet-oriented system.

Anticipating this effort, the Directorate for Plans and Programs in our office had prepared a list of seventy-four questions likely to be asked by the press after the announcement, and had distributed them to relevant sections of the Department of Defense for answers—to the Army, the Director of Defense Research and Engineering, the Assistant Secretaries of Defense for Systems Analysis and International Security Affairs, and elsewhere. Upon completion of the staffing, and after our deputies had approved the proposed replies, John Foster, Director of Defense Research and Engineering, and I went over each question and answer. My goal was to declassify as much as possible and to ensure that all replies calling for a philosophical treatment contained the McNamara philosophy and not the views of a Hawkish Army general who wanted a full-scale system, or a Dovish Deputy Assistant Secretary in Paul Warnke's International Security Affairs office who wanted no system at all. Dr. Foster's goal was to make certain that nothing was declassified which would be of technical value to the enemy and to ensure that responses were factually correct from an engineering standpoint. All proposed answers were then cleared with Secretary

McNamara, who had learned what many top officials of the
Executive Branch never learned—that a written response handed
a newspaperman by the brigadier general or colonel who was
Director of Defense Information in my office, or by a lieutenant
commander working for them, was an official position of the
Department of Defense and was transmitted in news stories
around the world as such.

There is no such thing as a casual, offhand reply by a junior
officer or lower-ranking civilian working in a Pentagon information office. A reporter receiving an answer from him will write,
quite justifiably: "The Department of Defense said today . . ."
Any Pentagon information officer speaking to a newspaperman
becomes the official voice of the Department of Defense. Occasionally this causes embarrassment, depending upon the astute-
ness of the officer and the degree of responsibility of the newsman. An inexperienced officer who had no personal knowledge
of a sensitive subject might say simply "No comment" to a reporter's question, and the reporter might then write: "Despite
the international importance of this incident, the Pentagon
stubbornly refused to comment." On the same issue, a more
astute officer would acknowledge that he had no personal knowledge of the situation but promise to check with his superiors, and
the more responsible reporter would avoid an immediate attack
upon the government's silence. The two stories would leave
vastly different impressions upon their readers.

As professionals, our plans people were able to anticipate all
important questions the press would ask on the ABM. Some were
as simple and factual as how much money had been included in
the Fiscal Year 1968 budget for ABM production, or when the
first and last batteries of missiles would be operational. Others,
while apparently simple, required great care in handling if we were
to establish from the beginning with the public, the Congress
and the military establishment that this was not a building block
toward a bigger deployment.

Example: "Can this system be used as a first step toward a
large-scale anti-Soviet system?"

The simple answer was "yes." Any ABM net costing $5 billion would contribute *something* toward a $40 billion system and could, therefore, "be used as a first step." But if the Director of Defense Information had given a short "yes," this story might have been written:

The Department of Defense today acknowledged that the Chinese-oriented antiballistic missile system announced yesterday in San Francisco by Secretary Robert S. McNamara could be a first step toward a massive $40 billion missile wall designed to protect the American people against an all-out Soviet attack.

That news lead, moving on the Associated Press or United Press International news ticker in Washington, would have drawn screams of outrage about the duplicity of McNamara from the Doves on Capitol Hill and cries of jubilation from the Hawks. More damaging, the word would have flashed through the entire United States Army that the door was wide open.

Our actual answers to the question posed above and two others along the same line were:

Q: Can this system be used as a first step toward a large-scale system?
A: There is no plan or intention to expand the system.
Q: Do you look upon this as a first step toward a large system?
A: Not in any way.
Q: Will this system be of any use whatever against a large-scale Soviet attack?
A: This system is not designed for such an attack, except for protection of Minuteman.

These were precisely the type of devious answers which infuriated me during my fifteen years as a Washington correspondent. Why could not the bureaucratic government give a simple "yes" if the simple answer was "yes"? Why was the Pentagon always trying to hide something?

Despite my personal knowledge of and sympathy with this reportional reaction, I found no way during my tour as Assistant Secretary to solve the problem. The simple yes-or-no answer which the newsmen want can be misleading in itself and can produce misleading stories. The antiballistic missile issue was too important to the government, domestically and internationally, to permit us to take that risk. The truth was that Robert McNamara did not intend this to be a first step; he did not intend to permit anyone to push ahead with a full-scale system; he did not believe that the one deployment would lead to the other, and he was prepared to use all his power to prevent that from happening. An official Pentagon answer which could have left any other impression would have been erroneous.

Yet members of the press, with some justification, still would retort that the government owed the people a simple answer. If it were true that this system could be used as a steppingstone, they would argue, then the answer should have been a straight "yes." How the press wrote the story was not the concern of the Pentagon.

Many in the Army—uniformed officers and civilian officials— eagerly desired a full-scale Soviet-oriented antiballistic missile system and definitely looked upon the San Francisco announcement as a step toward it. This was no secret to McNamara, his staff or the Pentagon press. For a decade or more the Army had fought for a thick system. In his book, *The Uncertain Trumpet*, published shortly after President Eisenhower left office, General Maxwell D. Taylor told of his efforts as Army Chief of Staff to get a green light for the old Nike-Zeus antimissile missile—an outgrowth of the Nike-Ajax antiaircraft missile with its conventional warhead and the longer-range antiaircraft Nike-Hercules wth its atomic warhead.

Nike-Zeus was overtaken by development as the years went by and as Presidents Eisenhower, Kennedy and Johnson all ruled against production and deployment of a large-scale ABM.

By 1967, more than $2 billion later, it was no longer recognizable and had turned into a program called Nike-X, involving greatly different missiles and radars. To the Army, the Nike-X research and development project unquestionably was a system to be used against the Soviet Union. While it had several different deployment plans at costs ranging from $3 billion to $20 billion (McNamara automatically doubled all these estimates, to be realistic), all were oriented toward the Soviet threat and all were steppingstones to a full-scale, nationwide defense against an all-out Soviet attack. Army press kits and all the public affairs policy guidance prepared by the Army described Nike-X in those terms. This had been done in the months and years before San Francisco, on the up-and-up, with approval of the Office of the Secretary of Defense, since the Nike-X program was, in fact, being developed primarily as an anti-Soviet weapon. With this kind of history and background, however, not only was the Army uninclined to accept Secretary McNamara's insistence that the deployment he announced was unrelated to a full-scale Soviet system; it was neither prepared nor structured to do so.

Necessarily, our office moved in to take over. To have the Secretary of Defense emphasizing that the new system was not a step toward a full-scale ABM while a large share of the Army was declaring that it was a step clearly could not be tolerated. We asked to see and approve every piece of paper the Army produced which might turn up in public print or affect material provided the public, whether a response to a newsman's query, a policy guidance message to an Army command or an unclassified letter to a member of Congress.

This, however, was not enough. McNamara's decision to build the thin, anti-Chinese system was not meant to affect continued *research* toward other systems, the objectives of which were to protect our people against large-scale attacks. As the Secretary pointed out in his speech, he was not opposed to the heavy shield because it cost $40 billion. If we could actually devise an impenetrable shield against a large-scale attack, it would be worth ten times $40 billion. Research toward this end was not to stop.

Thus the Army was moving ahead with part of a Nike-X *production* program which was to be deployed against a light Chinese attack and had virtually nothing to do with a Soviet attack against our cities, and also with a Nike-X *development and research* program designed to find an answer to just such a

Soviet attack. Even if the Army showed the purest intentions and genuinely tried to convince outsiders—and themselves—that the new ABM was not a building block, this situation on a sensitive matter was unacceptable from a public affairs standpoint.

Accordingly, we recommended to Secretary McNamara that the Chinese-oriented system be given a new name, so that we could separate all public affairs policy guidance related to the new system from guidance concerned with the old (and continuing) Nike-X program.

The Secretary agreed, and the thin ABM was rechristened the "Sentinel"—an Army choice. It made no difference to me what they called it, so long as the Army, the press and the public would begin to distinguish it from Nike-X.

In addition, McNamara ordered that the development and deployment of the Sentinel should be an entirely different project from the ongoing Nike-X. He designated a different general—Lieutenant General Alfred D. Starbird, USA, who had been serving as Director of the Defense Communications Agency—to be the Army's program manager for the Sentinel, to report directly to the Chief of Staff. The old Nike-X organization continued separately, with Lieutenant General Austin W. Betts, Army Chief of Research and Development, remaining responsible for it.

Had this divorce not been ordered, it would have been impossible to get across to the American people and to our allies that the Chinese-oriented system was to be exactly what McNamara had said it was and nothing more. Even with the divorce, some confusion and misunderstanding were inevitable.

An immediate official reaction of the United Kingdom, for example, dealt with the "adverse consequences" of the deployment. British officials told the press privately that this was a death blow to the treaty to prevent nonproliferation. They spoke of the new dimension being added to the arms race and of dangerous world-wide repercussions. The British government had both political and psychological problems because it could not afford to protect any of its people with even a limited ABM deployment.

From the West Germans came the same reaction. Helmut Schmidt, parliamentary leader of Germany's Social Democratic Party, told a Washington news conference: "In two years the question will be raised what happens to us Europeans with about 700 Soviet middle-range rockets targeted on us, when the superpowers are defended by their ABMs."

Secretary McNamara met the NATO problem head on. As we left Andrews Air Force Base for Ankara and the Nuclear Planning Group meeting at 7:15 A.M. a week after the speech, a few Pentagon press room reporters and a bank of television cameras were at planeside.

This exchange took place:

QUESTION: Do you expect our NATO allies to demand a share of the ABM system?

SECRETARY MCNAMARA: The anti-ballistic missile system we are planning for this country is directed at protecting it against an attack from China and really has no relationship to our commitments to the defense of Western Europe.

Nine hours later we landed the big C-135 at Ankara, where the news media were assembled, as always. And there was this exchange:

QUESTION: Will you recommend a missile defense system similar to what you're anticipating in the United States?

SECRETARY MCNAMARA: Well, I understand—I understand that this will be one of the subjects that will be discussed here but I think it's important to recognize that the anti-ballistic missile system that the United States in deploying has no relationship whatsoever to NATO. It's a system that is oriented toward the Chinese threat that will develop in the mid-1970s and is completely unrelated to the threat from the Soviet Union which of course is the threat that NATO is conscious of and directing its energies toward.

No single pattern emerged from the reaction at home, unless it was one of opposition from all sides. Yet we felt that our special educational operation had paid off. The initial news stories from the reporters seen by Henkin, Fryklund and Deputy Secretary Nitze were, almost without exception, objective and written intelligently. These were from the professionals in the Pentagon press corps—not all McNamara fans, but professional in their jobs. The comments by Sevareid and Chancellor were excellent—clear and accurate. Both the Washington *Post* and the *New York Times* printed the text. With one or two exceptions, the work of the columnists who had been invited in was rational—not necessarily favorable—and reflected the time McNamara had spent on Saturday.

We were off to a reasonable start. More importantly, we had demonstrated to ourselves that the government can communicate at least on a one-time basis with the press, if it tries hard enough to do so and if it has a case worth communicating. How much of that information was read by the people or understood by them is another issue.

From those with whom we had not made special contact came a mishmash of reaction.

The *New York Times* was gratified that we were not building a full-scale system, but felt that the genie had been let out of the bottle, that the President had thrown a $5 billion fish to the military-industrial-political cats, that this step was essentially a useless escalation of armament expenditures at home and that the effect on the Soviet Union was apt to be dangerous.

Senator J. William Fulbright (D.–Ark.) reacted with "deep regret." "Once this is started, there will be no stopping it, and its cost will be astronomical—comparable to the space program," he said. "I also have very grave doubts about its effectiveness."

The New York *Daily News* somehow thought McNamara was telling the Russians this: Anything you can do, we can do better. It added: "The U.S.S.R. started this latest chapter in the arms race by setting up its own ABM network. It has remained deaf to all efforts to negotiate a halt."

The Navy began lobbying for SAMBIS (sea-based antiballistic

missile intercept system). "Mr. Speaker," said Representative
William R. Anderson (R.–Tenn.), first skipper of the nuclear-
powered *Nautilus* submarine, "it has been estimated that Red
China will have a ballistic missile delivery capability in the early
1970s. When this happens we will have a most pressing need
for SAMBIS. The time to get going is now."

Representative Robert L. Sikes (D.–Fla.), Hawkish, called
the decision "little and late," and urged in the "strongest terms"
that there be "an immediate expansion of the planned ABM
system to insure fullest possible protection."

Newsweek found, but did not identify, "one of the government's top missile engineers." It quoted him: "If the election
were two years off, McNamara would not have made the decision.
He'd like to hold the line against the ABM forever."

Senator George S. McGovern (D.–S. Dak.), Dovish, called
it "one of the most wasteful and most dangerous proposals that
have been suggested in a long time."

The Dovish St. Louis *Post-Dispatch* assessed the decision as
"anything but rational."

The more Hawkish St. Louis *Globe-Democrat* typically went
in the other direction: "It is blind folly to sink our defense to
second place in the world. It is monstrous hazard to ignore an
ABM program, the absence of which endangers tens of millions
of our lives and invites the spread of Russia's design for total im-
perialism."

Senator Philip A. Hart (D.–Ind.), Dove, termed the system a
"campaign bauble," but Senator Strom Thurmond (R.–S. C.),
Hawk, renewed his call for "an ABM defense second to none"
and expressed displeasure at McNamara's "piecemeal approach."

The San Diego *Union* protested that it was too little and too
late, but Senator Frank Church (D.–Idaho) viewed it as "the
most extravagant and expensive sieve ever constructed."

Scarcely anyone was pleased with the Secretary of Defense,
which was par. It is difficult for me to name many "popular"
Cabinet officers, of any administration, even in the less sensitive
posts. The ABM issue is, like so many others before the Secretary

of Defense, highly charged with emotion. And it scarcely could be otherwise, involving billions of dollars, conceivably millions of lives, possibly a strong influence on our international alliances and, potentially, an impact on achieving a saner nuclear policy acceptable to both the United States and the Soviet Union. And beyond all of that, for opponents it represents money they think should be used for education and the ghetto and the other human problems of our times.

Nevertheless, the fact that we are not today saddled with the enormous cost of a "thick" ABM system is due to the inflexible stand of McNamara against it and his acceptance of an unwanted compromise that satisfied the administration on both political and defense grounds, and hobbled adequately the Hawks on Capitol Hill and elsewhere.

The Second Time Around

January, 1968

The second time we lost our hydrogen bombs all of us who were veterans of Palomares agreed at the start that we would turn in our news management buttons before enduring another eighty days and eighty nights of Spanish-type silence. From our Mediterranean experience we knew that the major public affairs problem would not be security, although security is always a sticky issue when nuclear weapons are involved, and that it would not be the safety of the population, although popular misconceptions on safety escalate rapidly when radioactivity is unleashed. The major public affairs issue would be the attitude of the host government.

This was again relevant, for again the operating arms of the Defense Establishment had chosen poorly. Again they had selected a territory outside the continental limits of the United States in which to misplace our megatons, and again the shots were to be called by a foreign government. The United States Air Force is proud of its ability to act and react anywhere in the world; all its aircraft and all their components are built and tested to endure the heat of the tropics at noon and the cold of the arctic that same midnight. In an unplanned demonstration of its general all-weather capability, this time the Air Force had lost our thermonuclear weapons in the frozen-most part of the frozen North.

It did this on January 21, 1968, when a B-52 bomber crashed

not too far from the North Pole at Thule, Greenland, where an Air Force base is located to support the operation of huge radar screens, the size of football fields, which are part of the Ballistic Missile Early Warning System.

The loss of a nuclear weapon anywhere can ruin your entire day, but I was particularly disconsolate at the news telephoned to my home that Sunday that our bombs were lost at Thule. Greenland belongs to Denmark, which has more of a thing about nuclear weapons than any nation on either side of the Iron Curtain. Denmark prohibits flights of aircraft carrying H-bombs over her territory, and Danish law forbids the stationing of atomic arms on her soil. As a reporter, I had encountered this sensitivity on one visit to the BMEWS site, when I had to agree in advance to submit my copy to the Danish censor, and on another to Denmark itself.

Our sometimes friendly allies at the Department of State were reluctant to believe my initial Sunday afternoon telephone messages that we had done it again. They also agreed that the nuclear-nervous Danes probably were going to be even more skittish than the Spanish, since Denmark was on the eve of parliamentary elections critical to the future of Premier Jens Otto Krag—a good friend, an ally of the United States and a solid supporter of the North Atlantic Treaty Organization. Many Danes were not our friends and solid supporters, and State decreed immediately that the United States would cooperate in every possible way with the existing government. We were asked, once again, to clamp a silence lid on the entire military establishment until we received a "go" signal from Denmark.

Internally, therefore, our first action that evening was again to send sharp messages throughout the military establishment ordering everyone to stay absolutely quiet about the crash itself until an announcement was authorized by the Assistant Secretary of Defense for Public Affairs. Telephone calls backing up those messages were made to the three elements most concerned: Strategic Air Command headquarters in Omaha, the base at Thule and the bomber's home base at Plattsburgh, New York—

the most likely source of a potential leak since so many on the base would know the plane was overdue.

Our second and third actions followed Henkin's Law: "Send someone."

To Thule we sent Colonel Willis L. Helmantoler, USAF, our prime floating troubleshooter, whose official title was Military Assistant to the Deputy Assistant Secretary of Defense. His orders identified him as my personal representative, however, and a coming-your-way message to Thule gave him complete authority to release information concerning the accident. From that moment on, no move of any kind concerning the press and the public could be made at Thule by any United States official of any rank without Colonel Helmantoler's permission. He flew in at once with the SAC investigation team.

To Copenhagen, from Stuttgart, we sent Lieutenant Colonel Dickson, who as information officer for the Defense Atomic Support Agency had been so involved in the perils of Palomares. He could give both the United States Ambassador and the Danish officials more inside information on how not to handle this crisis from a public affairs standpoint than any other individual, and also could serve better than anyone as a link between Denmark's scientists and her local public affairs officials.

With Helmantoler in Thule and Dickson in Copenhagen, I felt greatly comforted. Our office had inside representation at all times on both fronts; we had points of contact from whom we could receive unexpurgated information in instant telephone calls and to whom we could relay our desires and orders—and, as appropriate, those of the Secretary. Chains of command are essential, but Henkin's Law proved itself in the rapid deployment of Helmantoler and Dickson, as it always did.

In Washington that Sunday a proposed press release was drafted, based on recommendations from SAC, although details were scarce, as invariably they are at the beginning of a crisis. While skeptical about securing Denmark's approval that first night, we had learned from Palomares how important it was to push for action from the outset, and then to continue pushing.

After obtaining State's clearance by telephone, we received State's permission to have the draft carried by Pentagon messenger to the home of the Danish Ambassador.

Disappointed when the "go" signal was not given by Denmark on Sunday, but aware that losers can't be choosers, we began pressing again early Monday morning. With a 7 A.M. phone call, we urged State to remind the Danes that Air Force notification of the next-of-kin could not be delayed indefinitely and to re-emphasize the dangers to the Copenhagen government of wild and speculative news stories. State agreed, but before Denmark said "yes" the high-level international tug of war was ended abruptly by civil servants of the Canadian Transport Department's Air Traffic Control Center in Moncton, New Brunswick. At 9:07 Monday morning, these two paragraphs moved over the Associated Press wire:

MONCTON, N.B, (AP)—The Canadian Transport Department's Air Traffic Control Center here said today a U.S. Air Force B52 bomber crashed Sunday about seven miles from Thule, Greenland.

The aircraft was on a circuit flight from Plattsburgh, N.Y., and return. No details were available immediately.

In our office we were relieved that the news had surfaced, knowing that all who sought to conceal the loss of a B-52 for very long were living in fairyland. Later we used the case frequently as an example for public officials who refused to accept public affairs realities. Despite an agreement between two governments that nothing would be said yet, despite total silence in Denmark, in Thule, at Omaha, at Plattsburgh, throughout the State Department and throughout the Pentagon, the news of the crash popped out. It had not occurred to us to ask Moncton, New Brunswick, to keep still; indeed, we had been unaware that there was a Moncton, New Brunswick.

Clearly it no longer made any sense to delay the official announcement of the crash. I talked to my State Department counterpart, State talked to the Danish Ambassador about the draft release he had been given Sunday night, Denmark approved

it, and thirty-three minutes after the Moncton story had run
we read this release to the Pentagon press:

The Department of Defense today announced that a U.S. Air
Force B-52 bomber crashed at approximately 3:40 P.M. EST, Sunday,
January 21, on the ice of North Star Bay some seven miles southwest
of the runway at Thule defense area, Greenland. The aircraft was
attempting an emergency landing.

Seven crewmen were listed as being aboard the aircraft, which
was from the 380th Bomb Wing at Plattsburgh Air Force Base, New
York.

There were five known survivors, who parachuted from the aircraft. The body of a sixth crew member has been found. Search and
rescue operations are continuing for the seventh.

The aircraft was carrying nuclear weapons which are unarmed so
that there is no danger of a nuclear explosion at the crash site. There
is no known damage to civilian property.

The cause of the accident has not been determined. An investigation team has been sent to Thule from SAC Headquarters, Omaha,
Nebraska. There are no additional details available at this time.

The human tragedy of the story lay in the disclosure of the
loss of life. However, the significant paragraph, from an international standpoint, was the fourth. In our first announcement, the
antiatomic Danes had accepted a frank statement that nuclear
weapons had been aboard—putting us three days ahead of the
Palomares schedule and, more importantly, indicating that despite their nuclear nervousness the Danish understood that these
ugly matters really were going to get into the public domain,
however distasteful that was.

That the situation was difficult for them was clear. Three of
the four leftist parties in Denmark were opposed to Danish mem-
bership in NATO. The Soviets had charged periodically that
their government was planning to permit the United States to
bring nuclear arms to both Denmark and Greenland. Within
hours a group of Danes demonstrated in front of our embassy
in Copenhagen to protest the crash. Foreign Minister Hans
Tabor issued a statement defending and explaining his govern-

ment's position, but it was nonetheless more sympathetic to the United States than we had dared hope—and probably more sympathetic than we deserved.

An immediate issue for us was whether newsmen would be permitted at Thule. If the answer was "yes," we would arrange military transportation for them, since there were no commercial flights to that part of the polar icecap. But the word came back from State: the Danes said "no"—although we were not to blame them for that decision. As a result of this ruling, for several days the world was to be told the story exclusively through our news releases, with information coming primarily from Colonel Helmantoler. His around-the-clock communications with Dick Fryklund, who assumed full charge of the public affairs aspects of the story, were to put our office far ahead of the rest of the Pentagon on all Thule developments. And while government press releases never can begin to be a substitute for on-the-scene reporting and probing by a free press, the Fryklund-Helmantoler team nonetheless performed a remarkable public service. Helmantoler was a career professional information officer and one of the best in the business; Fryklund a lifelong newsman and a winner of national reporting awards who had specialized in military affairs and knew what the reporters wanted and needed.

Despite the incredible conditions at Thule, and due in large part to the outstanding cooperation from the Air Force, the State Department and the Danish government, our office was able to issue a second Department of Defense press release the same day as the first:

Following is additional information on the B-52 from Plattsburgh Air Force Base in New York which crashed in the North Star Bay Sunday:

The aircraft was approaching for an emergency landing after having declared an emergency because of a possible fire in the navigator's compartment and intensive smoke throughout the aircraft.

The aircraft impacted on the ice, which is about six to nine feet thick. Some wreckage burned, some is no longer visible on the surface

and may have burned into or through the ice and some has been
observed on the surface of the ice by helicopters. More detail will be
available as additional dog sled teams return.

The water depth of the Bay ranges up to 800 and 900 feet.

Thule is presently in polar darkness except for a period of sub-
twilight lasting from approximately 10 A.M. to 2 P.M. EST. The
temperature is 25 degrees below zero.

Flares are being used to assist helicopters and dog sled teams.

These search and rescue operations succeeded in finding the missing crew member. Search operations for the weapons aboard and
other equipment are continuing.

Teams of Air Force accident investigation experts have been sent
to Thule.

While this release did not say what had become of the hydrogen bombs, there was good reason for our silence on this point.
No one yet knew whether they had gone skittering down the ice
a mile or two, whether they were attached to wreckage around
which new ice had frozen, whether they were eight hundred feet
down, or whether all four had gone different ways.

Notwithstanding Fryklund's efforts to put out everything we
knew so as to discourage speculation, some newsmen went off
half-cocked. The first Associated Press story was written this way:

A B52 bomber crashed in Greenland yesterday, apparently dumping
several hydrogen bombs in the icy waters of a bay.

The Defense Department said the plane was carrying nuclear
weapons, but added they were unarmed "so that there is no danger
of a nuclear explosion at the crash site."

Other sources indicated that the big bomber was carrying about
four hydrogen bombs. It cracked through the ice, carrying the
bombs into freezing water.

The formal announcement did not say what happened to the nuclear weapons.

I was suspicious of any news story which proclaimed that unidentified "sources" had "indicated" that a bomber was carrying
"about four" hydrogen bombs. The odds favored that the source
was the reporter himself, who knew that the Palomares B-52

bore four weapons and assumed this one probably did, too. Perhaps I was unfair to the newsman, but I had done the same kind of thing many times as a reporter. In Washington political reporting, "a quick survey of Washington opinion" usually means the impressions of the writer and four of his friends and "observers here believe" usually means that the reporter writing the story believes.

But those were nit-picks. What troubled us most in the Associated Press story was the flat statement of apparent fact: "It cracked through the ice, carrying the bombs into freezing water." The location of the hydrogen bombs was the most important part of the episode; without that issue this was merely a routine, albeit tragic, airplane crash. No one possessed such knowledge, and Fryklund, advised by Helmantoler from the scene, had been careful in his press releases not to speculate. Yet a reporter, trying to meet the demands of the competitive system for instant fact, had created an unqualified declaration which appeared in newspapers over much of the world, was repeated thousands of times on radio and television and formed the basis for later editorial judgments. In the days ahead when it turned out that the bombs had not crashed through the ice into the bay, the government would be blamed for misleading and deceiving the public by the erroneous information it had "announced" the first day. This kind of reporting is responsible for a significant amount of the distrust between the government and the people, and contributes substantially to the communications problems between them. I do not wish to blame the press for the government's failures and failings, which are many, but neither can it escape blame. Most readers of that story would not differentiate between what the government had actually said and what the reporter was saying on his own. In the minds of most readers, the information that the aircraft had cracked through the ice and carried the bombs into freezing water was attributable to their government.

The actual fact was that two days later we still did not know what had become of our hydrogen bombs, but we did know that something had shaken loose on the polar ice. Reports from the first dog-sled survey team were received, telling of the first evidence of radioactivity. Working with State and with Dickson in Copenhagen, Fryklund and Helmantoler took only a day to clear with the Danes an announcement which included these paragraphs:

It is possible that the aircraft exploded as a result of the impact, according to the survey team, since most of the parts of the plane found by the team are in small fragments in and around the burn area. It was not determined whether any parts of the plane burned into or through the ice.

None of the parts located were identified as nuclear weapons or parts of nuclear weapons. A negligible amount of radioactivity was found in this first survey effort and was "light, fixed and closely confined." It was in an area 75 by 600 yards southwest from the impact point, roughly coincident with the burn area. The levels found are not considered hazardous.

The Air Force people, their Greenlander drivers and their Danish guide picked up what was described as "limited amount of low-level radioactivity" on their footgear. The radioactivity monitored at the scene was alpha particles which have extremely limited penetration ability.

The improvement over the winter of discontent at Palomares thus continued. In Spain we had not been permitted to mention radioactivity until forty-four days after the crash. Here it was little more than forty-four hours, and the governing factor for even that much delay was not Danish reluctance but rather the time taken by dog-sled travel through the arctic night. Later that day another dog-sled survey team returned, another report was received from Helmantoler, and Fryklund released additional detail—on radiation, on the installation at the scene of a wooden helicopter pad to reduce the amount of blowing snow and of the assembly there of a prefabricated building by pouring water over the joints and letting the water freeze. To counter the Associated Press story and to let the public know why we did not know more, these sentences also were included:

It still has not been determined whether parts of the plane or of the four nuclear weapons carried on the plane went into or through the ice. . . . Temperatures continue to be extremely low (minus 25F and lower), and darkness continues to hamper the men. Weather is deteriorating and a further search today was cancelled.

The Fryklund-Helmantoler reports to the public did not provide the color or atmosphere which made the weapons hunt on the arctic ice such a dramatic story, but they did provide facts as the Department of Defense knew them during that period when no newsmen were permitted in Thule. One week after the crash we were able to announce that parts of all four of the H-bombs had been found on the ice.

Due partly to the advice of Lieutenant Colonel Dickson in Copenhagen and the strong support of our ambassador there, the Danes reversed signals a few days after the crash and granted permission for newsmen to visit Thule. For a few dreadful hours consideration was given in Copenhagen to inviting Danish newsmen only, but the violent reaction of all elements of the U.S. government torpedoed that insanity. As a result, one aircraft left from Andrews Air Force Base outside Washington with twenty U.S. correspondents aboard and another from Copenhagen with eleven Danish newsmen and ten other reporters based in Europe. Helmantoler gathered them under his wing at the scene, giving them all as much access as possible to officials and to the crash site, and arranging frequent formal briefings on recovery operations by American Air Force generals, Danish authorities and nuclear experts from both countries. The briefings were taped and transmitted to Fryklund, who saw that they were made available for the Pentagon press and other Washington newsmen. Additionally, the Fryklund-Helmantoler team continued to turn out daily press summaries which were filed from Thule to our office and the American Embassy in Copenhagen.

The importance of internal communications in such cases is obvious. Authorities in Thule, Copenhagen and at both State and Defense in Washington had to know not only the facts but also what information was passing into the public domain. We did not want a major general at Thule refusing to comment on something that had already been cleared by higher headquarters in both Copenhagen and Washington. And we did want to ensure that answers given newsmen on the site, such as those following the announcement that parts of the weapon had been found, were disseminated at home and in Denmark. These included:

Q: What is the significance of this announcement?

A: It means that all four weapons did break up and that at least parts of all four are on the surface or frozen into the ice. Some of the ice at the crash site melted in the fire and refroze.

Q: Did any weapon parts go through the ice?

A: We cannot rule out that possibility at this time.

Q: Will the water in North Star Bay be checked for radioactivity?

A: Yes.

Q: Have all the surface fragments been located?

A: Probably not. The search is in its preliminary phases. It is probable that more weapon fragments will be found.

Q: Does the blowing snow carry radioactivity away from the crash site?

A: Checks by American and Danish scientific personnel at the scene show no radioactivity in the snow. In technical terms, the radioactive particles are "fixed," that is, are in the re-frozen ice, are in fragments of the plane or weapons or are held by their own weight to the surface where they were thrown by the explosion.

Q: How did the weapons fragment?

A: We do not know at this time. There are three possibilities. The weapons could have been broken up by the impact of the plane on the ice. They could have been blown apart by the explosion of the fuel on the aircraft after it crashed. The high-explosive (TNT) components of the weapons could have exploded during the crash or fire.

Q: Did the nuclear components explode?

A: No.

Q: How could the high-explosive (TNT) components explode without starting a nuclear or thermonuclear explosion?

A: Any piece of TNT, in or out of a nuclear weapon, can be exploded by shock or heat. Both shock and heat were present at the aircraft crash and a subsequent fire near Thule. The nuclear components of a weapon can be exploded, however, only by one specific kind of simultaneous explosion of all TNT components of the weapon. This can be achieved only by an intricate triggering process that cannot be activated by shock, fire or any other accidental process.

Q: Is the news of the finding of parts of all four bombs good news?
A: It is encouraging, because it indicates that fragments of weapons probably are confined to a relatively small area of the ice. It makes it impossible for one or more bombs to have gone through the ice and into the bay and it raises the possibility that no weapons fragments went through the ice. If this possibility is confirmed, then the clean-up problems will be greatly simplified, and the possibility of contamination of any wildlife will be sharply reduced. The water will be checked for contamination.
Q: Have parts of the nuclear or thermonuclear cores of the weapons been found?
A: We do not discuss particular components of the weapons.

Additionally, all queries submitted to Colonel Rodger R. Bankson's Directorate of Defense Information were cleared through Fryklund before answers were given the press. Since hundreds of them were routine, the extra clearance procedure was sometimes unnecessarily time-consuming, but accuracy was more important than speed. Many questions answered by Bankson at the Pentagon were worked by Fryklund through Helmantoler to the search, accident and radiation experts on the scene. Copies of final Pentagon answers were also sent Helmantoler so that he could keep Thule up to date.

The inspection and clean-up process continued for months, although general press interest was slight. Long after the crash, in August, 1968, the Danes and our people joined for an ecological survey to evaluate the environment again. Working from a fifty-four-foot motor ship, the *Aglantha*, the Danes sampled plant and animal life on the surface, while the U.S. checked the water below the crash site from the *Star III*, an oceanographic research submersible. In a joint statement, the two governments said: "Preliminary results confirm the earlier scientific findings that there is no danger to humans, plants, marine or animal life."

In tidying up, three shiploads of ice, snow and aircraft debris were removed, all sealed in containers and tanks, and put to rest with the soil from Palomares at the Savannah River burial ground.

Despite the personal tragedy for the crash victims and their families, the Thule disaster was considerably less of a public affairs catastrophe for the United States government than it might have been, and, for several reasons, it caused only a fraction of the criticism at home as Palomares.

One reason was the enlightened and cooperative attitude of the Danes, who permitted us to keep the people informed.

A second was that we now had a public affairs team of seasoned atomic losers. The Johnson administration had, after all, misplaced more hydrogen bombs than any administration in the history of the world. Having undergone the Palomares experience, we knew precisely how not to handle this kind of crisis.

A third was the professionalism of Fryklund in Washington, Helmantoler in Thule and Dickson in Copenhagen, along with the attitude of the Air Force and the cooperation of the State Department.

And a fourth was a Department of Defense diversionary operation off on the flank.

It was not easy to top the story of four hydrogen bombs missing on the polar icecap, of atomic technicians working by gasoline lantern and flashlight in snow igloos built as survival shelters alongside the frozen wreckage of a B-52 jet bomber, of Eskimo dog-sled teams carrying thermonuclear experts on a search for plutonium cores, of helicopters spidering their way through the eerie icy blackness.

It was not easy to drive from the front pages of every major newspaper in the world one of the most dramatic episodes of current history—the fight of man against a dark, frigid, radioactive arctic. But it was accomplished within forty-eight hours by the loss of the USS *Pueblo* to the North Koreans.

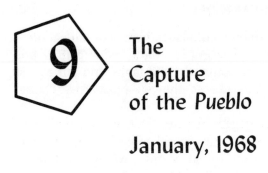

The
Capture
of the *Pueblo*

January, 1968

In our home for nearly four years were two gray telephones. One was cradled in the dining room, the other secured on the wall twelve inches from our bed. A good many times when I arrived home at nine o'clock at night I instructed the children not to answer the rings of the commercial apparatus belonging to the Chesapeake and Potomac Telephone Company. While this put rather a strain on their social life, especially since there are five of them, each of us must make some contribution to his country.

Not once, however, did I ignore the gray phones. They were difficult to ignore. A large red light blinked demandingly whenever they rang. They really did not ring at all; they yipped, in short staccato notes. All calls on the gray phones emanated from within the government. No inquiring newsman, however experienced or persistent, could crank himself into that net. Nor was I called by many members of my own office; our internal chain of command was established so that the colonels telephoned the admiral or general and the admiral or general telephoned Dick Fryklund or Dan Henkin, and one of them called me. And so, except on rare occasions, the voice at the other end of the gray phones would belong to one of my two top associates, to the Deputy Secretary of Defense or the Secretary, or to one of two or three men in the spook business whose problems were so private and/or urgent that they called me directly.

Shortly before one o'clock on the morning of January 23, 1968, the gray phone by our bed yelped and flashed until it awakened me.

It was Dan. We had, he said, a new problem in Thule. Whereas the Danish government had prohibited us from bringing in any members of the press corps to cover the H-bomb crash, a National Aeronautics and Space Administration aircraft returning home after observing the aurora borealis had landed for refueling with a newsman aboard.

Through sheer chance, this scientific-minded reporter had been plunked down into the biggest news story in the world, creating an unhappy situation. Hundreds of reporters and photographers had requested transportation to Thule, and several had made arrangements to charter their own planes as soon as we gave them permission to land. The Danes had not yet reversed themselves and allowed newsmen in. Therefore, because this was Danish territory, we had denied all requests. Now, in innocent violation of our regulation, a reporter had been unleashed in Thule—flown there by the United States government on its own aircraft.

This meant trouble with the State Department, trouble with the Danes, trouble with the entire American press corps, trouble with many foreign newsmen who were also trying to cover the dramatic story of missing hydrogen bombs in the frozen North, and trouble with the Congressmen who had intervened to seek free military airplane rides and access to Thule for their hometown or home-state newspaper friends. (I was shocked while in the government at how many reporters and editors ran to their Congressmen and Senators to appeal our decisions. The approach rarely worked, partly because we could not have survived had we bowed to Congressional pressures of this kind and partly because nine out of ten legislators made it clear that they were only going through the motions to maintain decent relations with their newspaper constituency and did not really expect us to grant them exceptions.)

I agreed with Dan: we did have a problem. We discussed the

solutions. We could call Thule and make certain that the reporter was locked up somewhere—somewhere warm and comfortable, preferably, but somewhere away from the H-bomb action and from all telephones, even if it were in an igloo. We would call NASA and instruct them to get their reporter off our base, cranking up one of our own planes and crews if they pleaded either equipment problems or pilot fatigue.

While we were talking, the Chesapeake and Potomac telephone rang on the other side of the bed. I asked Dan to hold on, tossed the gray phone on the pillow and crawled over, prepared to listen to some newsman's complaint.

But this was no reporter. It was Brigadier General Douglas Steakley, Director of the Joint Reconnaissance Center, an arm of the Joint Staff. He is an officer of great competence and professional skill, and is one of the nicest fellows I know. But his voice at the other end of a telephone always meant that something awful had happened. We regarded him as Mr. Disaster.

A United States ship, the general informed me, had just been boarded and seized by the North Koreans. Over an insecure telephone, there was no need for him to describe the type of ship.

My first question was the obvious one: "Where?" We were clearly in great trouble; his answer would give me a clue as to how great.

"Twenty-five miles from Wonsan."

Where the hell was Wonsan?

He told me, and identified the ship as the USS *Pueblo*.

The White House operator broke into the conversation to tell us Secretary McNamara was coming on the line. White House operators are the most efficient in the world, who can find anyone for you, any time, anywhere. The only problem is that they are so used to working for the President of the United States that they never ask you anything; they always tell you.

McNamara, Steakley and I talked for several minutes. Another operator broke in and Assistant Secretary of State William P. Bundy joined us. After a short additional conversation, McNamara instructed me to go directly to the Pentagon, get all of the facts from Steakley and the JRC people and write a suitable public statement for him to see at 7 A.M.

I was half-dressed before I noticed the gray phone on the pillow. Dan was still there.

"Your problem" I said, "has just gone away. Can you pick me up in fifteen minutes?"

(Later I learned that Dan quickly called back Helmantoler in Thule to say that he simply did not have time right then to deal with the H-bomb problem. When the colonel, who had thought he was handling the biggest news story in the world, recovered from his initial astonishment, he shot home a cable asking whether Washington was still in friendly hands. Nothing short of an invasion, the way he saw it, could relegate the missing H-bombs to second place.)

While waiting for Dan (he lived in nearby Silver Spring, Maryland; it was quicker to ride in with him than to rouse my own driver), I telephoned my executive assistant, Lieutenant Colonel Bruce Brown, USAF, to tell him we were en route. He would see that the secretaries and the front office administrative people were there to assist us.

We arrived at the Pentagon shortly after two and spent the next two hours with Steakley in the Joint Reconnaissance Center. While Steakley and one of his top officers worked with Dan and me, others went about their business, and decisions far removed from the Pueblo were put to the General. The major crisis does not eliminate the need for routine operational decisions, and world reconnaissance had not halted.

Dan and I went through the message traffic, item by item, culling out specific details we knew newsmen would want and trying to decipher exactly what had happened and when. While we had all the facts available in Washington to the United States government, we were having trouble keeping straight the sequence of events because of several pedestrian problems with time.

One was the relatively simple chore of handling time differences in three different parts of the world. Times on Navy messages are all in Greenwich Mean Time, at the zero meridian in England (called Zulu in military time-zone terminology), and we had to translate this into both Korean and Washington time to draw up an accurate chronology. It was necessary to keep in mind that 222345 Washington, 231345 Korea and 230445 Zulu were all the same time—January 22 at 11:45 P.M. (2345 military time) in the Pentagon, January 23 at 1:45 P.M. (1345 military time) at the *Pueblo* and January 23 at 4:45 A.M. (0445) at Greenwich in England.

Then we had to distinguish between the time an original message was dispatched as opposed to the receipt time by some station in the Pacific, and the subsequent time in Washington that the relay was received there. In the days ahead, one person would speak of a 9:15 message and another of a 9:35 message when they were discussing the same one.

A third confusing factor was the time of the incident described in a message as opposed to the time of the message itself. In her first "Sitrep" (situation report), for example, the *Pueblo* was discussing ship sightings and other incidents of the previous day.

And a fourth complication, both in time and wording, (similar to the *Liberty* case), was that a single *Pueblo* message would be picked up by several points in the Pacific and relayed back to Washington by more than one station. Some would send the original message verbatim; others would rephrase it in indirect quotations. "Initiating emergency destruction" was in one message with one time attached to it and "ship holding emergency destruction" in another message with another time attached— but both came from a single *Pueblo* transmission.

All of these appear to be minor points, and all were worked out easily by the professionals in the days ahead as fifty-two pages of messages relating to the *Pueblo* during those few hours were analyzed. But they were our major obstacles that night. We were not communications professionals; we were fighting the clock, and we needed a chronology immediately on which to base a statement for the United States government.

Not only did these relatively insignificant obstacles consume most of our time; they also were to become involved later in credibility discussions. President Johnson would use one set of times briefing Senate leaders at the White House, the Navy another set talking to favorite Congressmen, the Joint Staff a third filling in the Senate Armed Services Committee and the Secretary of Defense or our office a fourth in talking to the press. The Congress, the public and the press naturally became confused and suspicious.

The Assistant Secretary of Defense can standardize all times to be released to the public through official channels, whether the information is released in Honolulu, Saigon or Washington. But he has no control over the figures used by the Chief of Naval Operations in a classified discussion with the chairman of the House Armed Services Committee. Unless the reporter or the citizen is aware of these communications differences he can think erroneously that a twisted-tongue government is putting out two different stories.

In the Joint Reconnaissance Center, aided by Brigadier General Steakley, Dan and I pieced together this story:

The *Pueblo* departed Sasebo, Japan, on January 10, 1968, with orders to maintain radio silence unless she knew she had been seen. Her first transmission after leaving Sasebo was not until the morning of January 23 off Korea. (Our time confusion began with that first message, apparently dated at 6:15 P.M. on January 22 in Korea. We concluded finally that the message must have been drafted and dated at night but not dispatched until the next morning.) In that transmission the *Pueblo* reported that she had spotted two North Korean ships at ten thousand yards shortly after noon the previous day. The ships made two passes at her, coming as close as thirty yards. In late afternoon they drifted off and disappeared.

That was the complete message. Dan and I automatically considered the questions it opened up for the press. What kinds of ships? We don't know. What did they do? We don't know. Were they warships, fishing ships or merchant ships? We don't know. Did they signal the *Pueblo* in any way? We don't know. Did they warn her or order her farther out to sea? We don't know. Where was the *Pueblo* at this time? We don't know.

A half-dozen such answers could produce this kind of a news story: "The Department of Defense tonight disclosed that two North Korean ships had harassed the *Pueblo* 24 hours before she was seized. Pentagon officials refused to say whether the spy ship had been ordered out of Korean waters at that time."

The *Pueblo*'s next transmission, Sitrep (Situation Report) Number Two, was at 10:50 the morning of the twenty-third. During the night she had had eighteen contacts, the closest at three thousand yards. One contact, she reported, ignited a flare at 1:45 A.M. From that time on it was quiet. No attempts had been made to harass her.

Nothing in either message indicated the slightest concern. The commanding officer clearly was not upset or alarmed. There had been no incidents. Nearly twenty-four hours earlier two ships had come within thirty yards of her; that was not abnormal. She was breaking radio silence because she had now been observed, so one could assume that she had not been under surveillance until that time. That being so, her mission evidently was going well. Neither message suggested danger. Neither suggested that she had previously had cause to violate her instructions and move closer than thirteen miles from the shore. That she had hoarded the first Sitrep all night before sending it was evidence of her unconcern.

At 12:52 P.M. off the coast of North Korea, the USS *Pueblo* transmitted the first of eight messages which were to describe a contingency for which she and the United States were totally unprepared.

She reported that at noon she had encountered a North Korean patrol craft. Her position was 39 degrees, 25.3 minutes North latitude; 127 degrees, 55.0 minutes East longitude. After circling her twice, the ship asked by international flag signal for her identity. The *Pueblo* hoisted the American ensign and responded by international flags that she was a hydrographer. The patrol craft circled her a third time and ran up the flag hoist: "Heave to or I will open fire on you." The *Pueblo* replied by flag: "I am in international waters."

General Steakley, Dan and I noted the fifty-two-minute delay between the appearance of the patrol craft and the transmission. From that message we could not assess the feelings of the commanding officer. Again, from the standpoint of the press, many questions were unanswered.

How long did it take to exchange signals? We don't know. Was the *Pueblo* encircled immediately after the ship appeared or not until later? We don't know. Did the commanding officer wait too long before sending his message? The commanding officer used his best judgment; it would be unwise for us to speculate from here. Just when was the "open fire" threat made? We don't know. Well, how long would it usually take for a patrol craft to circle a ship three times and run up a couple of flag hoists? We prefer not to speculate.

We did not have these answers at five o'clock in the morning on January 23, nor were we to get them until nearly a year later when the crew was released. Working with Brigadier General Steakley in the Joint Reconnaissance Center, Dan and I were at the seat of the action in the Pentagon. The President was receiving no information not available to us. Unless the system had broken down, all important messages on the *Pueblo* were being passed in to the JRC, no matter what element of the government was receiving them.

As in the attack on the *Liberty* and in scores of other cases, however, we could not be certain how much was known in some corner of the world which had not yet been flashed back to Brigadier General Steakley. We had learned the hard way that public responses such as "Not to our knowledge at this time," or "Not that we know of" or "Not that I have heard" were safer than the flat "no."

The *Pueblo*'s next message was dated twenty-three minutes after the first, at 1:15 P.M. Three patrol craft had joined the first North Korean ship at 1 P.M. One sent a signal: "Follow in my wake; I have pilot aboard." Two MIG aircraft were circling off the starboard bow. One patrol craft approached the bow of the *Pueblo* with fenders rigged and an armed landing party on its bow, attempting to board. The *Pueblo* went ahead at one-third speed with the intention of departing the area.

Again, we could anticipate press questions for which we had no answers. How many men in the boarding party? Did the *Pueblo* offer any resistance at this point? What, precisely, did she mean by "attempting to board"? Why did the *Pueblo* say she was leaving the area at one-third speed; why didn't she move at top speed? What ever happened to the "open fire" warning of the last message—had the North Koreans now opened fire? If everyone was in international waters, why was there a pilot aboard the Korean ship? We don't know.

Fourteen minutes later the *Pueblo* reported her position again: 39-12 N; 128-21 E. She added one sentence: "They plan to open fire on us."

What had happened during that fourteen minutes? Did the *Pueblo* try to fire back? Had the North Koreans actually now opened fire? Had they fired shots across the bow? We don't know.

Later we learned that after that last message Rear Admiral Frank L. Johnson, Commander Naval Forces Japan, placed a call to the Fifth Air Force in Japan to request assistance. The Air Force commander, Lieutenant General Seth McKee, alerted the 18th Tactical Fighter Wing on Okinawa and initiated a call to Commander in Chief Pacific Air Force in Honolulu. Shortly before 3 P.M., the Fifth Air Force ordered several aircraft sent from Okinawa to Osan, South Korea, for reservicing there and deployment to the scene. The planes were launched shortly after 4 P.M., but while en route both the Fifth Air Force and Commander in Chief Pacific Air Force concluded that they could not reach the *Pueblo* before darkness nor while she was still in international waters. Flight time from Okinawa to the scene was one hour and thirty-three minutes; from Yokota, Japan, one hour and forty-five minutes. Sunset was at 5:36 P.M.

At 1:45 P.M., the *Pueblo's* next message was received. From different relay stations slightly different versions were received at the Joint Reconnaissance Center.

One read: "We are being boarded. Initiating emergency destruction of classified equipment. Request help: SOS."

A second: "We are being boarded. SOS. SOS. Ship holding emergency destruction of classified publications and equipment. Request help. SOS."

The press soon was to demand copies of all messages sent by the *Pueblo* and relevant to the *Pueblo* case. Their argument was not complicated: the American people had a right to know what had happened to the *Pueblo,* and they could not be certain that they were getting the full story unless the government released every message.

While I understand this viewpoint, there were several reasons why we thought it would be unwise to release all the messages.

One involved security and the reluctance of the communicators to disseminate word-for-word copies of encrypted messages because of the potential assistance to opposition cryptogrammatists, another the public confusion which would have been caused by the various versions of one original transmission, a third the difficulties in handling publicly the large volume of traffic involved and a fourth the fact that confidential recommendations of a commander to his superior are not necessarily any of the public's business. I cannot see that the public's right to know includes the right to all raw data and each military message. The full file—all fifty-two pages—was given to the appropriate committees of Congress, to be studied by Democrats and Republicans, friends of the administration and foes, Doves and Hawks. In my view, the House and the Senate adequately represented the people in this regard.

At 1:52 came the message: "We are being escorted into probably Wonsan."

At 2:03: "We have been requested to follow into Wonsan. Have three wounded and one man with leg blown off. Have not used weapons or uncovered .50-caliber machine guns. Destroying all key lists and as much electronics equipment as possible. How about some help? These guys mean business. Do not intend to offer any resistance."

Another version of this included two other sentences: "Have sustained small wound in rectum. Do not know how long will be able to keep up circuit and do not know if communications spaces will be entered."

Why had weapons not been used? How much of the classified gear was destroyed? Did the North Koreans get anything of value? How serious was the wound? Was it definitely the Captain who was wounded? How did the man lose his leg? We don't know.

The *Pueblo* reported next at 2:25 that almost everything had been destroyed and that she was keeping the communications circuit open as long as possible. She said further: "Have been directed to come to all stop at 230532Z [2:32 P.M. in Korea]. Destruct[ion] incomplete. Several pubs [publications] will be compromised."

Another version of that message included: "Being boarded at this time."

Were there two boardings, one reported in the 1:45 message and a second now at 2:25? Does this mean they were able to keep themselves locked up in the communications spaces for forty minutes while the Koreans were on the ship? Doesn't this indicate a hand-to-hand fight on the ship? How do you explain that she said once that almost everything had been destroyed and then that destruction was incomplete? We don't know.

The final message received from the *Pueblo* also included the 2:32 P.M. figure: "Four men injured and one critically. Going off air now. Time 230532Z. Destroying this gear."

How did the earlier message that she had been directed to come to all stop at 2:32 fit in with this message that she was going off the air at 2:32? We could not explain these possible inconsistencies to ourselves at that time, let alone to the public.

As Dan and I worked, our objective was not to try to tell the entire story in one hurried announcement. We were trying to get the main facts out as rapidly as possible, to be as certain as we could that our account was accurate, to avoid any misleading statements, to keep the release short enough so that newspapers would use the full text but long enough to pre-empt press speculation and to write it so that State would clear it without delay. And we wanted to provide the facts as we knew them before the North Koreans broke the story their way. Of course there were hundreds of unanswered questions, but we could not give the people information we did not have.

At 4:50 A.M., back in my own office with the background material for a press release, I took ten minutes out to telephone Julian Scheer, Assistant Administrator of the National Aeronautics and Space Administration, regarding his airplane and reporter in Thule. This was not absolutely necessary, but as long as we were up all night in the Pentagon it seemed fair that some of our government associates should share the dawn with us. Julian behaved like the professional that he is, and Lieutenant Colonel Brown arranged for him to use our communications system to talk to the senior NASA official aboard the plane in Thule. After that one conversation with him, I went back to the Pueblo and am not certain to this day what became of the reporter. Sooner or later, I presume, he was flown out on something. I certainly hope so.

At 6:25, while drafting the statement to meet his 7 A.M. deadline, I called Secretary McNamara at home to discuss with him whether we were going to identify the Pueblo as an intelligence collector, and whether he had asked Secretary Rusk if he wanted us to say that State had been in touch with the Soviet Union, as I knew it had.

At 7:10 the Secretary buzzed me on the hot line from his office and asked that I join him, bringing along the completed draft of the proposed release.

Again we discussed the identification of the ship. Both of us considered it essential that we tell the people, from the outset, that the Pueblo was in the intelligence business. McNamara's own inclination had been to identify the Liberty from the beginning, he had permitted himself to be talked out of it that time and he was not prepared to succumb to the same arguments this time. Neither was I.

There was, however, a powerful new argument against the identification. Eighty-three Americans were in the hands of the North Koreans. What would an official United States acknowledgment of the ship as an intelligence collector mean to them? Would it cost their lives? Might it cost their lives?

We had no way of knowing how the North Koreans would react, or what the crew was telling them already. It was possible that a flat announcement by the United States might help the crew members, perhaps causing the North Koreans to refrain from torturing them for information our government already had admitted publicly.

But it was fruitless for McNamara and me to try to approach the problem from the standpoint of the crew's safety. Too many unknowns were in the equation; we did not have the basis for even an intelligent estimate of what the Communists would do if we did declare the ship an intelligence collector or what they would do if we did not. That being so, we could weigh the decision only from the standpoint of the government, and we both felt strongly that we could not this time put out another *Liberty*-type cover story.

The Secretary agreed also on the necessity for speed, before the North Koreans came blasting forward with something that was one-quarter fact and three-quarters fiction. He made two changes in our draft of the proposed release, telephoned the Secretary of State to check additional points with him—thus saving several hours of low-echelon coordination and clearance —and informed the White House of what we were doing.

Under ordinary circumstances an important news release requires days of work and extensive coordination. If a Navy matter, the first draft would be prepared by the office of the admiral who was the Navy's Chief of Information, in conjunction with the relevant experts on that particular announcement—antisubmarine warfare, logistics, manpower or whatever. The Navy would decide how it wanted to tell the story, what points to emphasize, what background to include, what new information to release. Security would be a consideration in a statement about a new weapons system; international sensitivity in an announcement of a new foreign base for nuclear submarines; legal rights of an individual in a dramatic personnel case. If particularly important, the draft would be submitted to the Chief or Vice Chief of Naval Operations and, finally, to the Secretary of the Navy.

It would then be offered to our office, where it would be checked for accuracy, omissions, language and tone. Was the Navy leaving out something important simply because it did not want to acknowledge error? Did the wording suggest that this tragedy never would have happened if the Secretary of Defense had not cut the Navy's budget last year? Was the draft a gentle plug for expanding the bombing of North Vietnam or an indirect sales pitch for a weapon the Secretary of Defense already had disapproved? Was it, in brief, a Navy announcement or a Department of Defense announcement?

Our people would circulate the draft to appropriate civilians and military officers in the Office of the Secretary of Defense— Systems Analysis if it concerned force structures; International Security Affairs if other nations were affected; Research and Engineering if a new weapon was being announced. Acting first as coordinators and middlemen, our office would try to produce a draft satisfactory to the Navy and to all interested elements of OSD. This was sometimes impossible. Sometimes, in the end, my Director of Defense Information (or Director of Plans and Programs if this were a long-range project rather than a current news announcement) would rewrite the release as he thought best and distribute it internally in proposed final form.

The responsibility for the release of information in the Pentagon belonged to the Assistant Secretary of Defense (Public Affairs). The draft from the Navy was nothing more than a recommendation to us, even though the Chief of Naval Operations and Secretary of the Navy had approved it, just as the entire naval budget was nothing more than a recommendation to the Secretary of Defense. Relevant Assistant Secretaries of Defense could appeal to me if they were displeased with the final draft, and so could the Secretary of the Navy, but the decision was mine.

If any of these officials felt deeply enough, they could, of course, take the issue to the Secretary or Deputy Secretary of Defense, for whom we all worked. Rarely would they win, for if the matter were that important, I probably had already discussed it privately with the Secretary. One of the built-in advantages enjoyed by the Assistant Secretary of Defense for Public Affairs is that he is apt to see the Secretary and Deputy Secretary more often than any other high official in the building.

If the release involved our relations with another nation, as many did, our draft would be submitted to the Department of State for review and clearance. State's contribution would be confined to the international aspects of the release, over which they had the final say. Not until we heard from them would the announcement be released.

In practice, many of these coordination moves were made simultaneously. Our people would work informally with the Navy at lower echelons before a draft went to the Chief of Naval Operations. The Assistant Secretary of Defense (International Security Affairs) would be in touch with the Assistant Secretary of State for the geographic region involved, and I would be in touch with the Assistant Secretary of State (Public Affairs) during the drafting process. Mechanics of coordination were affected enormously by the importance of the release and the time factors. On an urgent matter, top officials became action officers and draftsmen. In our office, for example, Dick Fryklund was our high-level contact with the Navy and Marine Corps and Dan Henkin our contact with the Army and Air Force. In a crisis it was not unusual for Dick to meet around a table with the Secretary of the Navy or the Chief of Naval Operations and, after agreement or near-agreement, for them to walk together to the Deputy Secretary of Defense for final approval. The Deputy Secretary might then telephone the Under Secretary of State, read him the proposal and work out changes acceptable to both in a three-minute conversation.

While the high-level-crisis approach ensured the proper policy tone to a government press release, errors of fact were more likely to appear. Booby traps which normally would have been found by staff officers down the line went unnoticed.

If there had been time, input into the *Pueblo* release would have come from several elements of the Navy, the Joint Staff, the Joint Reconnaissance Center, the Assistant Secretary of Defense for International Security Affairs, my counterpart at State and his people, the Assistant Secretary of State for Far Eastern Affairs and others. A draft might have been sent to the United States Ambassador to South Korea for his comments and recommendations, and a copy to CINCPAC in Honolulu for his. Coordination of that nature was common on long-term releases.

But we could not wait on the *Pueblo*. In the Pentagon the only persons involved in the initial release were Brigadier General Steakley, Dan Henkin, the Secretary of Defense and I. At State only Secretary Rusk heard or saw the announcement before it was released.

I carried the approved draft from the Secretary's office to my own for retyping. Only a half-dozen secretaries in the building had seen enough of McNamara's left-handed scribble to be able to decipher it, and he had written in the corrections himself. The ability to read original McNamara was a secretarial status symbol in the Pentagon; it proved that one had been around long enough and worked closely enough with him to be someone of importance.

A stenographic error was made in the longitude on the first retyping, and the statement was rapidly typed again. Dan hovered over the news tickers in my office to watch for an announcement by North Korea. We did not wait for printing or mimeographing, but used Xerox machines for the first batch of copies. The press was waiting, having been alerted at home by telephone that an important statement was coming, and this announcement was given to them:

The USS PUEBLO, a Navy intelligence collection auxiliary ship, was surrounded by North Korean patrol boats and boarded by an armed party in international waters in the Sea of Japan shortly before midnight EST last night.

The United States Government acted immediately to establish contact with North Korea through the Soviet Union.

When the Pueblo was boarded, its reported position was approximately 25 miles from the mainland of North Korea.

The ship reported the boarding took place at 127 degrees, 54.3 minutes east longitude; 39 degrees, 25 minutes north latitude. The time was 11:45 P.M. EST.

The ship's complement consists of 83, including six officers and 75 enlisted men and two civilians.

At approximately 10 P.M. EST, a North Korean patrol boat approached the Pueblo. Using international signals, it requested the Pueblo's nationality. The Pueblo identified herself as a U.S. ship. Continuing to use flag signals, the patrol boat said: "Heave to or I will open fire on you." The Pueblo replied: "I am in international waters." The patrol boat circled the Pueblo.

Approximately one hour later, three additional patrol craft appeared. One of them ordered: "Follow in my wake; I have a pilot aboard." The four ships closed in on the Pueblo, taking different positions on her bow, beam and quarter. Two MIG aircraft were also sighted by the Pueblo circling off the starboard bow.

One of the patrol craft began backing toward the bow of the Pueblo with fenders rigged. An armed boarding party was standing on the bow.

The Pueblo radioed at 11:45 P.M. that she was being boarded by North Koreans.

At 12:10 A.M. EST today, the Pueblo reported that she had been requested to follow the North Korean ships into Wonsan and that she had not used any weapons.

The final message from the Pueblo was sent at 12:32 A.M. It reported that it had come to "all stop" and that it was "going off the air."

The Pueblo is designated the AGER-2. It is a modified auxiliary light cargo ship (AKL).

The Pueblo is 179 feet long and 33 feet wide, with displacement of 906 tons. It has a 10.2 foot draft. Its maximum speed is 12.2 knots.

In that initial announcement was a major error. It concerned, unfortunately, the single most important point—the location of the ship when captured.

The *Pueblo* was not 25 miles from the mainland when it was boarded, as the statement said. It was 25 miles from Wonsan. But Wonsan was on the westward inner side of a deep scoop into the coastline which is Wonsan Bay. The actual distance of the ship from the mainland when seized was 17 miles (16.3 nautical miles), not 25.

I was to blame. My first telephone conversation with Brigadier General Steakley had popped out of my mind as we drafted the statement at 6 A.M., despite the time we had spent during the night plotting and measuring figures on charts in the Joint Reconnaissance Center.

We did not catch the error until a reporter came to my office to point out the inconsistency between the twenty-five-mile figure in our announcement and the position he had plotted from our latitude and longitude figures. The announcement was corrected and the Pentagon press immediately advised of the error, but by then the figure of twenty-five miles had been rocketed around the world by the wire services, who were accurately quoting my inaccurate statement. The reporter, working for a morning newspaper, with no deadline for twelve hours, had time to plot his own position. The wire service reporters did not.

Having formally put the government of the United States on the record before the world with a major misstatement on an issue of international importance, I was sick.

While dreading the necessity of telling the Secretary, I had to let him know what I had done so he could fill in Secretary Rusk and the President. I walked back to his office, shocked and discouraged, and wondering how much damage I had caused. McNamara listened to the facts, interrupted my apology, noted that I had been up all night, pointed out that he had read and approved the statement personally, added that he was aware of the right mileage figure and should have corrected it, and accepted the full blame. In any case, he said, I had been wise enough to put the actual latitude and longitude figures in the statement, they showed clearly the exact position of the ship and the error was therefore unimportant. He dismissed it with a wave of his hand.

This was typical McNamara. The phrase "second-guess" is not in his vocabulary. He does not work personally with a great many people in his management of an organization, but he puts full trust and confidence in those with whom he does work, he will support them with 100 percent of his strength 100 percent of the time and he is, in dealings with them, the most gracious and compassionate of men. From a work standpoint, of course, he is some kind of a nut, but that is a different issue.

With a few exceptions, the Pentagon press was also understanding, sensing that our inclusion of the latitude and longitude indicated we were not trying to mislead them. But many other Washington newsmen were not as sympathetic, and the editorial writers seized upon the change from twenty-five miles to seventeen miles as evidence of our duplicity. I could not blame them.

(This error caused only a ripple compared with another to come later on the same basic point. I was, unfortunately, also responsible for it.)

Otherwise, the statement was a good one. Despite the haste with which it had been put together, it included the basic facts available to us from the *Pueblo*'s messages. Reporters, Congressmen, editorial writers and the public were not satisfied with that amount of information, which was natural enough, but we had little else of value from the ship. Such bits and pieces as there were—the timing of the calls for help, the various reports on injuries—were given out in response to inquiries. From the time of the 2:32 P.M. message until the crew of the USS *Pueblo* crossed the Bridge of No Return in Korea ten months later, however, we were to have no more information from the ship's company. That many newsmen chose not to believe this truth made it no less true.

We did beat the North Koreans with our announcement. They were out with their own version at 9:47, broadcast over Pyong

Yang radio and recorded by the United States. It said, in part:

Today a naval vessel of our People's Army captured an armed spy boat of the U.S. imperialist aggressor force which intruded . . . into the territorial waters of the Republic and was carrying out hostile activities.

This was our first alert that the Koreans were basing their case on intrusion into territorial waters.

It did not take long for speculation to begin on the course of action to be taken. The Associated Press wrote:

The range of actions under consideration was understood to include the possibility of retaliatory strike against a military target or targets in North Korea, although State Department officials generally soft-pedaled that speculation in the first hours after the seizure of the ship became known.

The AP thus raised the strawman of retaliation and disposed of it, all in the same sentence.

The press naturally wanted a list of the crew members. We promised that the Navy would produce one as soon as all next-of-kin had been notified, which raised an issue of constant controversy between the press and the military establishment. The military services feel that the next-of-kin should learn of injury, death or capture of a serviceman from the government, not from newspapers or television broadcasts. Some of the press argues that the Pentagon has no right to withhold the names of casualties when a disaster has occurred. On this point I backed the services in every instance over four years. The press, in my view, is wrong.

Another controversial personnel decision in the *Pueblo* case concerned how much information we would give the press on each of the detained crewmen. We accepted the Navy's recommendation and limited it to the information the men themselves might reveal under the prisoner-of-war code—name, rank and serial number.

Most members of the professional Pentagon press understood this, but many other newsmen around the country and their editors were extremely upset that we would not disclose more about the men—and many were abusive to the military information officers carrying out their orders.

The policy was adopted chiefly to protect the prisoner (or "detainee") and secondarily to protect his wife and family at home. If, abiding by the code, he was refusing to tell his captors that he had gone to Shaker Heights High School or that he had won the Science Award there, we felt it made no sense for the Pentagon to give the North Koreans this information via the U.S. press, enabling the jailers to say: "While you are being stupid and stubborn about your past, your superiors in Washington are handing out this information to the whole world." We felt also that any personal facts released by the Pentagon could make the interrogation harder on the prisoner. "Why won't you admit that you were an electronics specialist five years ago? We know it already. We know everything about you. We know that your wife is Joan and that your son Mark is four and your daughter Laura is eleven."

Additionally, we felt that widespread publication of lists of home towns, home addresses and wives' names could lead to harassment of the families—by well-wishers, crusaders, elements of the press and the despicable creatures who prey upon war widows and wives of servicemen overseas with obscene telephone calls and other unsavory approaches.

Editors and reporters who did not accept our reasoning argued that all this information was in the public domain, that it was bureacratic idiocy for the Department to pretend that the identification of a man's high school was classified information, and that we were, once again, managing the news and concealing legitimate information from the American people. While this was a minority view, included in that minority were some of the most influential newspaper and television news organizations.

Some of the press picked up the challenge, tracked down hometown information on the men and their families and printed it. We had no means of stopping them, but less of this material appeared than would have had we collected it all together and released it. I still regard our position as the correct one. We did not hide behind a security argument and claim that the information was classified; we simply declined to give it out on the grounds that it might be injurious to the men captured by the North Koreans.

The names of the men and their serial numbers were released to the press January 24, the day after the incident. Our announcement included the information that the name of one man had been withheld because of difficulty in locating his next-of-kin, and the name of another kept out at the specific request of his next-of-kin. Great interest, of course, was expressed by the press on casualties, and while we were even more interested than the newsmen, our information was scanty.

One message read:

"Have three men wounded and one man with leg blown off. Have not used weapons or uncovered .50-caliber mach. Destroying classified equipment."

An earlier version of that message, from another station:

"Have three men wounded and one man with leg blown off destroying classified equipment."

And a different message:

"Four men injured and one critically."

With two versions of one message and one of a second, we could not tell how many casualties the *Pueblo* had suffered. Were there three "wounded" plus a man with his leg blown off? Or was he one of the three? Were the four who were "injured" the same as the three who were "wounded," or was the *Pueblo* distinguishing between men hurt in combat and men hurt by other means? Did the man lose his leg while destroying classified equipment, perhaps in an explosion, or were those two unrelated facts and two separate sentences?

A credibility problem developed over that last point. As a result of a poor briefing given the House Armed Services Committee by a military officer—or inattention by some members of the committee—a few Congressmen received the impression that one man definitely had lost a leg through an explosion while he was getting rid of classified gear. This was soon leaked to the press by members of the committee. The reporters, therefore, were hearing privately from senior Congressmen that some equipment had been blown up and that one brave crew member had lost a leg in the process, while our people were insisting publicly that we could not verify any such report.

While responding in writing to scores of queries from newsmen that first day, the Secretary, the Deputy Secretary and I all deliberately avoided a face-to-face meeting with the press. It was a marginal decision. More than a hundred reporters naturally were demanding that someone from the Pentagon see them and that someone appear before the television cameras. In our minds was the question of whether the United States government would gain or lose from a press conference. This was an international crisis. Plans involving military force were being considered. The lives of the crew were at stake. We did not ourselves have answers to many of the most pertinent inquiries. Many touchy international questions required careful coordination with State before they could be answered. Many military questions involving the disposition of our forces could be answered if we were not going to retaliate, but should not be answered if we were going to take military action.

The issue was not whether press conferences and personal confrontations between government officials and the press are desirable but whether there need be immediate personal confrontations at the time of every major news event at the desire of the press and on the timetable of the press. The press has a responsibility to the people, but so does the government.

Rightly or wrongly, we decided against an early press conference, relying instead on dozens of written responses to the reporters' questions which were issued that first afternoon and evening by Colonel Bankson, who had succeeded Brigadier General Sidle as Director of Defense Information. Among the individual questions and answers were these:

Q: What instructions did Pueblo ask and what instructions did it receive?

A: None.

Q: Did the commander of the Pueblo request instructions before permitting the North Koreans to board the vessel without resistance?

A: The commander requested no instructions. The circumstances of the boarding are not known.

Q: At whose instruction did the skipper of Pueblo surrender to North Koreans and permit the craft to be boarded?

A: The circumstances of the seizure of the Pueblo and the subsequent actions are not known.

Q: Was the Pueblo under control of the Seventh Fleet Commander or was she under JSC [Joint Chiefs of Staff], DoD [Department of Defense], DIA [Defense Intelligence Agency] or NSA [National Security Agency] control?

A: She was under CINCPAC [Commander in Chief Pacific] control exercised through the normal chain of command for Pacific naval forces.

Q: Who does the ship operate for? Navy? National Security Agency? Other?

A: Navy.

Q: Did the Pueblo skipper ask permission to scuttle?

A: No.

Q: Who ordered the Pueblo to submit to capture?

A: No one. The ship was boarded.

Q: Why did Pueblo not use weapons to order patrol craft from area?

A: We have no information on this.

Q: When did Pueblo report it had been accosted by the North Koreans patrol boat? To whom did she report? Did the Pueblo ask for help? Was help dispatched? If not, why not?

A: The Pueblo made periodic reports to higher naval authorities. She asked for help at the time of the boarding.

Q: Did the Pueblo resist? If not, why not?

A: The Pueblo reported she did not fire weapons. We have no further information on this point.

Q: (a) Were the civilians aboard the Pueblo NSA technicians? (b) Was the ship being operated by the Navy for NSA? (c) What was the Pueblo position when the first North Korean patrol boat made contact at 10 P.M.?

A: (a) No, Navy employees—hydrographers. (b) No, for the Navy. (c) Virtually the same location as the one announced.

Q: How far out from shore do the North Koreans claim as territorial waters?

A. Twelve miles.

Q: Why was no attempt made by the men of the Pueblo to scuttle their boat or to destroy what must be highly secret gear?

A: No comment.

Q: Do you have names of skipper, home town, etc., and for crew? Will you release this information now?

A: When the next-of-kin have all been notified.

Q: What were the specific missions assigned to the Pueblo?

A: No additional comment beyond "intelligence collection."

Q: How many people were there in the boarding party? How were they armed?

A: We have no information on this.

Q: Is there any information to indicate that the crewmen or officers of the USS Pueblo had any contact with the Japanese peace group Beheiren while in a Japanese port?

A: None to our knowledge.

Q: Did the North Korean ships open fire and did the Pueblo crew sustain any casualties? If so, how many and what type?

A: Messages from the Captain do not specifically refer to gunfire. However, one message did refer to four injured crew members, one critically. In another message, he referred to them as wounded. There is no additonal information. We do not know the identity of the men or the cause of the injuries.

Q: After the USS Liberty incident last June, were procedures for our "radio research"—vessels in the sense of operating distances of standing instructions regarding resistance—changed? If so, can any of these changes be outlined generally?

A: No comment.

Q: What air and naval strength could hit Wonsan?

A: Classified information.

Q: Was the President alerted? When?

A: (Referred to White House.)

Q: How long had the Pueblo been in the Sea of Japan?

A: Since January 8.

Q: Were there any U.S. aircraft available to reach the area during incident?

A: No comment.

Q: Were any vessels or submarine or aircraft from the Soviet Union reported in the vicinity by the USS Pueblo in the 24 hours preceding the incident? If so, what type and when?

A: No comment.

Q: Has it been clearly established that the Pueblo was in international waters at all times? And is there any disagreement between North Korea–South Korea–U.S. as to boundaries of international waters there?

A: At no time did the Pueblo violate territorial waters.

Q: Does Pueblo and/or other intelligence ships regularly patrol the general area of the incident?

A: No comment.

Q: Did the U.S. Eighth Army [in Korea] assume alert status?

A: No comment.

Q: Who got word first on the incident?

A: No comment.

Q: What are the names of other ships in this class?

A: No comment.

Q: What are the Navy regulations or orders on defending a United States ship?

A: Rules of engagement are classified.

In retrospect, some of those answers were weak, but, under the circumstances, most were satisfactory. Consider the "No comments":

We could not discuss with the press changes in operating procedures for intelligence-collection ships. . . . The dispatching of the aircraft was highly classified, since military actions were still being considered. . . . We did not want to pinpoint publicly the location of our carriers. . . . It did not seem wise to discuss the alert status of the Eighth Army; the alert status of any unit is always classified. . . . The intelligence people were opposed to giving out names of other ships in the *Pueblo's* class.

There was no sound reason for not having disclosed who was notified first; probably our people did not know whether General Wheeler was notified before or after Secretary McNamara, and someone did not consider it important enough to track down the first day. Generally speaking, however, the answers and the statement covered the basic facts.

But one of them was disastrous, and its release was a dreadful mistake which did great damage to the United States.

The sentence was given to newsmen by the Director of Defense Information. But while the Assistant Secretary sees very few of the answers to the 35,000 queries handled by his staff each year, this one was an exception. I saw the exact language which had been prepared for the response and I approved it personally before it was released to the press. The sentence was this:

"At no time did the *Pueblo* violate territorial waters."

I have no satisfactory explanation as to why it was made; certainly there was no pressure from the Secretary of Defense, the White House or any individual or agency to make it.

The factor most responsible was our concentration upon the immediate problem and my failure to think beyond it. It is fair to recall, I believe, that the basic question in the minds of almost everyone that day, inside and outside the government, was the one I had asked General Steakley in the middle of the night many hours earlier: "Where was it?" Was this piracy or was it not? Was this as outrageous as it appeared or was there a better explanation? Had these people really come out into international waters with their ten-cent gunboats and taken over a ship of the United States Navy, or were we getting only half of the story?

My own initial reaction as Dan and I drove to the Pentagon in the middle of the night was that we were missing some essential information. I was not overly impressed by the first reports to General Steakley. First reports, as I have mentioned, are invariably erroneous and incomplete. Someone had fouled up somewhere, and we were going to have to dig deeply enough to find out who and where. The preliminary account didn't make sense. Even Communist countries, even fifth-rate Communist countries, did not behave this way.

After two hours in the Joint Reconnaissance Center I had changed my mind. We had much more than a fragmentary first report from an upper-echelon commander; we had a series of classified messages from the ship itself.

The *Pueblo* was in international waters when approached by the Korean ships that morning and when seized. We were convinced of that. The commanding officer had radioed his position, and we had no reason to think that he was lying deliberately or that he was incapable of knowing his true position. In addition, we were in possession of independent evidence which was to be disclosed to the public within twenty-four hours, after the Secretary of Defense made a policy decision which stunned the intelligence community. While the people and the press were not aware of that additional evidence the first day, we were.

Another possibility seen by the public was that the *Pueblo* had been in territorial waters on a highly secret mission under highly secret orders, had been discovered and was fleeing with the North Koreans in pursuit at the time of the seizure. This was not the case; no such secret orders had been issued. Again, the press and public could not be certain of this, but we could.

A third possibility was that the *Pueblo* had drifted accidentally into territorial waters, or had entered them indiscreetly on its own initiative, and was racing seaward when boarded. This did not fit the known facts. The commanding officer had reported the initial encounter with two ships the day before, after which he had reported another eighteen contacts during the night. In a series of messages, he had then reported the seizure. It was inconceivable that in between these messages he would have transgressed into territorial waters, thus triggering the boarding, without also reporting that transgression. The public might wonder whether we had received such additional messages, but we knew that we had not.

And so all night and all day the questioning and answering in our minds went this way: Was the ship in international waters when seized? Yes. Are you certain? Yes. Could you be wrong? No. Was she chased into international waters? No. Are you certain? Yes. Then we can say that at no time was the *Pueblo* in territorial waters? Yes.

No. That is where we went so wrong. A "yes" answer from the United States government to that final question was unforgivable. We had not heard from the *Pueblo* for thirteen days, we had no way of knowing where she had been for those thirteen days, and we had no justification whatever for stating to the public that at no moment during those days had she, in any way, by any error, come within twelve miles of North Korea.

We knew that there was not a grain of evidence to suggest that she had done so, and that her orders forbade her to do so, and that no radio messages had been sent by either the *Pueblo* or the North Koreans indicating that she had done so, and that the commanding officer would have been a fool to have done so. We were as confident as a nation could be that she had been in international waters when seized and that she had not violated territorial waters the day of the seizure, when she was sending messages. But we could not make the flat statement—which I made—that at no time had she violated territorial waters.

So far as we knew a year later, it was a valid and true statement, but that was not the point. It should not have been made. It could not have been defended before the press, the public, the Congress or the Communists. If anyone at the time had asked the simple question, "How do you know?" we would have had no answer.

In fact, no one did ask that simple question. Not even the North Koreans asked it, in their propaganda broadcasts, or the Russians at the Security Council. They, too, apparently were thinking in terms of the day of the seizure; they were contending that the *Pueblo* was confronted only 7.6 miles from land. That was the point at issue; that was the charge we were fighting. Our statement was not challenged those first few days because everyone's attention was centered on January 23, and not the two prior weeks. None of that made the statement any more acceptable.

Not until shortly after midnight that first night, checking back over scores of answers released that day and evening, did I notice what we had done. My first thought was that in the morning we could issue a straightforward correction: "The Department of Defense erred yesterday when it stated that at no time had the USS *Pueblo* violated the territorial waters of North Vietnam.

We cannot be certain that there was no intrusion because we have insufficient evidence."

On reflection, I realized that we could not release such a statement because of its potential danger to the crew. Coming so quickly after the seizure, with emotions aroused and the North Koreans probably uncertain as to their own next actions, an official United States "admission" of any kind might result in the execution of eighty-three men. Inevitably, a statement of that type would have led to headlines around the world of this nature: "U.S. Reverses Itself On Pueblo"; "Pueblo Guilt Possible, U.S. Admits"; "Pentagon Says Spy Ship May Have Intruded." The North Koreans might not have reacted to them at all. But they also might have seized upon them, linked them to a false "confession" from one of the crew and used both as their rationale for cruel or deadly action. We dared not deliberately open that door in those first emotional hours, when neither country knew what it would do next.

While we did not have a wispy, gossamer suggestion of evidence that the ship had penetrated North Korean territorial waters during those thirteen days, clearly we could not repeat a statement which we could neither prove nor defend. I instructed the Director of Defense Information not to use the answer again and to inform me personally if the question was asked again. It was not. Additionally, we attempted to walk back the cat a little by writing two sentences into a new statement issued the next day to counter an alleged "confession" by the Pueblo's commanding officer. We said: "The Pueblo was under orders from the beginning of its mission to stay at least thirteen miles from North Korean territory. There is no evidence to suggest that these orders were disobeyed."

That did not constitute much of a correction, but at least it was a slight move in the right direction. The press paid no attention to the difference between that statement and the flat denial of the previous night, chiefly because they were concentrating on the seizure, possible retaliation, why no help was sent, what we might do to get back the crew and who was at fault. Secretary of State Rusk was reported in the press as telling the Senate Foreign Relations Committee that "the ship was in international waters at all times, according to every indication we have." The State Department press officer took a hard line. So did Arthur Goldberg, U.S. Ambassador to the United Nations. The Department of Defense must bear the responsibility for any statements within the government which left the impression that we knew there had never been a violation. After all, it was our ship and our information. And for the release of the initial "denial," the full responsibility was mine.

The record remained incorrect for ten days. Then, when the opening of the door seemed no longer a problem for the crew, the Secretary of Defense straightened it out. Appearing on Lawrence Spivak's *Meet the Press* program, McNamara was asked this question by Max Frankel, an outstanding newsman who was to become Washington Bureau Chief of the *New York Times*:

Q: Secretary McNamara, does the Navy know for sure that the *Pueblo* at no time entered North Korean waters?

A: No. I think we cannot say beyond a shadow of a doubt at no time during its voyage it entered North Korean waters. We can say this: I think it bears on the answer. First, the commander had the strictest of instructions to stay in international waters. We believe he did. Second, at the time of seizure we are quite positive it was in international waters. Thirdly, there was a period of radio silence appropriate to its mission from the period of roughly January 10 to January 21, and it is in that period that we lack knowledge of that until the crew and the commander are released.

Secretary Rusk, who was also on the program, added:

Well, I think we can say on that that we cannot be one thousand percent sure until we get our officers and crew back and we have a chance to interrogate them and look at the log of the ship. This was a ship peculiarly qualified to navigate with accuracy. Now it would not disturb us to let everybody know that when we get them back if we discover that they were at any point within a 12-mile limit, for example, as claimed by North Korea, despite the fact that we recognize only a three-mile limit, that we will make those facts available. We will make them available.

But we cannot do that on the basis of the testimony that we get from men who are held prisoner, or from spliced tapes of broadcasts that they are alleged to have made. We have got to get access to hard information.

And I would add that we have not a single scrap of information from any source whatever that this vessel was inside the 12-mile limit at any time during its voyage.

The press reaction was as anticipated. The Washington *Post* headline: "PUEBLO'S INTRUSION POSSIBLE, U.S. SAYS"; the lead: "The administration said for the first time yesterday that it cannot be absolutely sure that the U.S. Navy intelligence ship Pueblo did not intrude into North Korean territorial waters."

The *New York Times* also had a page one story; the headline: "US IS UNCERTAIN IF PUEBLO STAYED BEYOND 12 MILES"; and the lead: "The United States is unable to rule out the possibility that the intelligence ship Pueblo entered North Korean territorial waters at some point before she was captured, two senior Administration officials said today."

I could not quarrel with either story, and was gratified that the record had been cleared. The criticism we received was deserved. Credibility stories months later quoted our twenty-five miles versus our seventeen miles and my one-time answer versus McNamara's statement. The writers could not be faulted. The record spoke for itself; we could clarify it, as McNamara did, but we could not rewrite it. I do not know how many hundreds of thousands of words I spoke officially as Deputy Assistant Secretary of Defense and Assistant Secretary, but if I could unspeak twenty-seven, they would be eighteen in the sentence dictated to Miss Jackie Grant shortly after six o'clock on the morning of January 23, 1968—"When the *Pueblo* was boarded, its reported position was approximately twenty-five miles from the mainland of North Korea"—and nine in the one sentence I approved sometime after eight o'clock that same night—"At no time did the *Pueblo* violate territorial waters."

The facts that the latter statement was issued innocently, that it turned out to be accurate, that there was no intention to mislead the public and that the record was corrected ten days later by the Secretary himself—playing it in high key on national television—can be considered by charitable judges, but they do not erase the failure.

If we were uncertain about a prior transgression at the time, we were not certain about the location of the ship when boarded, for that information came not only from the *Pueblo* but from the North Korean vessels attacking it.

Military intelligence, as one would suspect, is a highly classified area, and within that area few activities are more closely guarded than the electronic interception of enemy messages and signals. Thousands of individuals—tens of thousands—who hold other high-security clearances are permitted no knowledge about these intercepts. They know nothing of the methods or equipment used, and they are denied access to the information collected by this means. All the rules applying to the handling of top-secret material are supplemented in this area by a huge new batch of regulations.

The reasons are obvious. The enemy or potential enemy clearly knows that we are trying to listen to his internal radio communications. That is not a secret. Therefore, he goes to a good bit of trouble to guarantee that we do not hear correctly or that we do not understand what we hear. We always want him to think he has succeeded perfectly. The less he knows about how much we know, the better off we are and the more we are going to learn about him.

The press corps, like a wife, is always more difficult when you have no logical explanation to give it for the statement you make or the position at which you have arrived. I can recall scores of instances, some minor and many major, when the government could not prove publicly the statements it knew to be true because it would not discuss the source of its information.

But so important was it to convince the people that the *Pueblo* was in international waters when unlawfully boarded and seized that Secretary McNamara ripped the classification labels from the intercepts of North Korean communications. For the only time that I can recall during my years in the Pentagon, the government decided not only to acknowledge that it had collected this information and not only to use parts of it publicly but even to quote some of it directly.

The *Pueblo*'s first-encounter message at 12:52 gave her position as 25 nautical miles from Wonsan, 16.3 nautical miles from the nearest point on the North Korean mainland on the peninsula of Hodo-Pando, 15.3 nautical miles from the Island of Ung-do. Her position, you will recall, was 39–25.3 N; 127–55.0 E.

At exactly the same time, the North Korean submarine chaser which was challenging the *Pueblo* reported her own position over her own radio to be 39 degrees, 25 minutes North latitude; 127 degrees, 56 minutes East longitude.

The two positions were within one mile of one another—the one sent to U.S. stations by the U.S. ship and the one sent to North Korean stations by the North Korean ship. And the North Korean ship put the encounter one mile farther out to sea, farther from land and farther into international waters than the U.S. ship did.

Nearly an hour later, at 1:50 P.M., the North Korean vessels reported their position as 39 degrees, 26 minutes North; 128 degrees, 02 minutes East—or about 21.3 miles from the nearest North Korean land. This was within five minutes of the time when the *Pueblo* sent word that she was being boarded.

Earlier messages from the Korean submarine chaser had been monitored, so that we knew where she had been long before the encounter began. But in no message, either by voice radio or code, did she mention the *Pueblo* until she radioed that she was approaching a three-hundred-ton American ship.

She subsequently sent this message, roughly translated in the field: "By talking this way, it will be enough to understand according to present instructions we will close down the radio, tie up the personnel, tow it and enter port at Wonsan. At present, we are on our way to boarding. We are coming in."

This intercept information was not all processed and in the Joint Reconnaissance Center those early hours that first night, and when it was available the task of responding accurately to questions from the press became more rather than less difficult, as it always did when communications intelligence was involved.

For example:

In this instance, the *Pueblo* did tell us that she was "probably" being taken to Wonsan. But assume that she had not, and that our only knowledge of where she was going had come from our intercept of the North Korean message. Under ordinary circumstances, without McNamara's decision to declassify, we could not have used that information publicly. What, then, would our choices have been to demands from the press as to what had become of our eighty-three Americans?

"No comment" would have been unsatisfactory. The President could not have lived with such a response.

"We don't know" would have been misleading, if not an outright lie, and would have done nothing to inform our people.

"We know, but we won't tell you" would have been politically impossible. Furthermore, this would have alerted the North Koreans that we were successfully intercepting their communications.

Probably the answer which would have given the best guidance to the press and still protected security would have been something like: "The incident was only twenty-five miles from Wonsan, as you know. Wonsan is the logical place for the ship to have been taken. We assume that is where it is."

That is a kindergarten example, but suggests the kind of problems the government can have in dealing with the press and public with information obtained by sensitive means.

Partly as a result of McNamara's decision to release communications intelligence, within three days the press and the people knew as much about the seizure of the *Pueblo* as the government.

To the press, three hours is a long time, leading to a missed deadline, a missed edition or a missed network news show, and three days is an eternity. But to the government, three hours usually is without real significance and three days is a short time. The collection of information in the Department of Defense is not a rapid task—and should not be. As indicated earlier, the coordination required within the government prior to the release of information is time-consuming. The bigger the crisis, the greater the public interest and the more the demand for speed. But the bigger the crisis, the more necessary is the input from the highest and busiest officials of the government—the Secretary of Defense, the Secretary of State and the President, and their closest advisers. Also, the bigger the crisis, the more elements of both State and Defense are involved.

Once the seizure story of high-seas hijacking had been told, the *Pueblo* incident became one in which State had more of a primary interest than Defense. A task force was established within the State Department to handle all aspects of the case, with representatives of the Assistant Secretaries of Defense for International Affairs and for Public Affairs assigned to it. From that point on, answers to all questions were cleared through that task force, whether the questions originated from newsmen at the Pentagon, the White House or the State Department. It was a sensible move, keeping together a band of experts working solely on the *Pueblo*, and helping prevent State, Defense and the White House from giving three different offhand answers to the same question—all based on the same facts, but each with a slightly different interpretation of those facts.

But the task force, oriented more toward the substantive view of what the country was going to do next than to responding to the press, necessarily functioned much more slowly on public affairs matters than we did that first night when the action officers on our announcement were the head of the Joint Reconnaissance Center, a Deputy Assistant Secretary of Defense, an Assistant Secretary of Defense, the Secretary of Defense and, through the telephone call to him, the Secretary of State.

Interest of the press and the people those first few days went far beyond details of the seizure and involved questions of mission approval, conduct of the commanding officer, potential military reaction and whether our world-wide defense forces were stretched too thin by Vietnam. Opinions of the top officials of the Defense Department, including Secretary McNamara and General Wheeler, were given on these issues, but not in the first seventy-two hours. On many points, they did not have before them personally in seventy-two hours all the facts on which to base opinions.

Yet the Pentagon's silence on just such issues resulted in a great many critical news stories. A typical one, in the *Wall Street Journal* of January 25, said in part:

WASHINGTON—Two days after the event, the Administration was acting as if it were in a state of complete confusion over how to respond to North Korea's seizing of the U.S. Navy's spy ship Pueblo.

At the Pentagon, Defense Department officials still were unable or unwilling to answer a host of pertinent questions about the event. They wouldn't even confirm that the 179-foot long vessel in fact rests in Wonsan harbor, even though the military has dozens of reconnaissance planes based in South Korea that presumably could locate it. They noted only that the North Koreans said it was in Wonsan Harbor.

The facts of the story were inaccurate and the military judgment of its author questionable. We did not have dozens of reconnaissance aircraft in South Korea, and if we had had, the wisdom of intruding into North Korea's air space with unarmed reconnaissance aircraft was dubious, since the North Koreans had scores of jets standing ready on their landing fields and their antiaircraft defense net was on top alert. But more important than the writer's lack of military expertise was the fact that the current system almost demands stories of this kind if government answers are not produced immediately. Instant answers make television news shows more interesting and satisfy hungry managing editors. Often as a reporter I was pressed for instant answers and often, I am sure, stories of mine were in the same vein as the one in the *Wall Street Journal*. However, I wonder whether the people might not prefer to wait a few days for more comprehensive responses. The United States government cannot avoid responsibility for its acts; there always will be time for criticism, blame and finger-pointing.

But the government today too often is pressured into shooting from the hip instead of reviewing the situation carefully and speaking more slowly with more fact, knowledge and logic. I believe leaders of the press might consider re-examining their approach in this respect. Perhaps they would conclude that they should not expect serious government answers to all the serious questions in the first forty-eight or ninety-six hours of a crisis. The government, of course, can do a better job of resisting those pressures, but it needs help. If some of the pressure were eased, as a result of more understanding from the news media, it would be less apt to blurt out answers too quickly and the public would benefit.

Consider, for example, the *Pueblo* question of who had recommended the mission, who was responsible for it and whether it was actually necessary. This was a logical question, and the public had every right to know whether approval of these sensitive operations came from a rear admiral in the field or top officials in Washington.

What were the facts?

The *Pueblo* mission was recommended by field commanders, approved by the military commander in the Pacific theater, and then considered by a committee composed of top officials of the State Department, Defense Department and intelligence agencies. These men examined the information which was to be obtained, heard intelligence officials present their assessment of the probable risk, asked themselves whether the potential gain was worth the probable risk, decided affirmatively and authorized the operation. Other missions examined by the same group at that same meeting were rejected.

Opinions may differ as to whether the group exercised sound judgment or spent sufficient time examining each case, but the approval procedures themselves were adequate, with the mission recommended at the lower levels in the field and authorized at the highest levels in Washington. A satisfactory system had been established, and the *Pueblo* mission was handled within that system.

Secretary McNamara felt that he and his counterparts bore full responsibility for the mission. While he did not personally sit with the committee which had approved it, his personal representative was there—and McNamara pointed out that he could have been there himself if he had wanted to.

Among points considered by members of the group in arriving at their decision were the current objectives of North Korea. General Wheeler believed that the Communist government was trying to pressure Seoul in every way, seeking to demonstrate how vulnerable the South Koreans were to North Korean activity, causing dissension in the South and weakening the control of the Seoul government. Two dramatic acts indicated how far the Communists were prepared to go. One was the seizure of the *Pueblo*; the other, two days earlier, was the invasion of Seoul by a party of armed raiders infiltrated from the North with the admitted assignment of assassinating the President of South Korea in the Presidential Palace.

The *Pueblo* mission was related primarily to the defense forces of North Korea. Appropriate leaders of our government felt it was important for us to know how those forces reacted, how extensive they were, what their radar coverage was like. None of the government elements assessing the mission—intelligence, uniformed military, civilian military, State—considered it of such high risk that extraordinary precautions were needed or extraordinary plans required to meet the contingency that occurred.

All this information on mission responsibility was put before the public. No secret was made of it, nor was there any effort to make a secret of it. But it was not all available within forty-eight hours. The same persons who were most involved in the approval of the mission were involved in how and whether we were going to react militarily—and in the conduct of the war in Vietnam. There would be time later for them to review the past.

Other issues were whether the *Pueblo* should have been more heavily armed, escorted by other naval ships, covered by an air cap of combat aircraft or replaced for the mission by a destroyer. Again, these were all legitimate questions, but answers to them involved examination of such additional questions as these: Could any noncombat ship be armed adequately to defend itself against opposition submarine chasers or torpedo boats? Would arming it heavily have been more or less provocative? Could the mission have been accomplished had the ship's presence been advertised from the start by escort warships? Similarly, could a destroyer, with its visibility, have accomplished the mission? How provocative would it have been to North Korea, Red China and the Soviet Union if we had deployed destroyers thirteen miles off the shoreline? What is the basic doctrine of the high seas? Dare we at any time give the impression that we acknowledge the authority of another country to control international waters? Would the sending of an escort have been a dramatic departure from the practice traditionally followed by both the United States and the Soviet Union? Might that in itself have increased the possibilities of an international incident? How would the North Koreans or other nations have reacted to an air cover? Could the ship then have performed its mission? Might the North Koreans or the Soviet Union have misunderstood the presence of U.S. jet fighters circling thirteen miles offshore? Was there a risk that the Communists might have assumed we were going to launch air strikes against them?

Opinions of McNamara, Wheeler and others in the government were made public on these points. General Wheeler was to say:

In the first place, this was clearly an act of piracy on the high seas, hijacking, and one cannot foresee such an illegal act happening. We have supported the freedom of the seas for over 100 years. In fact, one of our first wars was fought on that very principle. To escort the vessel of that type would be provocative. In terms of the requirements for forces to escort vessels such as this all over the world, the cost would be extremely high and, as a matter of fact, would require in

some cases carrier task forces deployed thousands of miles from our
shores in order to protect the vessel which should be able to proceed
freely on the high seas in accordance with international law.

But neither General Wheeler nor Secretary McNamara was
available and prepared to present publicly all his views in the first
forty-eight hours, and I was not prepared to speak for them that
quickly, either on those issues or on hundreds of others raised the
first two or three days. In time, I believe that every major question was answered by the top officials of the government for committees of Congress, and nearly every one for the public. When
the record had been completed—much of it necessarily awaited
the return of the crew—there was little or none of the story
which the people did not have from their government.

Public interest in the Pueblo incident has continued, and I still
am asked frequently about it by nongovernment friends and
associates. Was the ship really and truly in territorial waters?
Should the mission have been approved in the first place? What
about the conduct of the commanding officer? Why didn't we
send help at the beginning? Why was not more done the next
ten months?

The first question is the easiest. When I left the government
on January 20, 1969, we had learned absolutely nothing to indicate that the Pueblo was for a single instant in the territorial
waters of North Korea from the moment it left Japan until after
it was boarded and taken there by the North Koreans.

This bears on the second question: Should the mission have
been approved? Inasmuch as the ship did not intrude, the real
issue then is whether the United States government should have
anticipated piracy. In retrospect, having suffered both the Pueblo
case and the unwarranted action against a reconnaissance aircraft more than a year later, perhaps we should have—if our
intelligence had been better. It was better intelligence, of course,
that we were seeking.

Obviously, the administration misjudged the temper of the
North Koreans, and obviously the Pueblo mission should not

have been approved—although if I had been a member of the State-Defense-intelligence group assessing the gain against the risk, unquestionably I would have voted to approve it.

So far as the commanding officer is concerned, I have nothing to add to the discussion of the extremely complex issues involved in second-guessing the courses of action he chose. All the facts have been made public. Any man who risks his life for his country has my gratitude, and any man imprisoned by the North Korean Communists my compassion.

While I had little time for travel except when accompanying the Secretary, in a few public appearances around the country in 1968 I found audiences more interested in the *Pueblo* than in anything except Vietnam. And I learned something of the value of face-to-face communications with the people.

Pueblo questions were always hostile. What was the government doing about the *Pueblo* case and why weren't we doing more to get back the men? My answer was always a candid review of the decision which the administration had to make once the crew had been captured. What was the top priority? Was it retaliatory action or was it the safe return of the crew? Strong arguments were made within the government for each course. Some persons—not limited to the admirals and generals, and not by any means all of the admirals and generals—believed that it was more important to our national security to demonstrate that nations could not get away with this piracy than to secure the release of the crew. Others, including Robert McNamara, Clark Clifford and President Johnson, did not. The objective of the administration in 1968 was the safe return of the men.

Once that was established, military retaliatory action or punishment became impossible. While many military actions were proposed, some of them exotic, no one produced a military plan which would free the men. Since our objective was to get them back alive, and since we found no military means of accomplishing that, the only route left was the tedious and sometimes humiliating diplomatic one. It would take time. In past cases it had taken a year or more. But we were hopeful that it would work.

It was my opinion, I told questioners, that the President had chosen wisely. Not once did I find a critical questioner who did not nod his head in understanding and agreement. Their frustration, of course, remained, and often their anger that the ship had been sent there in the first place.

I was also convinced personally that no military response on the day of the seizure could have rescued the men. With instant reaction, we might have been able to sink the *Pueblo* before it docked in Wonsan, at the cost of the lives of the crew, a probable air war with North Korean jets stationed there and possibly a greatly expanded military action in Korea, but I could not see how that would have been to our advantage.

It was a tragic incident, and the one most certain fact is that the United States was not prepared for the event which took place. We were not prepared for the seizure of this ship, operating legally and in international waters, as similar ships of our nation had operated for a decade and a half and as similar ships of the Soviet Union were operating in many areas of the world at that instant. If we had been wiser, we might have been prepared, but we were not.

No one in government attempted to convince the press or the people otherwise. Robert McNamara was perfectly candid on that major issue. "I think the point is that we don't maintain contingency plans to react to hijacking on the high seas in all the situations in which that is possible, and there wasn't such a plan here," he said.

All these statements and views were to become part of the public record—but not in the first twenty-four or forty-eight or seventy-two hours.

It is my belief that the Department of Defense did present the facts of the *Pueblo* to the people in a responsible, accurate and reasonably rapid manner. I know that it did not attempt to mislead the people. With the exception of my own two errors, and particularly the second, I believe it did not mislead them.

It told as much as it knew as quickly as it could. It acted wisely in disclosing the communications intercepts. It presented the views of its highest-ranking officials on all the major issues.

I do not know whether my conclusions in this regard are shared by a majority of interested and objective citizens. My guess would be that they are not. I fear that we communicated to the people neither our candor nor the facts of our case. And while we must assume full responsibility for our failure, I believe contributing external reasons for it were the impatience of the press and the insistence by the press upon too many answers to too many serious and complex questions too quickly, and the intolerant reaction of some of the press when those answers were not given soon enough to please them.

Clark Clifford
and the Beginning
of Disengagement

February, 1968-January, 1969

It is not an exaggeration to say that President Johnson's designation of Clark McAdams Clifford as Secretary of Defense to succeed Robert S. McNamara was accepted without enthusiasm by the McNamara people in the Pentagon. This was not entirely because it was Clark Clifford; no replacement for McNamara would have been really welcome except for Cyrus Vance, automatically assumed by us to be McNamara's own personal first choice, but known by all of us to be prevented from returning to Washington for full-time service at that time by an excruciatingly painful back, a desire to rejoin his family after six and a half years of government service and professional commitments to his law firm. Our second choice was Paul Nitze, respected as Deputy Secretary and eminently qualified by international experience, administrative background and military knowledge to run the Defense Establishment. But no other name would have pleased us; we were McNamara men. Many of us had been with him the entire seven years, and we had all been brought into the Department by him and were serving because he had recommended us to the President.

The tenure of McNamara civilians in the Pentagon was an all-time record. As a reporter during the Eisenhower administration, I wrote a story commenting on the short service of the top presidential appointees, service which at that time averaged only seventeen months in the Pentagon. But in early 1968 when

McNamara left, a large percentage of the people holding the highest civilian offices had been there the entire time since 1961. Part of this was due to his insistence on a minimum four-year commitment from his early appointees, part because he promoted from within whenever feasible, part because of the fascination of the times and part because he was held in such esteem by the men working for him.

Many of us believed that Robert McNamara was the most brilliant man in the government; all of us considered him as dedicated a person as we knew; none of us had met anyone with more integrity. He had earned several hundred thousand dollars a year as a manager, and was worth it. His value in this regard existed entirely apart from his views on bombing North Vietnam, the North Atlantic Treaty Organization or strategic nuclear warfare; it resided in his ability to organize and run a $75-billion-a-year operation.

He is a man of compassion and deep emotion, magnificent instincts and great humor. Many who worked for him would resign their present posts and report back immediately if he returned to government and asked them to serve. The farewell gift selected for him by a group of extremely practical, tough, hardheaded officials was a beautiful piece of crystal, with the miniature sword Excalibur in it, and on the attached card were these lines from *The Canterbury Tales:*

> A Knight their was, and that a worthy man,
> That fro the tyme that he first bigan
> To ryden out, he loved chivalrye,
> Trouthe and honour, fredom and curteisye. . . .
> He was a verray parfit gentil Knight.

Millions of televiewers watched Bob McNamara unable to respond at the White House ceremony at which President Johnson honored him with the Freedom Medal, and at least a dozen of us were affected with similar emotion at our private farewell. The Congress, the press and the people have made their contemporary assessment of McNamara as a Secretary of Defense. Many have called him the greatest Cabinet officer in our national history. Some blame him for Vietnam, for which they will never forgive him. Among retired military personnel are men who regarded his managerial changes as disastrous for the armed forces. Each person obviously is entitled to his own judgment; we who worked closely with him had ours.

I missed McNamara's farewell telephone call the afternoon of his final day, for after public departure ceremonies and a private buffet luncheon I left the Pentagon in the early afternoon to walk in the rain. Crossing Memorial Bridge into Washington in a cold winter drizzle, I went down Pennsylvania Avenue, past the White House and the nearby Albee Building at Fifteenth and G streets where the *Plain Dealer* office had been, stopping occasionally for a drink or a cup of coffee. I am not a walker, but that day I ambled about the city alone in the rain until after nine o'clock in the evening. My thoughts were diffuse and my dominant emotion was sadness, feeling that the nation had lost one of its great public officials, regretting that the people had so little understanding of his stature as a human being, damning the darkness of Vietnam for having obscured so much of what he had accomplished. Selfishly, I thought, too, of the unique period ending in my own life, knowing that I would not again have the opportunity of working so closely with men of the caliber of Cyrus Vance and Bob McNamara.

And who had the President named to replace Robert McNamara? He had picked an intimate friend; a personal crony; a fabulously successful Washington attorney with, the newsmen wrote, fabulously successful connections. He had picked a man who, it seemed, had never really run anything except his law firm—a firm which, however successful financially, consisted of only a handful of lawyers.

True, the man was not totally ignorant of defense matters. For several years he had worked closely with two Presidents as a personal adviser on a great many issues, some of them involving the military establishment. He had served as a member and chairman of the Foreign Intelligence Advisory Board. During his White House tour with President Truman twenty years earlier, he was the architect of the original legislation creating the Department of Defense, and his friends and associates for two decades had been men at the highest levels of government wrestling with defense and international problems.

Compared to a Nitze, a Vance or a Harold Brown, however, his current defense background fell woefully short. But even this was not the prime concern of those of us on the McNamara team. What frightened us most was that Clark Clifford was believed to have Neanderthal ideas on the war in Vietnam.

The Republican State Chairman of Connecticut charged that the Defense Department had been turned over to a "political operator" who had "no apparent qualifications for the job."

Darrell Garwood, one of UPI's Pentagon reporters, wrote that he was "regarded as more Hawkish than McNamara."

The Associated Press described him as "reputedly a hard liner on the Vietnam war."

While not influenced by the comments of Radio Prague, we noted them: "Contrary to his predecessor, Clifford does not doubt the morals, methods or purpose of the Vietnam War; he is a Hawk in the fullest sense of the word."

Neil Sheehan of the *New York Times* quoted an unidentified "senior military leader": "He is a lawyer and a political operator, and I would expect him to behave like a lawyer and a political operator."

In his "Personality Parade" in the Sunday supplement, *Parade*, Walter Scott wrote:

> Clark Clifford is a handsome man of great charm and courtly courtesy. Beneath the veneer, however, lies a calculating and pragmatic mind. Clifford started out as an idealist in the administration of Harry Truman but was subsequently seduced by money, security and creature comforts. . . . Several years ago a pair of Hollywood writers decided to write a screenplay inspired by Clifford's life. It was entitled, "Mr. Smooth."

William Randolph Hearst, Jr., said in a column: "And on the value of American bombing of North Vietnam, Clifford clearly feels more strongly than McNamara that it serves a vital purpose in reducing the flow of Communist manpower and matériel from North Vietnam into the south."

The McNamara men in the Pentagon did not want a Washington political operator, a man reportedly seduced by money, security and creature comforts or a Mr. Smooth. And above all, those of us who had been involved in the Senate air-power hearings with McNamara did not want a hard-line Hawk and did not want as Secretary someone who put his faith in the bombing of North Vietnam as a solution to the war.

My first meeting with Clark Clifford at the Pentagon was lunch on February 8 in the Secretary's dining room with McNamara, Nitze and the other Assistant Secretaries of Defense. It had been planned that we would go around the table, with each of us filling in Clifford on how our offices operated, where they fit into the pattern and what our major problems were. By the accident of seating order, the first two men were Dr. Alain Enthoven, Assistant Secretary for Systems Analysis, and Dr. John Foster, Director of Defense Research and Engineering. The entire lunchtime—more than two hours—was spent on those two alone, which was just as well from my standpoint since I had laryngitis and could not speak.

But I could watch, and sitting there I compared the outgoing Secretary of Defense and his successor. The word for the new man was elegance—elegance of movement, style and manners. This was a silent screen star, with his handsome profile and his evenly waved hair. He reminded me of the automobile advertisements in Fortune magazine thirty-five or forty years ago—the millionaire in a smoking jacket sitting in his paneled library, the first editions on one wall and gun cases on another, accepting a drink from the silver tray held by a manservant, while beneath the picture, in dignified type so as not to disturb the mood, were the only words on the page: "He drives a Deusenberg."

His double-breasted suit was magnificently tailored; the shirt and tie blended perfectly with it; the amount of French cuff showing must have been exactly the amount that should have been shown that year. Clark Clifford looked, sounded and acted as smooth as everyone had said he was.

Sitting across from him was McNamara—needing a haircut as he so often did, wearing a frayed, white, button-down oxford shirt with a sewn tear over the pocket. He had, I knew, just put on the suit coat before coming to lunch, since he worked always in shirt sleeves (and also peeled off his tie whenever feasible).

Clifford asked all the right questions. Everything about him was proper, courteous, courtly, friendly and gracious. His ignorance of many current defense matters was colossal, a point he himself made immediately, but he used his time well. Clearly he was intelligent; clearly he was able.

From my own standpoint, however, he had walked into the wrong dining room for the wrong job. My personal inclination had been to leave the government when McNamara left, particularly since Cyrus Vance was gone, but after talking to McNamara and Vance I had decided to stay on at least long enough to help the new Secretary get settled—if, of course, he wanted me to do so. My acceptance of his invitation to remain led me into the most interesting and personally worthwhile year of my life.

For all our fears were groundless. Misled perhaps by the long lapels, the peripheral government activity as a confidant of Presidents or the courtly Old World manner, we had formed an impression of Clifford as a kind of political dilettante. No image could have been more in error. One of the most important things not said by the press about Clark Clifford was that he was a worker—a worker, God help us, in the McNamara tradition, pouring out at the age of sixty-one every gram of his strength into the position he had accepted from the President of the United States. Not many men of any age are inclined to keep up with a group of McNamara-picked zealots, but Clifford, almost double the age of some 1961 Whiz Kids and years senior to any top-level civilian in the building except Paul Nitze, was both disposed to and capable of matching hours with any of us. His primary purpose in coming aboard was not to mend fences on Capitol Hill or to sit as caretaker or to paste the Department together with a more publicly acceptable glue until after the summer presidential convention and the fall election. He was interested not in the title of Secretary of Defense but in the job. And in speculating on how he would do the job, another major error was made by those who assumed that a Great Conciliator was, by definition, an indecisive man. There is not, in Clark Clifford, an indecisive bone.

All of this could have been abominable, of course, if the determination, industry and strength of Clark Clifford had been channeled in the wrong direction. More important by far was the Clifford philosophy, and particularly the Clifford view on Vietnam. For some of us, the intense satisfaction of 1968 resulted from the fact that the Washington political operator who was "Mr. Smooth," the hard-line Hawk, was within five days convinced that the war in Vietnam could not be won by additional bombing of the North or additional troops, within fifteen days convinced that it could not be won in a reasonable time period under any military circumstances, within thirty days convinced that the only sane way out was through negotiations and within sixty days convinced that the effort was no longer essential to the national security of the United States.

Furthermore, unlike Bob McNamara, whose internal government objective and external public one were to teach and inform so that man's brain and man's logic would bring him to the right conclusion, Clark Clifford's aim was to persuade. "Our objective is not to prove to anyone how wrong he is," he would say. "Our objective is to get them to do it our way."

Clark Clifford's first decision of importance to the public affairs operation and to my personal relationship with him was whether to continue the morning meetings with which McNamara, the Deputy Secretary and I had begun each day. These meetings were built around summaries of interesting defense news stories and commentary from newspapers, network news shows and magazines. Members of my staff came in at about

5 A.M. to check all the news items, select those most pertinent to the Defense Department, prepare one-or-two-sentence summaries of each, reproduce the items themselves and have the package ready for my arrival shortly after seven. I would read the pieces and dictate personal comments on each to McNamara and the Deputy Secretary. To save time, I scanned the Washington *Post* while being driven to work, choosing the columns, editorials and news stories of significance and dictating my comments into a portable machine in the automobile. These were typed by our secretaries while I was working on the summaries of clips from the *New York Times*, Baltimore *Sun*, *Wall Street Journal* and other papers, plus transcripts which had been prepared of early morning radio and television newscasts and those of the prior night.

Other members of the staff, working under the rear admiral or brigadier general who was my military assistant, would use this same time to check out internal message traffic and classified reports dealing with the subjects raised in the news stories. Before going upstairs to meet with McNamara, I would attempt to have in hand the essential facts of each situation as well as the newspaper version. If a column by Joseph Alsop dealt with infiltration from North Vietnam, for example, our people would collect the latest classified material on infiltration from the Defense Intelligence Agency, read the latest internal messages from Saigon on the subject and brief me quickly. Sometimes such a column would be extremely accurate; sometimes wholly inaccurate. Later in the day, if the issue was important enough, Dan, Dick and I would call in the relevant intelligence experts for a ten-minute or two-hour briefing, depending on our time and needs. Whenever feasible, however, I wanted basic facts on the major stories prior to my morning meeting with the Secretary. In noncrisis situations this was not difficult, since we would have personal knowledge of 95 percent of the items and had ample skilled manpower to check out the other 5 percent rapidly enough to give me some kind of a reading prior to the 7:50 A.M. session.

No single activity was more important to me as Assistant Secretary of Defense under McNamara than the daily morning meeting, at which we would use the news items as a basis to discuss every major issue confronting the Department. From the discussion would come my advice on how to handle certain matters publicly. On the column dealing with infiltration, for example, we might decide that the issue had now become so confused in the public mind that we had better forfeit some security and jeopardize some intelligence-collection sources in order to lay out more detail for the press—or the Secretary might damn the unknown official who had leaked highly classified information and decide that the sources were so sensitive and the information from them so important to us that we could not risk further disclosure and would decline any comment. If a story dealt indirectly with McNamara's attitude on strategic nuclear talks with the Soviet Union, we would discuss the progress of secret preliminary probings and whether the national interest would be served or hampered by deliberate diffusion of that attitude—by the Secretary publicly at a news conference or by me, quietly, with a half-dozen columnists.

The meetings also gave us an opportunity to discuss the maneuverings of the military services or other internal special-interest pleaders, perhaps in the Office of the Assistant Secretary of Defense (International Security Affairs) or of the Director of Research and Engineering. We knew the positions held by most persons and most elements of the building on the most important issues well enough so that we could tell that the Army was bounding off the reservation on this subject or someone in Dr. Enthoven's Systems Analysis shop on that one, and at the morning meeting could agree on what action should be taken, internally and externally, to rein them back in again.

In addition, my office could not have functioned efficiently without the updated information I learned from the Secretary at the morning sessions. The Assistant Secretary of Defense for Public Affairs must have full knowledge of all important events taking place within the Defense Establishment. With only the rarest exceptions, all message traffic from overseas was made immediately available to me, and copies of all internal Pentagon memoranda to the Secretary were sent to my office (many of them for my personal reading only), but even this was not good enough. Under any regime, unless the Assistant Secretary of Defense for Public Affairs is up to date on the current thinking and decisions of his Secretary, the Secretary of State and the President, he and his world-wide empire are, unwittingly, apt to do horrendous damage. The same is true, of course, of his counterpart in State and of the White House News Secretary.

If Clifford should discontinue the morning meetings and fail to substitute something similar to them, it would mean that he intended to use the Assistant Secretary as the head of a routine information office, albeit the largest in the world, rather than as a personal adviser and confidant. That early morning session had been the foundation of my working day and of my working relationship with McNamara.

Clark Clifford did decide to keep up the morning sessions, initially in the same pattern, and I used the news critiques to explain how our office was structured, to acquaint him immediately with the Department's major public affairs problems, to warn him of the most dangerous personal pitfalls (for example, any discussion of the circumstances under which nuclear weapons might be used), to brief him on how our office maintained control over information policies in Saigon or Stuttgart, and to inform him of the necessity of public affairs coordination among State, Defense and the White House. From the first day I was deliberately frank and, sometimes, impertinent, but from my own selfish standpoint I wanted to ascertain quickly how candid he would be with me, personally and professionally. I had been working with intimate friends; he was a stranger.

The first test in candor came quickly on the first item discussed on the morning of the first routine meeting, March 2, 1968. Several news stories that day mentioned that he would be only a "caretaker" Secretary. My dictated comment on this said, in part:

Your first personal problem, and one that could become a management problem, is the "caretaker" theme. There has been little of it to date, but more will develop. You should expect to be asked about it at your first meeting with the press, whether that be a press conference or a more informal session. . . .

Clifford informed me at once that he had not come on a "caretaker" basis, that he had severed all connection with his law firm and that he expected to stay on as long as the President wanted him. Privately, he said, that meant at least through 1969 and 1970 if President Johnson was re-elected. We agreed that the problem was more internal than external; it was important for the military establishment to realize that the new Secretary was not a short-termer. He authorized me to spread that word informally among the other Assistant Secretaries, the service Secretaries and the top military people, and later to let it seep out to the press. Without wanting to make a production of it, we did want the world to know that he had come to stay.

The morning items were of many different types. One news story told of an enemy ship laden with Vietcong supplies that was permitted to escape off Vietnam because it was outside the twelve-mile limit. My comment explained that public explanations on such matters were made in Saigon without specific guidance from Washington. Another story from Southeast Asia involved looting in Hué by Marine troops. I advised him that this also was a field problem for General Westmoreland to handle, both operationally and from a public affairs standpoint. The Secretary of Defense should not involve himself with it; the military command would deal harshly with looters. A third item from the war zone reported that a current battle proved that South Vietnamese conscripts, not just the elite troops, could fight well against heavy odds when properly led. This one I used to inform him of my personal views on an internal government dispute on publicizing the ARVN (Army of the Republic of Vietnam), saying in my dictated comment:

Plus piece for the ARVN. When the ARVN does perform well, the reporters on the scene will discover it and gradually write about it. When the ARVN is ineffective, all of the trumpeting in the world will not disguise that fact. We should be alert to point out their good work, but too many are too quick to attempt to sell the press that all ARVN are white knights. This can only backfire.

With some items, I tried to bring the new Secretary up to date on less important issues on which he might be buttonholed by others in the government. One story, for example, dealt with a recent ruling by McNamara against Department of Defense participation in the 1969 Paris Air Show. My comment:

Bob cancelled Defense participation in the Air Show on our recommendation. Harold Brown supported us strongly. Commerce, State and Ed Welsh of the Space Council are all prodding the Vice-President, who has told Commerce to circulate plans which include our participation. The trade press is against us; the small amount of editorial comment in the daily press has supported our nonparticipation decision. We will have a piece of paper up to you in a few days for your review. It is a boondoggle, but you may not consider it worth an early fight with the Vice-President. We are not certain how strongly he feels personally; Commerce is using his name very freely. There would be more press interest than usual in your action since a change would be your first reversal of Bob.

On a story about the use of Army troops for riots, I recommended that he sit down with Dan Henkin, who had gone to Detroit with Cy Vance when the President sent Vance there during the rioting as his personal representative. On a draft piece, I noted that there was no public affairs action to be taken but recommended an early substantive briefing for him by the Assistant Secretary of Defense (Manpower), Alfred Fitt. On a story quoting the reaction to his appointment by unidentified admirals and generals, I said:

The building is waiting to see how much leeway you will give the Services in your image as the "Great Compromiser" and "Reconciliator." They are straining at the leash and will make the most out of any sign of unleashing.

One item was about the Navy's attitude toward racial and religious minorities; I commented on the Navy's penchant for living in a world of its own. On another involving the Fractional Orbital Bombardment System, I recommended that he request one briefing by the Director of Research and Engineering and another by the Assistant Secretary for Systems Analysis. On a story concerning the Tonkin Gulf resolution, I filled him in on an understanding which had been reached between a Congressional committee and his legislative liaison people.

The critiques included my comments on personal problems he would face if news stories continued to refer to him as a "soother and smoother," advice on how to handle a particular four-star general and brief remarks on some of the newsmen with whom he would be dealing. Among the latter:

"A miserable untrustworthy SOB. This is basically a plus column for you, but beware of [Reporter X] under all circumstances."

And:

"Typically thorough and objective piece by Don May of UPI, one of the pluses in the Pentagon press room."

And:

"Ashworth [George Ashworth of the *Christian Science Monitor*], who is relatively new to the Pentagon, is doing some of the best interpretative reporting out of this building, and this piece is typical."

Many of my comments contained classified information, many were libelous and many extremely blunt on specific individuals, in and out of government, and in and out of the Pentagon. Some of the military personnel I had known fifteen years, most of the top-level civilians several years as both poacher and gamekeeper, and many of the highest-level civilians intimately for three years.

My early concern about my relationship with the new Secretary of Defense was short-lived. Some points that first morning involved his personal affairs; others official conversations between him and the President. In each instance, he explained the background and the facts, and we then discussed what course he should take. Some of the problems were in the public domain;

others involved things he should do internally within the Pentagon. We quickly established an effective working relationship, which grew into an association of full trust and, within a few weeks, into a close friendship. I am not predisposed to instant friendship, but the associations of people in government, wrestling with the infinitely complex problems man has made for himself, are unique.

Within a month or so, Clifford expanded the morning meeting beyond himself, Deputy Secretary Nitze and me. He added one other presidential appointee, Paul Warnke, and his own two top personal aides—George Elsey, who had worked with him in the White House under President Truman and joined him in the Pentagon on leave of absence from Pullman, Inc., as his Special Assistant; and Colonel (later Brigadier General) Robert E. Pursley, USAF, one of the most broad-gauged military officers (or people) I know, his Military Assistant.

The two Secretaries for whom I worked utilized their top people in very different ways. Paul Warnke once remarked that McNamara used them as a corporation executive and Clifford as the head of one of the country's most successful law firms. McNamara, for the most part, would call upon us for advice in our own areas of special competence. He wanted public affairs advice from me, not international advice; international advice from Warnke, not systems analysis advice. While the lines obviously often were hazy, especially regarding my office, since we swept across the board into everyone's business, McNamara's technique was to keep the production manager in the production business and the sales manager in the sales business—as, I am told, a corporation executive is apt to do. Clark Clifford, however, gathered around him each day five of us to serve as his top strategy board on all important matters—which, I understand, is the way the head of a law firm often works with his senior partners on the most delicate and important topics.

Each of us sat in the same place around Clifford's desk each morning as we dicussed all the latest developments in roundtable fashion—Vietnam, nuclear-powered warships, the ABM,

the qualifications of potential successors to General Westmoreland, the *Pueblo*, the newest problem of NATO, strategic talks
with the Soviets or a pending appearance before the Fulbright
committee. On his standing orders, all the most important
memoranda and messages the Secretary saw were reproduced so
that each of us had a copy to study. Clifford would review the
facts without disclosing his own reaction and then go around
the room, requesting an opinion and supporting evidence from
each: Paul Nitze, Paul Warnke, me, George Elsey and Bob
Pursley. Rank was nonexistent—Colonel Pursley did not hesitate
to challenge the Secretary or Deputy Secretary of Defense; areas
of specialty were crossed—George Elsey's opinion on a public
affairs matter was sought along with mine, or my opinion on
Spanish-base negotiations along with Warnke's.

Clifford would open a typical session with such a comment as:
"Walt Rostow and I had a long talk last night to exchange views
on where we go from here. Now I want to go over with each of
you the points he made and get your reaction. . . ."

Security was tight in what has been called the Executive
Council, the Advisory Council and the Strategy Group, but
which Clifford referred to simply as the "8:30 Group." No others
in the Pentagon had knowledge of some matters discussed; only
General Wheeler of others. Each man expressed his opinions
without reservation and without fear that he would see them in
print or that he would be quoted to others in the government. I
am aware of no instance of internal or external leak from the
8:30 Group.

The morning meeting nearly always lasted one hour and often
ran close to two. Perhaps 75 percent of the time was spent on
Vietnam, which was approximately the percentage of his total
time Clifford devoted to Vietnam while he was Secretary. He did
not run the Department of Defense totally, as McNamara had
run it; Paul Nitze was the day-to-day operating chief, working
incredibly long hours and personally handling most of the decisions which had been shared formerly by the Secretary and
the Deputy Secretary. Only the most important—and there were

scores even of those—did Nitze put before Clifford for final decision.

Sharp differences of opinion on many issues were held within the 8:30 Group, from the long-range objectives of the Soviet Union in different parts of the world to the exact nature of our obligations to the South Vietnamese or the government course on the *Pueblo* case. Paul Nitze had spent most of his lifetime in government in international affairs; Bob Pursley had had a career in the military. Paul Warnke's outside interests had been in education and civil rights before Vance and McNamara lured him into the Pentagon from an outstanding Washington law firm; Elsey, a long-time Washingtonian, was politically sensitive and understood Congressional and Executive Branch infighting.

The different reactions produced by our different backgrounds and experience were exactly what Clifford wanted and what were most helpful to him. But before long there was general agreement among the four veterans and the two newcomers on many of the major issues related to the war in Vietnam, including these points:

Bombing the North was not going to win the war, deploying even twice as many American troops was not going to win the war, and, in fact, no acceptable military actions were going to win the war in the classical sense within a time period satisfactory to us or the American people.

Bombing all or part of North Vietnam was not going to limit infiltration, expanding the bombing was not going to increase the safety of our men in the South and halting it was not going to decrease their safety, if Hanoi would not take advantage of the halt by utilizing the DMZ or otherwise.

Continuation of the American involvement at the current level for as long as two years was totally unacceptable even if the American people would stand for it—which was doubtful.

Negotiations, therefore, offered the most intelligent route toward disengagement. In those negotiations, military aspects of a potential settlement could be worked out between the North Vietnamese and the United States, and the Saigon government could not be allowed a veto over such a settlement. Political aspects of the settlement could be worked out between Saigon and the National Liberation Front, and should not be imposed upon them by us.

As indicated in the chapter, "McNamara's Fight for De-escalation," the sentiments on bombing and the need for negotiations were not new to the four of us who had worked with McNamara. What so satisfied us and so surprised many was that Clark Clifford reached the same views so soon through his own examination of the facts and then, despite contrary thoughts of others in government, galloped past us so rapidly.

He had come to the Pentagon believing that our military presence in Southeast Asia had been warranted at the time of our original involvement. While assisting President-elect Kennedy in the transition from the Eisenhower administration, he had heard the outgoing President emphasize the strategic importance of Southeast Asia to the cause of freedom, including both Laos and Vietnam. That had impressed him. Two years later he had heard President Kennedy say that withdrawal from Vietnam would mean the doom of Thailand and the collapse of the entire Southeast Asian area. That had impressed him. Having watched the Korean War, he believed that the fate averted there through American and United Nations intervention would overtake Southeast Asia if we stood aside while subversion and terrorism in the South were sponsored by the North.

Entering the government in March, 1968, Clifford still felt that the national interest of the United States was intimately involved with Southeast Asia, that our commitment there was just and that we would have been derelict in our obligation to our own people had we not taken part in that struggle.

He told us in March (and, after his departure from government the next year, wrote publicly) that this conviction had been somewhat shaded by impressions gathered on a 1967 trip he took to the Western Pacific and Southeast Asia with General Maxwell D. Taylor at the request of the President. Their main mission was to see whether the countries in this area would make a greater contribution to the war that was so close to them, but by the time he arrived home he was convinced they did not share our degree of concern about it.

Australia bothered him particularly. On many occasions during our eleven months he pointed out that in World War II Australia had more than 300,000 troops in the various theaters, many as far away as North Africa, but that she had sent only 7,800 to South Vietnam. New Zealand had 70,000 in World War II and 575 in Vietnam; Thailand, a nation next door with 30 million people, had 2,500 in Vietnam (later increased to 11,000). This lack of major involvement from nations in that part of the world deeply disturbed him and caused his first doubts.

It was on this same trip, to digress, that Clifford met for the first time one particularly difficult American Ambassador. After an initial session at the embassy, General Taylor asked his impression of the man. Clifford delayed answering for a moment, then responded with a question: "Am I correct that we are dining with the Ambassador at his residence this evening?"

He was.

"And we are due there at seven-thirty?"

"That is correct," said Taylor.

Clifford was silent another moment before saying, "Sometime between seven-thirty, when we arrive, and the time we sit down at the table, I intend to pop him right in the mouth."

Clark Clifford's first assignment from the President as Secretary of Defense was to head a committee to review a military request for additional troops for Vietnam. Shortly after the Tet offensive of late January and early February, the President had sent General Wheeler to Southeast Asia to find out what General Westmoreland needed and to take an on-the-spot look at the situation. Wheeler returned to Washington the morning of February 28, bringing with him a request for a substantial increase in American forces. We were at that time building toward a ceiling of an announced 525,000, although the number actually in South Vietnam was about 516,000.

The Clifford task force met at the Pentagon in the Secretary's dining room. It included the Secretaries of State and Treasury; the Deputy Secretary of Defense and Under Secretary of State; the Chairman of the Joint Chiefs of Staff; the Director of the Central Intelligence Agency; the President's Special Assistant for National Security Affairs; and three or four others, including Paul Warnke and me.

It has been widely written in newspapers and magazines that General Westmoreland asked for 205,000 or 206,000 more troops. But the record is distorted by that flat statement, which leaves the impression of Westmoreland reeling in panic after the Tet offensive and rushing to Washington with a distress call for a 40 percent increase in his total force.

I am not privileged to quote from the documents, which presumably are still top-secret, but I can say that it did not happen quite that way. It was more that Washington asked Westmoreland this kind of question:

We understand that you would like to have more troops. We share, of course, your conviction that nothing must be allowed to put into additional jeopardy the lives of the men already under your command or in the pipeline. You are in the best position to tell us how many more are required. If necessary, assume a Reserve call-up and additional draft calls. How many extra men do you want within ninety days, how many by the end of the year and how many by June 30, 1969?

Those are my words, designed to describe a tone, not to paraphrase a message. Perhaps they are a little overly generous to Westmoreland, but they do present a more accurate picture of the give-and-take between Washington and Saigon than the unmodified statement that General Wheeler brought back with him a bald request from General Westmoreland for 206,000 men. Nonetheless, the basic fact is that an additional long-term deployment of that size was proposed and was considered, seriously and in detail, by the Clifford task force which spent many sandwich-and-coffee days in the Secretary's dining room in early March.

These March meetings were of tremendous importance to Clark Clifford because out of them came his great disillusionment with the war effort and his conviction that in the spring of 1968 the United States was on the wrong path, whatever the case might have been at any given point in the past.

While the 8:30 Group had not yet coalesced those first few days, Clifford, Nitze, Warnke and I met frequently before and after the task force sessions. Among the points most troubling to the new Secretary were these:

With the military emphasizing that the Tet offensive had been handled satisfactorily and at an appalling cost in casualties to the enemy, and since there had been no stated need for additional troops before Tet, why are so many additional troops required now?

Accepting the possibility of another Communist nationwide offensive in March or April before full recovery from the Tet attacks, and the possible need for emergency reinforcements, how do troops which cannot reach Vietnam until early summer at the earliest help meet such immediate needs?

Will the deployment of another 200,000 men to Southeast Asia hasten the end of the war? If so, why can no one explain how and by how much?

Cannot the North Vietnamese add 50,000 or 100,000 more men of their own and thus offset the new build-up? What would we do then? Would we need another 200,000?

In summary, what do we gain by this 40 percent increase in our commitment and all the other steps which must be taken to achieve it—a Reserve call-up of 250,000 men, higher draft calls, a total increase in the armed forces of nearly a half-million men, additional spending of $12 billion a year and possibly financial controls on the home economy?

Clark Clifford did not find satisfactory answers to these questions.

Because he did not find them, and because he did find in the South Vietnamese leadership a great reluctance both toward peace negotiations and toward a lessening of the United States commitment, Clifford became a vehement proponent of de-escalation during his eleven months in office, arguing within the government with great vigor for the de-escalatory position at which the President arrived in both March and October and fighting with equal vigor against the escalatory proposals which were considered seriously by the White House during the year.

Out of the March review, which began at the Pentagon and continued later in the month with meetings I did not attend at the State Department and the White House, came the President's speech of March 31—the speech which signaled the turning point of United States involvement in Southeast Asia.

In addition to the surprise announcement of his decision not to run for re-election in November, in that address to the nation the President made three major points regarding the war.

One involved the bombing, a second troop deployment and the third the South Vietnamese armed forces.

On the bombing, the President said:

We are prepared to move immediately toward peace through negotiations. So tonight, in the hope that this action will lead to early talks, I am taking the first step to de-escalate the conflict. We are reducing—substantially reducing—the present level of hostilities, and we are doing so unilaterally and at once.

Tonight I have ordered our aircraft and our naval vessels to make no attacks on North Vietnam except in the area north of the De-militarized Zone where the continuing enemy build-up directly threatens allied forward positions and where the movement of their troops and supplies are clearly related to that threat.

The area in which we are stopping our attacks includes almost 90 percent of North Vietnam's population and most of its territory. Thus there will be no attacks around the principal populated areas, or in the food-producing areas of North Vietnam.

Even this very limited bombing of the North could come to an early end—if our restraint is matched by restraint in Hanoi. But I cannot in good conscience stop all bombing so long as to do so would immediately and directly endanger the lives of our men and our allies. Whether a complete bombing halt becomes possible in the future will be determined by events.

Our purpose in this action is to bring about a reduction in the level of violence that now exists.

The President's second major point involved troop deployments. He said:

On many occasions I have told the American people that we would send to Vietnam those forces that are required to accomplish our mission there. So with that as our guide we have previously authorized a force level of approximately 525,000.

Some weeks ago to help meet the enemy's new offensive we sent to Vietnam about 11,000 additional Marine and airborne troops. They were deployed by air in 48 hours on an emergency basis. But the artillery and the tank and the aircraft and medical and other units that were needed to work with and support these infantry troops in combat could not then accompany them by air on that short notice.

In order that these forces may reach maximum combat effectiveness, the Joint Chiefs of Staff have recommended to me that we should prepare to send during the next five months the support troops totaling approximately 13,500 men.

A portion of these men will be made available from our active forces. The balance will come from reserve component units, which will be called up for service.

The President's third principal point involved the Army of the Republic of Vietnam. Noting that President Thieu had ordered the mobilization of another 135,000 South Vietnamese toward a total military strength of 800,000 men, that all men in the South Vietnamese armed forces now had their tours of duty extended to the duration of the war, that reserves were being called for immediate active duty, that the government had started drafting nineteen-year-olds in March and would begin drafting eighteen-year-olds in May, President Johnson said:

We applaud this evidence of determination on the part of South Vietnam. Our first priority will be to support their effort. We shall accelerate the re-equipment of South Vietnam's armed forces in order to meet the enemy's increased firepower. And this will enable them progressively to undertake a large share of combat operations against the Communist invaders.

Aside from the play given the President's personal political decision, most of the news stories on the speech highlighted the bombing cutback. Had I been reporting, I also would have stressed the bombing issue, which was the most dramatic and represented a signal step toward peace talks. It is likely, however, that the deployment announcement, constituting a possible major departure from past policy, was of even greater potential importance.

"For the first time," said one member of the 8:30 Group, "there is a lid on the bottomless pit."

The metaphor could be faulted, but the meaning was clear. Never before had the President turned down a request for additional troops for Vietnam. The potential importance of his decision was scarcely measurable. For the first time there was at least the suggestion to the military, the hard-liners and the South Vietnamese: this much and no more. For the first time there was a suggestion to the people of the United States that our commitment was limited.

I emphasize that there was only a suggestion of these points, because the speech of the President did not impose a limit on troop deployment. He did not say that this was the end. Pending requests from the military of 200,000 were not mentioned; future deployment plans were left wide open. The President had announced that we were sending 13,500 more troops to support 11,000 which had been rushed to Vietnam during Tet, but he had announced no new ceiling and no decision not to send others.

It was on this point that Clark Clifford launched his public campaign for disengagement from South Vietnam.

That campaign was to last as long as Clifford was in office. It was a deliberate effort, based upon the simple premise that the only sane and logical way out of the entire tragic Southeast Asian mess was through negotiations with the other side. It was essential, therefore, to defend all de-escalatory actions taken by the President, prevent all escalatory actions proposed by others and ensure that nothing was permitted to interfere with or threaten the success of such negotiations.

All proposals from within the United States government or the South Vietnamese government which might hamper or terminate negotiations were bad; all proposals from any source which might advance or keep alive negotiations were good. The Clifford course for 1968 was almost that simple.

Internally, he fought with total singleness of purpose and with the incredible skill he possesses for marshaling facts, advocating a position, splintering opponents, winning supporters—and, through a remarkable ability to sense the moods of an old and intimate friend, cajoling, convincing and persuading the President.

Externally, he demonstrated an uncanny talent for communicating to the specific audience he most wanted to reach at each potential turning point. Speaking to seventy-five or a hundred newsmen slouched in the unfinished audio-visual studio on the second floor of the Pentagon, he would address his remarks to the American people one month, the South Vietnamese government another, the military leaders a third and the President of the United States a fourth.

There was one indispensable principle to which he adhered in his public campaign. Not once did he oppose the President publicly. Not once did he suggest error in a past presidential decision. Not once did he undercut a move the President was making or contemplating. And on every occasion possible he presented the President as the man in the world who had given more of himself to the quest for peace than any other. When he felt at a news conference that he could not support a presidential policy or decision personally, he would, with exquisite delicacy, turn his response so that he presented to the public the President's case in the President's own words.

But while scrupulously refraining from burrowing under the ground on which the President presently stood, Clark Clifford consistently and skillfully moved in public to occupy the ground the President had not yet reached.

The troop-deployment "limitation" was the first major campaign.

The Pentagon press was told at a background session the day

after the speech that a limitation had been placed upon deployments at this time. The world "limitation" was used deliberately —although President Johnson had spoken of no limitation.

Ten days later Clifford held a news conference, and again sounded the "limitation" theme. "I might add . . . that when these additional forces go, the total in . . . South Vietnam will be brought up to some 549,500, and it is the President's intention at this time not to increase those forces," he said.

Again, at another point in the news conference: "This is part and parcel, I believe, of the President's decision to place a limitation at this time upon our troop level at a point not exceeding 550,000."

No public statements by Clifford were accidental. We had discussed in the 8:30 Group the desirability of shutting off all talk of deploying 200,000 more men to Vietnam by hammering at the point that the limit had been reached. We had a half-dozen different audiences: to the U.S. military and the Hawkish U.S. Embassy in Saigon, the message was that they should stop dreaming about another 200,000 men; it was not going to happen. To the South Vietnamese we wanted to say: this is it, dig in, do more yourselves. To the North Vietnamese the signal was a different one: we are leveling off for the long haul. Do not expect erosion of our public support to continue; our people now know this is no longer a bottomless pit.

Some believed that Hanoi would be encouraged by the U.S. decision to send only 13,500 at this time. We in the 8:30 Group did not; Paul Warnke and I, particularly, argued that the girding-for-the-long-pull approach should be bad news for Hanoi and should discourage her.

If you are at a high enough level of government and say something often enough, it becomes government policy—unless the President himself chooses to step in and contradict you. This, over the next few months, was the case with the troop-limitation issue. At this early juncture, Clifford worded his limitation talk carefully, specifically including the phrase "at this time" in discussing the ceiling, yet seeking generally to create a mood of a permanent limit in at least three capital cities: Washington, Hanoi and Saigon—and, later, Paris.

It worked admirably. The *New York Times* story after his first postspeech press conference began:

> Secretary of Defense Clark M. Clifford announced today a ceiling of 549,500 on the American troop strength in Vietnam. . . .
>
> He linked the . . . policy to a decision by President Johnson to treat the level of 549,500 men, which was previously announced, as a ceiling beyond which the Administration does not intend to go at this time. . . .
>
> Mr. Clifford was careful not to make his remarks sound like an ultimatum to Saigon. . . .
>
> The implications of his remarks, however, were that the United States was telling Saigon for the first time that it could not look forward to an unending flow of American reinforcements. If more troops are needed, Mr. Clifford was saying in effect, Saigon must supply them.

That was exactly what he was saying. And, by design, we followed up on the same theme at his next news conference, June 20. When a reporter asked whether our commander in Vietnam would ask for additional troops in the light of estimates that the North Vietnamese were sending south twenty thousand troops a month, he replied: "I do not believe that we will be asked for more troops by our American commander in the field. It is my belief that he feels he has adequate troops to take care of the present situation."

At another point in the news conference, he recalled—not perfectly accurately—that one of the President's March 31 points was that "he was not going to send another massive number of troops to Vietnam."

On August 15 the Secretary of Defense put the troop limitation of 549,500 in hard cement—again using a news conference to do it.

For some time in Vietnam there had been a program of hiring local civilian labor to do some of the work being performed by U.S. military personnel—work such as cargo handling. When the original ceiling of 525,000 had been set, it was planned that several thousand troops would be replaced by civilians and freed for combat or combat support duties. But problems were encountered finding people good enough to hire, and the military were proposing that they be allowed a few thousand extra troops above the 549,500 to compensate for the civilians they could not get. Their proposal was eminently fair; without the increase the 549,500 total would give them less manpower than they had been promised.

It was the unanimous agreement of the 8:30 Group, however, that even this legitimate leak in the dike could not be permitted. Whatever the justification for a few thousand extra men, it was not as important as holding to the troop limitation.

At this same time there was considerable speculation also about the possibility of a new Communist offensive. On a trip we took to Vietnam in July, Clifford had discussed this with his troop commanders, all of whom were confident that any offensive could be handled without additional U.S. manpower.

I suggested at an 8:30 meeting that the Secretary open his next news conference with a firm and final troop-limitation statement, designed to inform everyone everywhere that there had been no change in the March "ceiling," that no change was contemplated and that the issue was closed. After group discussion, Clifford agreed, and he began a session with the press on August 15 this way:

Good morning, gentlemen.

From time to time in the press conferences I might try a different approach to the problem that you men have of keeping up with the news.

This morning I have three brief memoranda which I shall refer to that touch upon subjects that have been in the news to some extent since the last conference that I had with you here.

The first has to do with the ceiling regarding the number of American troops in South Vietnam. You will all be aware of the fact that MACV [Military Assistance Command, Vietnam] has indicated that the total of American troops is now approaching the limit of 549,500 which has previously been set.

The total last Thursday was 538,000 and the total today is 543,000. You will recall that the ceiling of 549,500 was based upon MACV estimates of the number of American servicemen who were needed to handle the foreseeable contingencies in South Vietnam, and was also due to the decision that was made by President Johnson that our contribution to the effort there would not be unlimited.

You are aware of the fact that we are faced with the possibility of a new offensive in South Vietnam. When General Wheeler and I were there a few weeks ago we discussed this in detail with General Abrams. General Abrams informed us that he believes that the Allies have the ability to cope with the enemy threat.

In view of his attitude in this regard, it remains our intention to limit American troops in South Vietnam to the total of 549,500.

The President, of course, could have overruled Clifford at any time. But he did not, and in the absence of any affirmative action before he left office on January 20, 1969, the tentative decision he had made nearly a year earlier to send only a few thousand troops instead of 206,000 had been transformed by public statements of the Secretary of Defense into government policy.

On the second major point of the President's March 31 speech, the bombing limitation, Clifford followed the same formula, using news conferences and other public appearances month after month to communicate his feelings and to interpret the administration position according to his own de-escalatory predilections. In his statements on bombing, as in the troop ceiling remarks, he suggested no differences at any time with decisions already taken by the President, but whenever the cutback was threatened, internally or externally, he re-emphasized publicly why the President had ordered the de-escalation, praised the President's decision, pointed out how resumption of full bombing would be contradictory to the President's position and explained why resumption was not warranted by present conditions. Many of the President's advisers dissented strongly from this viewpoint; many were recommending escalation during the summer and fall. While they were doing so, Clifford made public statements on what folly this would be—without, of course, referring to them or to the internal debate.

From a public affairs standpoint, the initial bombing reduction announcement had been handled disastrously. The issue in late March was whether the President would specify in his speech that he was limiting the bombing to the area south of the 20th Parallel. Paul Warnke and I felt very deeply that he should, and won the support of the rest of the 8:30 Group, including the Secretary. We argued that the newsmen were certain to learn that the line was the 20th and that we would take unnecessary "credibility" losses by not being forthright. Additionally, we were concerned that nonspecific language would be misunderstood and interpreted different ways by different individuals.

Most of the support for vague, indefinite language came from the State Department, which apparently believed that the President would have more future flexibility if he did not publicly pin himself to a particular dividing line.

It could not work, since there was no way to keep the public uninformed. The public affairs realities were that the orders to the military to attack only beneath the 20th Parallel would, without question, leak to the press, and that the press, without question, would write the story. As time passed, and as Saigon newsmen noted from MACV announcements that all missions were south of the 20th Parallel, it would become accepted throughout the world that the President had drawn the line there. Any attempt to take advantage of the "flexibility" by bombing north of the 20th would be regarded as escalation and looked upon as a retreat from the March 31 speech just as certainly as if the 20th Parallel announcement had been made formally.

Clifford urged the White House to specify publicly the cutoff line, but was unsuccessful in selling our case. In the final draft of the speech, the President generalized, saying that he was limiting attacks to "the area north of the Demilitarized Zone where the continuing enemy build-up directly threatens allied forward positions and where the movement of their troops and supplies are clearly related to that threat."

While he added that the attack-free area included almost 90

percent of the population of North Vietnam and most of its territory, the deliberately vague language unfortunately left him extremely vulnerable to misinterpretation.

On Monday the reaction to the President's speech was heart-warming, as a nation hungering for an end to the war clearly believed that we had stopped the bombing, except for an area near the DMZ, and praised him for this step toward peace.

On Tuesday newsmen in Saigon were briefed as usual on the air strikes flown. All were south of the 20th Parallel, a point the reporters immediately noted, but some were in Thanh Hoa Province only two miles from the 20th Parallel—and, because of North Vietnam's long narrow Panhandle, more than two hundred miles deep into her territory.

That night and Wednesday morning the Doves panicked. They had, in their view, been misled and deceived again. The warmonger in the White House had not changed his stripes. He had promised one act and ordered another—or, worse yet, the militarists in the Pentagon were running unbridled and refusing to obey his orders.

The *New York Times* said editorially:

American air attacks on North Vietnam in the past two days have blown a 200-mile gap in the credibility of President Johnson's latest peace initiative, seriously diminishing prospects for reconciliation at home and accommodation abroad. . . . Unfortunately, American military action since the President spoke has already undermined the widely accepted implication of his words.

The Washington *Post* took the same tack, saying in part:

In short, one gathered that the pause was a genuine effort to elicit some sort of response from Hanoi—either an agreement to negotiate or a reciprocal de-escalatory act. And if this is in fact the point of the exercise, then it would seem logical, at the outset at least, to give the effort the best possible test by erring on the side of restraint.

Instead, not much more than four hours after the President's plea for "restraint" by Hanoi, American aircraft were attacking targets in an area where, it seems safe to say, very few if any of Mr. John-

son's Sunday night listeners would have expected them to be. . . .
A bombing pause which does not appear to be much of a pause
at all is no fair test of enemy intentions.

Discussing these editorials in the 8:30 Group, we disagreed
among ourselves on whether, given the President's decision, the
military should have bombed so far north the first few days. My
view was that they had been correct, militarily and psychologically. By a few immediate token strikes that far north, they had
carved out the limits in which they were going to operate. Had
they remained close to the DMZ at the outset, as the *Post* and
other critics were now proposing, then strikes farther north at a
later time would have been regarded as escalation and might
have jeopardized peace talks.

We were all bitter over the editorial reaction because we
thought the newspapers were allowing their disappointment and
astonishment—fully understandable though it was after the President's language—to interfere with their judgment and their
assessment of the facts. The bombing cutback at the 20th Parallel
was a major de-escalatory step of enormous significance. The
fact was that some 90 percent of the people of North Vietnam
were free from attack. To suggest that this was not much of a
ban at all, largely because it was less of a ban than they had anticipated, was, we felt, grossly misleading and inaccurate.

An additional reaction was a personal one, of grief and sympathy for the President. He had moved so far toward the beginning
of a way to peace, but a public affairs error was depriving him of
the credit he so deserved, and the Doves, who should have been
rushing to telephone their support for the de-escalation, were
instead attacking him for not having gone far enough.

It was necessary on Tuesday afternoon to straighten the record
and say what should have been said Sunday night. Even some
State Department officials, according to the press, were contending that the Air Force had "sabotaged" the peace initiative. I
issued a statement under my name announcing (too late) that
the limit was the 20th Parallel, explaining that all raids since the
speech had been south of the 20th Parallel, affirming that these

raids were all within the framework of the President's instructions, pointing out again how much of North Vietnam was free from attack, and stating (as we had hoped the *Times* and *Post* would state) that the President of the United States had moved unilaterally to "reduce significantly the level of violence."

One Washington writer noted that I was "taking the unusual step of offering an explanation of what the President meant in his speech." I certainly was, and it certainly was unusual. It was also, of course, planned that way within the government, and each word had been cleared at the necessary level. An Assistant Secretary of Defense appointed by the President does not offer official explanations of that President's meaning in cavalier fashion.

Not everyone regarded the bombing limitation as a "pause which does not appear to be much of a pause at all" or as something which was "seriously diminishing prospects for reconciliation at home and accommodation abroad." A few hours after those critical editorials were read at the breakfast table Wednesday morning, Hanoi announced that it would like to talk.

The President's decision on the air attacks was, unfortunately, not irrevocable. It was threatened internally throughout 1968 by advisers who had been lukewarm initially and others who had opposed it from the start on grounds that the Communists understood only force and additional military pressure. All these high-level attempts to persuade the President to ease the restriction were watched carefully by the 8:30 Group, and on many occasions Paul Warnke and I worked together for the Secretary on rebuttals to memoranda submitted to the President by officials desiring a return to full-scale bombing or some lesser escalation. And Clifford missed no public opportunity to discredit such arguments.

Throughout the summer and fall, infiltration was a major concern of the press and the public in their consideration of the advantages and disadvantages of the bombing cutback. Despite the McNamara testimony of the prior year, and the lack of any subsequent evidence that bombing could halt or reduce infiltration, some influential Americans declined to reject the correlation of the two. At his first postspeech news conference on April 11, 1968, Clifford was asked whether infiltration had increased since the limitation. His pointed response was that we had no evidence of an increase, that our efforts south of the 20th Parallel were concentrated in the narrowest part of the Panhandle and that this permitted us to carry out an active effort against the flow south.

Another topic at the 8:30 meeting during this period was Saigon's reaction to the March 31 speech and the United States probe for peace talks. Foreign Minister Tran Van Do said: "I feel no qualms about the future as long as the fighting continues. I look forward to negotiations with serious misgivings." And Senator Bui Van Giai was quoted this way: "We are not yet ready for peace negotiations. We are still too weak—not only to cope with the Communists but also to cope with the Americans."

This attitude on the part of the South Vietnamese became one of the keys to Clifford's behavior for the rest of the year. Not at this time—not for certain until we went to Vietnam in midsummer—but in time, slowly and inexorably, Clark Clifford came to believe that the Saigon government leaders had reached the firm decision that it was not in their interest or their country's interest to end the war quickly at the negotiating table. And once he became convinced of this, he lost all sympathy for their position.

That position was perhaps not unreasonable from Saigon's own standpoint. The South Vietnamese armed forces gradually were growing stronger. Their government was also growing more stable and somewhat more mature, even if national political progress was slight. The enemy was growing weaker each day—not at a rate that would cause him to capitulate in the foreseeable future, but undoubtedly weaker. President Thieu and Vice President Ky could, and in my view did, calculate that they could get a better settlement in the summer of 1969 than the summer of 1968, and a better settlement in 1970 than in 1969—so long as the

United States continued to fight, to carry the brunt of the war and to expend vast sums of money in South Vietnam.

But while that course might have been in the best interests of the Saigon government, it assuredly was not in the best interests of the United States.

There was no doubt in my mind that Clifford was right, both in his conviction that the Thieu government did not want to end the war at that time and that it would never agree to a settlement until and unless it was convinced that we were serious about our own disengagement.

In June the Communists stepped up their attacks on Saigon, and pressures within the U.S. government for escalating the bombing rose again. Clifford attempted to damp them down, pointing out at a news conference that we had to expect the North Vietnamese to apply additional military pressure in the South to win an advantage at the negotiating table. The United States, after all, was doing exactly the same thing: we had ordered our commanders in the South to go all out.

At the June news conference newsmen also again linked bombing and infiltration. A reporter asked this question: "In view of North Vietnam's success in infiltrating important numbers of troops into the South, do you think the time may arise soon when it might be necessary to reconsider the bombing plan and authorize attacks throughout military areas of North Vietnam?"

Clifford responded as firmly as he could, noting first that the final decision on resumption would be up to the President himself, and then giving his personal position: ". . . it is my feeling that as long as there continues to be some hope that results will occur at the Paris conferences, it is my notion that the President is likely to continue to keep in effect this present restriction in the hope that that will lead the North Vietnamese to come forward with a reciprocal act of restraint on their part."

The Secretary of Defense was making national policy.

Convinced that it would be disastrous to resume additional bombing, Clifford would not yield an inch on that issue between

March 31 and November. The day before we left for Vietnam in
July, one newsman reached back to the prior August to quote
the Chief of Staff of the Air Force, General J. P. McConnell.
The reporter asked: "Mr. Secretary, last August during the hearings on the air war, General McConnell was asked: 'What is
your assessment of what the impact of halting the bombing north
of the 20th Parallel would be, what impact would that have on
the war in the South?' He said: 'Concentrating your bombing
in that particular area, in my opinion, after a short period of
time would certainly be disastrous.' We have stopped it now for
three months. Has a disaster occurred?"

Clifford answered: "I think it has not occurred. I have not
discussed it particularly with General McConnell, but I believe
that General McConnell would not now take the position that
the result has been disastrous. While we have ceased the bombing north of the 20th Parallel, we have concentrated our efforts
at this particular time on the interdiction of the roads in the
Panhandle, south of the 20th. I believe our efforts have been
very effective there. In some respects, possibly the concentration
of our efforts on a more limited target has produced more divi-
dends and rewards than if the bombing were spread over a larger
area."

It should be noted that this statement was accepted with very
little controversy or rebuttal, whereas it would have created a
storm a year earlier, prior to McNamara's testimony before the
Stennis Senate subcommittee. This was exactly the situation for
which McNamara had established the foundation.

All summer and fall Clifford made the same points: The bombing limitation does not put our men into jeopardy; it does not
affect the amount of infiltration. He said in an August news
conference:

If their [North Vietnamese] losses go up in the process of moving,
then apparently they just move more men and more supplies. So they
have moved the men they chose to move to get them into South
Vietnam. As far as the restriction on the bombing and its effect, there

have been approximately the same number of missions because our target is more concentrated down in the Panhandle. I think it has probably been more effective from an attrition standpoint. . . .

I do not believe that by cutting the bombing back to the 20th Parallel we have jeopardized the lives of our troops or allied troops in Vietnam.

Some critics of the de-escalation were pointing out that the North Vietnamese were busy repairing earlier bomb damage north of the 20th Parallel. Acknowledging this but immediately dismissing the importance of it, Clifford said: "They are making considerable progress in repairing bomb damage. They are engaged in rebuilding bridges and rebuilding some plants and repairing highways, and so forth—just about what you would expect that they do. It is my opinion that this does not bear much of an effect upon the progress of the war. They have found different ways of getting men and supplies down."

When Clifford arrived in the Pentagon, he was concerned about public support for the war, believing in March that it was eroding so rapidly that it might force withdrawal in a fashion damaging to American interests. As he examined the situation from within the government, he decided that the growing public disenchantment with the scale of our military effort was entirely sound, and that it should be reflected in a policy looking toward disengagement. The problem, of course, was how to disengage; the answer, he thought, was not the immediate withdrawal of a half-million men.

"I am willing," he told the 8:30 Group on April 22, "to consider any reasonable approach that will let us cut down in great measure the contribution we are making."

Disengagement continued to be his objective; Paris was the best route to disengagement; the bombing limitation had brought the negotiators to Paris. Clifford was unwilling to take any escalatory step with the bombing that might hamper or even break off the peace talks. Of course the talks were moving slowly, but the alternative was a return to a path he considered hopeless.

Publicly, therefore, he was always the optimist on the talks, the soother of emotions, the pleader for patience. Neither the President nor the public could be permitted to abandon Paris.

As early as June he told newsmen that he was hopeful about Paris, that he believed both the North Vietnamese and United States negotiators were there to try and arrange an ultimate disposition of the conflict. He saw "bits and straws" that indicated some movement, however slight. Asked for proof of the "bits and straws," his answer was necessarily vague.

"They would be nothing more than what you also have noticed in the papers. For instance, in the early days the sessions were consisting solely of diatribes from one side or the other. After a bit, they decided to have a recess during the course of the discussions. I noticed that the recesses are getting longer. There are indications that now, instead of just pleasantries taking place, perhaps subjects are being touched that might be peripheral to ultimately starting some additional kind of contact other than the public propaganda that has been flowing."

Not everyone in the government was pleased with Clifford's public optimism. Some high-ranking officials felt in the summer that progress was not being made in Paris, that we should not arouse false hopes, that the morale of the South Vietnamese was falling because of the bombing limitation, that since Communist attacks on Saigon were continuing we should consider retaliating against Hanoi. That course, in Clifford's view, would have been catastrophic.

"I am opposed to the school of thought that the talks are valueless and nothing is to be gained from them," he told a staff meeting of the service Secretaries, the Chiefs of Staff and the Assistant Secretaries of Defense. "I feel very strongly that the talks must continue and that every element of them must be investigated. If the talks break down, we go back to March 31. I have the deepest concern for the attitude of our people in this country and what we would then do to get a settlement in Southeast Asia."

In July he maintained his public optimism, pointing out to

the press that Ambassador Harriman had said the day before that there were "straws in the wind" that could point to some possible progress in the future, noting that there had been "some diminution of the level of combat in South Vietnam" and stating that some would look at that as "possibly a hopeful sign."

At an August 15 news conference, the Secretary moved to set the stage for future negotiations by citing his desire for "limited peace" in Vietnam. Asked whether we were winning the war and whether there was progress, he responded:

> Yes, we are making progress. I don't know, and I have never been quite sure, what the word "winning" means. I have never had in mind . . . that in the traditional sense we are going to win the war, and then sit down on the deck of the battleship *Missouri* and sign a peace. I don't think it is that way. We are fighting a limited war, and I think we are likely to end up with what might be a limited peace.
>
> By that [I mean] an arrangement that will accomplish our major purpose, and that is to prevent the subjugation of South Vietnam by North Vietnam; an arrangement whereby we can continue to be the shield that prevents that [subjugation] until a political settlement is agreed upon. I think we have made substantial progress toward the obtaining of that ultimate political settlement.

In a post-mortem session—both McNamara and Clifford always held them after any meeting with the press or public—I mistakenly advised him that his remark would capture the headlines and bring the Hawks down upon him. In fact, it went almost unnoticed. We were disappointed that it did not cause more of a flap, because we wanted the public to think more about "limited peace" and less about "winning the war."

Usually our post-mortems were in the Secretary's office on the third floor of the Pentagon, although on a few occasions they were in mine. Customarily I escorted the Secretary to the second-floor audio-visual studio in which news conferences were held and back—partly as a courtesy, partly to advise him of any last-minute developments before the session and partly to steer him through newsmen after it. Most reporters will not intercept a

Cabinet officer after he has given them thirty minutes at a news conference, but a few always try to get him alone for another question as he walks out of the room or down the corridor. We preferred that the Secretary courteously sidestep such private interrogation, both because we would have no record of what he was saying and because it was unfair to the other newsmen who did not pursue him down the hall. On those occasions when the questioner was persistent enough and the Secretary interested enough so that he did say something substantive, I would take my own notes and pass them along to the Director of Defense Information for distribution to the rest of the Pentagon press corps.

In the Executive Branch of the government the regrettable tendency is to approach any session with the press with a somewhat negative attitude. The thought most on our minds was usually not how many points we had scored or what constructive steps we had taken, but rather how much damage had been done, what misstatements had been made, what problems had been caused for the State Department, the President, the peace negotiators or ourselves. With both Secretaries of Defense for whom I worked, with both Deputy Secretaries and with almost every other top official, military or civilian, the first postconference questions were: "What did I do wrong? What trouble are we in?"

Invariably, there was at least one misstep. Twenty-nine minutes of thoughtful, informative, well-planned responses could go down the drain with one too-rapid exchange with a single reporter. We looked upon news conferences as potential booby traps and excellent opportunities for disaster. Any sentence could be picked up and disseminated around the world. One remark spoken too hastily or taken out of context could plague a top official his entire time in office—or for the rest of his life. This is not meant solely as a criticism of the press; even if every newsman present writes with accuracy, responsibility and objectivity, a political opponent or a Congressional critic scrutinizing the transcript can pounce upon an error or deliberately misinterpret a comment or, having missed an inflection or an intonation, honestly misunderstand an answer.

This is why both Clifford and McNamara spent so much time preparing for news conferences. There are always alive at any one time a dozen sensitive international issues, a dozen sensitive Congressional issues, a dozen sensitive political issues, and a dozen sensitive internal Department of Defense issues. Any Secretary of Defense who appears before the press without having thought out how he is going to respond to the five most difficult questions on each of those sensitive issues is doing himself and his President a disservice. Too much is at stake.

While McNamara took several hours preparing for a major news conference, Clifford spent perhaps twice as long. It was not uncommon for us to work together for eight or ten hours prior to a session with the Pentagon press, and twenty or more hours getting ready for a Sunday panel show on national television.

One obvious reason why Clifford's preparation for the press— not for the Congress—was even lengthier than McNamara's was that at the time of his first few conferences he had been Secretary of Defense for only a few weeks and was not as familiar with all of the issues, particularly the minor issues, as McNamara had been after seven years. A second reason was the difference in their personalities. McNamara packs sixty seconds of work into every sixty seconds of work time (and relaxes for each sixty seconds of relaxation time), whereas Clifford is more leisurely during working hours. A third was that McNamara plunged into discussion of the decision at issue, spending no time on review, whereas Clifford invariably followed the technique used by lawyers preparing for oral argument and talked out the full background of the situation. While ensuring the success of his communications, this technique was time-consuming. Finally, Clifford deliberately used the sessions with the correspondents to press his points on Vietnam, and a great deal of behind-the-scenes work went into some of his public answers which seemed to the press to be offhand responses to their questions. McNamara preferred to communicate to the people through prepared speeches, such as the San Francisco ABM address, and formal testimony, such as the 1967 Senate bombing hearing. He felt, I believe, that he was too often misinterpreted by the press. While he understood that the wire-service reporter was dictating on the telephone five minutes after a news conference ended, and recognized that the system demanded this kind of quick reporting, he considered it a risky means of communicating major ideas. McNamara never said "can" when he meant "will"; when he said he was "not unduly alarmed," he did not mean he was not alarmed at all; when he declared there were no "significant differences" between himself and General Wheeler on an issue, he did not mean there were no differences.

In my opinion, McNamara was correct in preferring not to use the news conference as a major method of communicating his ideas on important issues. Too often his unusual precision was lost in the transmission process as the reporter shortened one of his comments into an indirect quotation, a copy editor sharpened that language to make it more readable and a headline writer colored it with attention-attracting verbs. Reporters themselves are sensitive about telegraph editors trimming out the important explanatory paragraphs in their stories or copy editors altering their leads or headline writers missing the nuances of their writing. But a reporter, after silent cursing or registration of a futile formal protest, forgets it and goes on with the next day's story. The official whose views are being communicated improperly cannot dismiss it that lightly.

I am not suggesting that McNamara should have held fewer news conferences; most high officials in the Executive Branch would help their own causes if they held many more instead of abandoning the stage to the opposition. News conferences are useful to keep the record straight, to stomp out brush fires, to prevent erroneous notions and false rumors from reproducing themselves and spreading. But for a man as analytical and precise as Robert McNamara, the news conference was not the best vehicle for transmitting major ideas. He did far better on live television, in fact, where the public heard exactly what he said, than he did via the press.

For Clark Clifford, the news conference was a natural.

He treated the press—and the public beyond the press—as a jury, aware always that his objective was communication. When it served him best to do so, he oversimplified and spoke in generalities, although in language most carefully chosen. But when he wanted to make a major point, he took the reporter and the televiewer by the hand and led them slowly down the road, assuming that they had no knowledge of the past, walking with them from the beginning, ensuring at each milestone that they were alongside him before moving ahead with them to the next, until together they reached the final Clifford position. The time-consuming rehearsal had been in his office; this was the performing technique of the lawyer in oral argument. Clark Clifford was a trial lawyer in St. Louis for sixteen years, and while I never heard him in court, there is no doubt in my mind that his jury received the message he wanted it to receive, couched in convincing and cogent terms. He can sense an unexpected impasse and, having prepared his case carefully, will instantly abandon a point which is not getting through and press forward with double strength and persuasion on another point designed to accomplish a similar result.

Before any sessions with the press, he would work with all the 8:30 Group—which often met additionally at noon or 7:00 P.M. or 11:30 A.M. Sunday—on the position he wanted to take, and the approach and words to employ in taking it. Rarely, after a Clifford press conference, did major news stories report his position inaccurately. The price he paid in time was a high one, but where Vietnam was concerned he considered that price well worth it.

Despite all the advance work, however, and the importance he placed upon the message he was trying to get across to the public, Clifford's initial postconference reaction was also the negative one: "What mistakes did we make?" Only after he could be assured there were none, or that they were minor, could he relax enough to examine whether he had advanced our own Vietnam campaign.

One excellent platform for advancing it was the Sunday afternoon news panel program presented by each of the three major television networks. A Secretary of Defense enjoys an open invitation to appear, and Clifford supplemented his news conferences in the fall and early winter with appearances on all three, doing *Meet the Press* in September, *Issues and Answers* in November and *Face the Nation* in December.

On Larry Spivak's unrehearsed September program, he spoke again of the importance of the South Vietnamese taking over more of the war and restated his confidence in Paris, saying, "I believe that our main hope right now, as far as Vietnam is concerned, is in Paris. It is my belief that North Vietnam does wish to find a basis for concluding the conflict. I know that we do, and I believe that if they [Harriman and Vance] stay with this frustrating task they have, ultimately they will find the means to bring peace."

For more than five months in Paris in 1968 the main obstacles to substantive talks had been Hanoi's refusal to let the Saigon government sit with it at a peace table, Hanoi's insistence upon an unconditional bombing halt and our insistence that there would be no halt until we knew what kind of reciprocal action they would take.

Finally, in mid-October, Harriman and Vance brought about a break in the negotiations, arriving at an understanding with Hanoi. After two weeks of intense activity in Paris, Washington and Saigon, the President announced on October 31 that he was stopping the bombing, that peace talks would begin promptly, and that Saigon had been assured a place at the conference table.

Clifford was elated, as we all were. But within hours Saigon declared that it was not sending a delegation to Paris after all and suggested that the President had acted on the eve of the presidential election for political reasons without their knowledge or consent.

For months there had been little rapport between the United

States Secretary of Defense and the government of the Republic of Vietnam. From this point on there was none. He was incensed, not only because President Thieu's government was endangering the peace talks but also because he felt the South Vietnamese were behaving in an unpardonable fashion toward President Johnson. Calmly and with extraordinary deliberation, Clifford publicly exploded. He disclosed to the Pentagon press on November 12 that Saigon had been kept informed of our efforts in Paris at every step and that there had even been agreement before October 31 on the exact language of the communiqué which was to have announced the beginning of the talks.

He said:

He [the President] worked through 5½ months to reach an agreement that he thought could be a major step toward peace, and then in the last out of the 9th inning, why suddenly they say, "No, we can't go along."

I think the President felt he had to proceed with his plan. He was committed. He had made the commitment to Hanoi. Vance and Harriman had put their word on the line, and I think he felt he had to go ahead.

In addition to that, after all we have done in that country, after the enormous contribution that's been made, with the knowledge that we had gotten to the point where we had the sort of agreement that we had been working toward, I believe the President was absolutely right in not giving Saigon a veto on the plan.

I do not believe that you can work along with your partner up to the very last instant, with the understanding full and complete as to what the arrangement is, and then suddenly have Saigon change its mind and decide not to go ahead.

I think the President owed it, under his constitutional duty, I think he owed it to the American people to proceed with the talks."

The Saigon government was displeased with the Secretary of Defense and retaliated with a personal attack upon him. But what caused them more anguish by far than Clifford's scolding was his flat declaration that the President should go right ahead and begin the substantive talks in Paris without them.

Now, I say that I believe we should make every reasonable effort to demonstrate to Saigon why it should come in and join the talks. At the same time, if they choose not to, I believe the President has the constitutional responsibility of proceeding with the talks.

There are a great many subjects that can be covered between the United States and Hanoi of a military nature and that's our real function. We have been there as a military shield for South Vietnam. I have not anticipated that we would get into the political settlement of South Vietnam. That is up to South Vietnam and Hanoi.

But we can work out arrangements with Hanoi in Paris that could be very valuable. We could work out steps that could lead to a diminution in the level of the combat, which we all desire very much.

I would like to see our casualties go down. I believe we can work out arrangements in that regard. I believe that we can sit down with Hanoi and begin to work out programs that would call for the withdrawal, both of North Vietnamese forces and of American forces.

So the President has all this in his mind when he has to make that decision on Thursday. I say to you that I felt he acted with courage and he acted with forthrightness, and I don't know when I have ever been as proud of a President as I was of President Johnson on Thursday when he had to face up to this question with all the political implications and pressures that were bearing on him.

Mind you, he did not pick the day to announce this. This had been brought about by the decision on the part of Hanoi that they now felt that there should be a break and that we ought to get on with it.

When the offer was made and the offer was accepted, it was up to the President to proceed with it because the opportunity of ending the war was of infinitely greater importance than any possible political consideration.

That was the end of the Clifford–South Vietnam relationship, which had really come to a private ending in Saigon in July when the Secretary spent much of his time informing both our embassy and the South Vietnamese leadership that the American people were about as fed up with the war as they could be and that Saigon had better take this truth into account in their future planning. Inasmuch as Warnke and I were carrying the same message to most of the same officials, all three of us felt when we left the country that we were *personae non gratae* with both the U.S. Embassy and South Vietnamese leaders.

The warm glow of international cooperation was not rekindled in December, at which time peace talks were not yet under way and the Saigon government was quibbling over table shapes and which delegation was to speak first. CBS News Correspondent Stephen Rowan asked Clifford on *Face the Nation* whether the talks might be wrecked before they ever began by the attitude of the South Vietnamese. The Secretary replied:

Well, I would hope not. I would hope that some of these objections that are being raised about the seating and all could be determined very quickly. I think what they have to think about in reaching this agreement is, each day and each week that they delay, more men are dying on the battlefield in South Vietnam. We are losing somewhere in the neighborhood of 200 men a week. The South Vietnamese are losing slightly more than that. The North Vietnamese are losing somewhere around 1,500 a week. I would hope that they would stop squabbling over these details and get to the substance so that we could stop the killing in South Vietnam.

A little later on in the same program he said:

I am becoming inordinately impatient with the continued deaths of American boys in Vietnam. I would like to get going at the Paris conference. I would like to get started on these plans to lower the level of combat. This isn't difficult to do. I would like to start getting our troops out of there. I would like to see a cease-fire. All of that can take place while these lengthy negotiations on a political settlement can also be handled by the parties. . . .

Ambassador Harriman and Ambassador Vance—whom I might say have done a superb task—have said, "We are ready to sit down at any kind of table." It is Hanoi and Saigon that have raised the questions about these details, and it seems to me that there ought to be sufficient pressure of world opinion on them to get them going on the talks.

Until the end then, Clifford put his hopes in Paris.

While nearly all the McNamara team stayed on with Clark Clifford, because of his concentrated use of the 8:30 Group on all major matters there were only a few of us who worked intimately with both Secretaries of Defense—chiefly Nitze, Warnke and I among the civilians and General Wheeler and Colonel Pursley among the military. Because my job put me in such close contact with both men, many persons have asked whether I thought the same events would have taken place in 1968 if McNamara had remained as head of the Department of Defense. Would there have been the bombing limitation of March, the measured response to the military's request for troops, the new troop ceiling, the successful campaign against re-escalation all summer and fall and, finally, the bombing halt of October?

I do not know the answer. No one knows it. Certainly McNamara favored each of these moves with the same intensity as Clifford, and had already recommended them, but he operated in such a vastly different manner that it is impossible to theorize intelligently on what would have happened if he had remained Secretary.

What I do believe is that the principal reason for the removal of Robert McNamara as Secretary of Defense was that he was trying to achieve those objectives. In fairness to President Johnson, McNamara and the reader, I emphasize that this is merely a belief, representing reportorial speculation rather than official information or even logic based on official insight. I cannot produce a grain of direct evidence to offer as proof and do not presume to possess any confidential knowledge of the President's thinking in November of 1967 when he nominated McNamara President of the World Bank. But I can cite the reasons for my own personal opinion.

McNamara had been at odds with the bombing policy throughout 1967, having attempted, as I have outlined, both to limit and halt the attacks against the North. In the South he felt that there was progress but no great promise of bringing the North Vietnamese and the Vietcong visibly closer to collapse within a practical time period. Seeking negotiations, he had urged stabilization

—by halting the bombing, by refusing to expand ground operations and by announcing that we would not send one man beyond the 525,000 already committed. But he had lost his de-escalation case at the White House.

While his testimony in August before the Senate Preparedness Subcommittee had supported all past presidential decisions, and had avoided all references to his own earlier recommendations, it must have been disappointing to the President. On many minor points—attacking Phuc Yen and other targets on the list of fifty-seven—he was overruled within a few days or weeks. Around the Tuesday luncheon table at the White House, where major policy decisions on Vietnam were made, his voice in 1967 was the only one that was off-key. Anyone aware of McNamara's positions needed only to read the public statements of the other officials to know that.

In my view, the World Bank opening offered a unique escape hatch for the administration in late 1967, inasmuch as it was one of the two or three positions in which McNamara was genuinely interested and the only one the President could control. There is no question that Mr. Johnson had the highest personal and professional regard for his Secretary of Defense and was determined to give him anything within his power to give. I cannot believe, however, that the President of the United States, a retiring American head of the World Bank and the relevant officials of other nations could not have arranged for the post to be filled twelve months later by Robert McNamara if the President of the United States had desired it. It is my conclusion, therefore, that Mr. Johnson wanted a different Secretary of Defense and that the prestigious, humanitarian and challenging job at the bank presented him the ideal means of both rewarding McNamara and removing him.

The President, of course, had every right to take this action. Indeed, one could argue that from his point of view he had an obligation to do so if he thought his administration and the country would fare better under a change. On the fringes, too, above and beyond McNamara's views on Vietnam, Mr. Johnson could have seen a good many supporting reasons for a new Secretary. McNamara had become a highly controversial figure, particularly on Capitol Hill, where he was being attacked by both Hawks and Doves, and 1968 was to be a political year.

In retrospect, my own opinion is that the President acted wisely and that he should have also chosen a new Secretary of State his final year in office. Despite my personal sorrow at McNamara's departure and my admiration for the courage and dedication of Secretary Rusk, I think no man should serve in either post as long as seven years.

In any case, would 1968 have been different with McNamara as Secretary of Defense?

Certainly he would have reacted as strongly as Clifford to the shocking request for 206,000 more men. And it was that figure, leaked by stunned officials and printed by the press, which, in the wake of the psychological impact of the Tet offensive, caused such a reaction at home. I know that McNamara would have contested the increase vigorously, and I am convinced that if the President had approved any significant additional deployment, McNamara would have resigned.

He would not have fought for de-escalation in the same manner as Clifford in 1968. By that time he would not have been as effective with the President. His views were known in the White House and his voice was stale. Clifford was the President's special friend, his last major Cabinet appointee, selected by the President from the bosom of his personal family. Inevitably this new voice, uttering sentiments the President could not have expected to hear from it, made more of an impression upon him than the same old tired refrain from McNamara.

Furthermore, McNamara's techniques would have been totally dissimilar. Never would he have veered off publicly from the course set by the Department of State by issuing his own optimistic assessments of Paris; never would he have suggested publicly that we proceed with peace talks without Saigon's presence nor publicly blasted the Thieu government for squabbling while men were dying. He would have made each of these points within our government, in more of his strong secret memoranda to the President, but he would not have been out in front of both State and the White House in public.

(He was out in front of the government with his antiballistic missile speech in San Francisco, but nuclear strategy was his special area of competence, about which he probably knew more than any living man. Additionally, each word of that address had been read and approved in advance by both the State Department and the White House. He was formulating national policy, but with the knowledge and consent of the President. The cases are, therefore, not comparable.)

McNamara's relationship with Secretary Rusk and the President was also entirely different, and that, too, would have had an effect in 1968. Knowing that the President detested split recommendations from his two top advisers, he always tried to reach common ground with Rusk before they went to the White House. He did not always succeed, but always tried. For seven years the two men worked intimately together, sharing at that highest level of government incredible experiences, some of them —the Berlin crises, the Cuban missile crisis—of total importance to every human being.

Clifford's hand, then, was much freer than McNamara's could have been in 1968. Of the President's Washington advisers on Vietnam, he alone had no personal commitment to the war. Unencumbered by that involvement, and as a close personal friend and confidant of the President, his position was unique.

The companion question to whether events would have been the same under McNamara was this one: Is it true, as many have said, that Clark Clifford was more responsible than any other man for the change of the government's war policy in 1968?

That the policy did change is undeniable. When 1968 began, the bombing of the North was continuing at an unbelievable pace. Within the administration the issue still was whether to expand it, and by how much. While no requests for additional troops were on the table, it still was being said that General Westmoreland would be given whatever forces he needed. The lack of communications between the two sides fighting the war was total: neither the United States nor Saigon spoke in any way to either Hanoi or the Vietcong. Since we were unable even to talk about talking, nothing appeared to lie ahead but more of the same. With the exception of McNamara, who was leaving, all the President's closest advisers believed that the answer lay in the continued tightening of the screw.

By the end of 1968 the bombing of the North had stopped. Resumption, even at a low level, was unthinkable. By his act of unilateral restraint in halting attacks on 80 percent of North Vietnamese territory earlier that year, the President had brought together Communist and U.S. negotiators in Paris. Months of secret talks, in which Cyrus Vance played the major U.S. role, had set the stage for all four parties to meet; we finally had persuaded Hanoi to permit Saigon to sit at a peace table. The troop ceiling was in cement, General Creighton Abrams had stated publicly that he needed no additional men, and an increased deployment of U.S. troops in the future was as unthinkable as a resumption of the bombing. The South Vietnamese were taking over more of the combat burden, more slowly than we wished but somewhat more rapidly than previously now that they finally were compelled to realize that the American escalator had come to a stop. We were ready and anxious to talk to Hanoi about a mutual withdrawal of foreign forces, which could be accomplished by the United States and the North Vietnamese while the government of President Thieu began working out a political settlement with Hanoi and the National Liberation Front.

It had been a long hot summer and a perilous fall, and on more than one occasion the escalator had been within a blink of moving upward again. But the President had always decided against it, and the question is whether Clark McAdams Clifford was the man responsible for those presidential decisions.

Having been so closely associated with Clifford in his effort to turn around the war, all of us in the 8:30 Group like to think that he was. Moreover, I believe it, although assuredly I cannot testify to it.

Many men in addition to the McNamara Doves in the Pentagon shared Clifford's views during 1968, and some of them—Averell Harriman and Cyrus Vance in Paris are the most obvious examples—were in a position to contribute enormously to the turnaround of the war. Vance and the President were especially close; and at times when Clifford was most in need of support, Vance's brief return trips from Paris and his lengthy intimate conversations with the President—he was usually a White House overnight guest—were critical. One must also go back a year: there could not have been a bombing limitation or a bombing halt in 1968 had Robert McNamara not fought so hard to prevent further escalation in 1967. Many individuals who had less direct contact with the President played essential roles behind the scenes—Nitze, Warnke and Under Secretary of State Katzenbach are the three principal examples. And while their motives were to stop the erosion of support rather than to disengage, the roles of Generals Wheeler and Abrams were important. In my opinion the President would not have decided as he did in March had not General Wheeler been so aware of the public feeling nor as he did in October had not both generals personally endorsed the full bombing stop.

But no other proponent of a reduction in our Vietnam involvement had Clifford's day-to-day access to the President's ear. Of the small circle of close presidential advisers, Clifford alone was advocating a limitation on our military efforts, as McNamara had before him. Of these men, it was he who most persistently urged negotiations as the way to extricate ourselves from a situation for which no military solution was attainable at any price we should be willing to pay.

Apart from Clifford, those who met with the President that year to decide major Vietnam policy issues believed strongly that unrelenting military pressure would see us through. The President's decisions in 1968 to take a step back and to stand down the bombing of North Vietnam thus are in themselves the best testimony as to whose voice was most influential. In the final analysis, of course, the single man most responsible for the turn in the war in 1968 can only be the President himself—who listened to Clifford's views and to the views of other equally dedicated men who felt differently, and who then moved with great personal courage to seek a way out of the bog.

As this is written in the fall of 1969, the war is still on and the casualty lists are still long. Eight months have passed since I have read the intelligence reports or the messages from Saigon and Paris with their new code-word designations. I do not know where we are, or whether there are bits and straws, or whether an entire foundation for peace is being built silently.

Clark Clifford has urged publicly the removal of 100,000 troops by the end of 1969 and the removal of all U.S. combat ground forces by the end of 1970. President Nixon has ordered the withdrawal of 60,000 men. The voices of the Hawks, so dominant within and outside the government for so long, are nearly stilled. While I have no privileged information on the internal administration debates, one cannot conceive of renewed bombing or additional troop deployment. The desire of the people to terminate this tragic involvement is patent.

Looking back, we know now, as we knew then, that not enough had been accomplished by January 20, 1969, despite the earlier groundwork of McNamara, the campaign of Clifford, the resolute struggle in Paris and Washington of Harriman and Vance and the March and October decisions of the President. Military disengagement on satisfactory terms was the objective, and while disengagement in the North was effected, the casualty rates in the South were no lower when Clifford and his 8:30 Group left the Pentagon than they had been a year before. But the progress from one January to the next was nonetheless of immeasurable importance to the disengagement which inevitably will follow, and while we did not come far enough, we can take some consolation for having come so much further than any of us believed possible on March 1, 1968.

Postscript

The crisis business ended for me on January 20, 1969, when a brand-new administration full of brand-new people, some of whom were to preside over brand-new crises, came to town. All presidential appointees who wanted to leave the government had been asked to submit their resignations to President Johnson; I had done so in a formal note and he had accepted in a formal note.

In December and January I had two or three good talks with Melvin Laird, an old friend from a decade earlier when, as a Republican-oriented reporter, I had covered Congress and the Defense Appropriations Subcommittee on which he served. I had no desire to stay with the new administration and he, so far as I know, had no desire for me to do so. But he knew me perhaps better than any other civilian official in the Pentagon and I willingly talked candidly to him on personnel matters. He, of course, was to spend weeks talking to dozens of others before making his decisions on the top appointees. In addition to responding to his questions about a few men who wanted to stay on, I suggested that there were seven who definitely should be replaced, despite my high regard for most of them (and most of whom had already accepted new jobs in any case). These were the Deputy Secretary, because a new administration should have its own man in the Number Two post; the three service Secretaries, for political expediency and to bring in new faces; the brilliant and valuable Alain Enthoven, who had become too controversial with both the military and the Congress; and Paul Warnke and me, because we both had been so involved with Clifford on policy decisions and because our names were fairly well known to the public in association with the "old" McNamara-Clifford regimes.

I also strongly urged the Secretary-designate to persuade the President-elect to nominate Dan Henkin as my successor. In this campaign I had powerful allies, including the Chairmen of the Joint Chiefs of Staff and both previous Secretaries of Defense. To their credit, Mr. Nixon and Laird had the great good sense to withstand heavy Republican political pressure, and Dan, a McNamara appointee and lifetime Democrat, became their Assistant Secretary of Defense for Public Affairs.

For the good of the government, it was time that I left that office. One certain sign of this was my vulnerability to criticism. President Truman's advice, that those who did not like the heat should stay out of the kitchen, was, in my view, incomplete. Many men will never learn to like the heat of criticism, and assuredly I am among them. So is Robert McNamara, although he probably would not admit it. The test is not whether one likes the heat, however, but rather one's ability to withstand heat and still perform effectively. For me, the criticism which had been merely annoying in 1965 and 1966 was affecting my judgment and performance by 1969. When one becomes supersensitive to a Congressional or offhand reportorial comment, or begins to dread the prospect of appearing before a testy Congressional committee, it is time to leave the government. I had reached that point. Furthermore, I had begun to regard nearly every news story about me and/or the Department as biased, inaccurate and saturated with controversy and conflict. With a few old-friend exceptions, I had begun to view all reporters as irresponsible enemies. Despite eighteen years as a newspaperman, these feelings persisted for several months, and the first draft of this book was violently antipress—and was petty and unfair.

The problem was that the battle with catastrophe and crisis had left me physically and mentally exhausted by January 20, 1969. While I would not have given up a day of the four-year experience—miserable, enervating, frustrating, embittering and infuriating though it was—neither would I have continued under any circumstance save one. That would have been the return of Cyrus Vance to the Department, this time as Secretary, and his insistence that I could have the public affairs job but no other. Clark Clifford and I had discussed the future, and he understood this. If Vice President Humphrey had won the election in 1968, Clifford would have remained if asked to do so. In that event I would have stayed with him, but in another capacity—not in the crisis business.

For as long as I can remember, my dream was to become a newspaperman in Washington. That dream was realized a dozen years before my earliest hopes, at the age of twenty-nine, and for the next decade or more no salary could have lured me into other work. I was doing what I most wanted to do for a newspaper which then believed that informing the people was more important than crusading for them or amusing them. It was a stimulating career, full of memorable experiences. One does not forget an hour spent alone with Senator Robert A. Taft the night after he was not nominated for the presidency, or the sight of Alan B. Shepard strapped into a tiny box atop a huge torch at Cape Canaveral, or the face of the young Attorney General standing alongside the young widow that interminable weekend. The challenge was to try to tell those stories quickly against the clock, and to tell them as honestly as they deserved to be told while being overwhelmed by the same emotions affecting millions of others. However rarely one succeeded, that was the challenge.

Despite the excitements and satisfactions of those newspaper years, the high point of my professional life has been my service in the Defense Department. It is far more rewarding to be a participant than an observer. Helping one's government grapple with its awesome problems, sometimes in a very minor way and sometimes, as in the 8:30 Group, more significantly, was an incredible experience. And the deepest gratification came from the people. No three men differ more than Robert McNamara, Clark Clifford and Cyrus Vance, but the facet of my government experience which was most meaningful to me was the closeness of my relationship with all three—and with others such as Paul Nitze, Paul Warnke and, of course, the two I had known so long, Dan Henkin and Dick Fryklund. McNamara believed that nowhere in the world—in government, business, university, church or other institution—was there such a collection of integrity, dedication and ability. Certainly I had not worked with so many persons of such caliber before, nor do I expect to again.

Index

Vietnam War, bombing of North
(Cont.)
Phu Ly, 76-77, 78, 80
Phu Xa, 77-78
power plant sites, 192-193
Salisbury series on, 52-92, 146, 172
San Antonio formula, 175, 179-
180, 210-211, 212
textile plant near Gia Lam, 66
Thanh Hoa Province, 335
tonnage dropped (1966), 90
20th Parallel proposal for, 177,
179, 186, 204, 210, 213
Van Dien vehicle depot, 57-61, 80
Yen Vien railroad complex, 57-61
cost of, 53
de-escalation efforts
of Clifford, 84, 306-358
of McNamara, 168-213, 322, 357
foreign troop committments, 323
Hué looting, 316
National Liberation Front, 322, 356
number of U.S. troops in, 172, 322,
323
Paris peace talks, 170, 341-342, 349-
354, 356, 357, 358
Saigon government and, 349-350,
351, 354
Tet offensive, 323, 324, 325, 328,
354
Thailand and, 50-51, 147-148, 322
thirty-seven-day pause, 178, 213
troop withdrawals, 258

Turkestan incident, 139-152
20th Parallel
Clifford's cutback to, 335-338, 340
McNamara's proposal on, 177,
179, 186, 204, 210, 213

Wall Street Journal, 230, 298, 313
Warnke, Paul C., 177, 184-185, 210,
319, 320, 321, 325, 330, 337,
351, 352, 357, 359, 361
Washington Evening Star, 8, 63, 133,
147-148, 230
Washington Post, 4, 63, 115, 127-128,
134, 164, 203, 217-218, 220,
221, 230, 236, 246, 293, 313,
335-336, 337
Welsh, Ed, 317
Westmoreland, William C., 68, 82,
153, 316, 320, 353
request for 206,000 troops, 323-324
Wheeler, Earle G., 104, 142, 145, 191,
194, 208, 287, 298, 300, 301-
302, 320, 322, 333, 347, 352,
357
White, William S., 218
Wicker, Tom, 218, 220
Wilson, Charles E., 118
Wilson, George, 115
World War II, 91, 141, 143, 197, 198,
322

Yen Vien railroad complex, 57-61

About the author

PHIL GOULDING was graduated from Hamilton College, Clinton, New York, in 1943, and spent the next three years in the Navy. At the end of the war he joined the Cleveland *Plain Dealer* and, after three years as a reporter in Cleveland, was assigned to the Washington Bureau. For seven years, he concentrated on Congress, the White House and politics. From 1958 on, he specialized in military affairs, based in the Pentagon but traveling overseas quite extensively. He also covered all manned space shots at the Cape until his entry into the government, and for the entire fifteen Washington newspaper years covered all presidential nominating conventions and campaigns. In 1965, Robert McNamara named Mr. Goulding Deputy Assistant Secretary of Defense (Public Affairs). In January, 1967, upon the departure of Arthur Sylvester, President Johnson appointed him Assistant Secretary, a post he held under McNamara and then under Clark Clifford until the new administration came in.

Mr. Goulding spent 1969 as a Scholar-in-Residence at the Aspen Institute for Humanistic Studies in Aspen, Colorado, where he wrote most of *Confirm or Deny*. His wife, Anne Wright Goulding, is a professional interior decorator in Washington, and an artist. They have five children.

70 71 72 9 8 7 6 5 4 3 2 1